BEYOND A DREAM DEFERRED

Foreword by

DERRICK BELL

BEYOND A DREAM DEFERRED

MULTICULTURAL

EDUCATION

and the **POLITICS**

of **EXCELLENCE**

UNIVERSITY OF MINNESOTA PRESS

MINNEAPOLIS

LONDON

EDITORS

BECKY W. THOMPSON

and **SANGEETA TYAGI**

Langston Hughes, "Harlem," from Langston Hughes, *The Panther and the Lash*, copyright 1951 by Langston Hughes, reprinted by permission of Alfred A. Knopf, Inc., and Harold Ober Associates, Inc. Kate Rushin, "The Bridge Poem," reprinted from *This Bridge Called My Back: Writings by Radical Women of Color*, copyright 1983 by Kate Rushin, used by the permission of the author and Kitchen Table: Women of Color Press, PO Box 908, Latham, NY 12110. Chapter 2, Cornel West, "The New Cultural Politics of Difference," first appeared in *Out There: Marginalization and Contemporary Cultures*, edited by Russell Ferguson, Martha Gever, Trinh T. Minh-ha, and Cornel West (Cambridge, Mass.: MIT Press, 1990), reprinted by permission. Chapter 3, Chandra Talpade Mohanty, "On Race and Voice: Challenges for Liberal Education in the 1990s," first appeared in *Cultural Critique*, no. 14 (Winter 1989-90): 179-208, copyright 1989, *Cultural Critique*, reprinted by permission. Chapter 6, Ian Haney López, "Community Ties and Law School Faculty Hiring: The Case for Professors Who Don't Think White," first appeared as "Community Ties, Race, and Faculty Hiring: The Case for Professors Who Don't Think White," in *Reconstruction* 1, no. 3 (1991), copyright *Reconstruction* journal, reprinted by permission.

Published by the University of Minnesota Press
2037 University Avenue Southeast, Minneapolis, MN 55455-3092
Printed in the United States of America on acid-free paper

Library of Congress Cataloging-in-Publication Data

Beyond a dream deferred : multicultural education and the politics of
  excellence / Becky W. Thompson and Sangeeta Tyagi, editors.
      p.   cm.
    Includes bibliographical references and index.
    ISBN 0-8166-2267-1 (alk. paper). — ISBN 0-8166-2269-8 (pbk. :
  alk. paper)
    1. Intercultural education—United States.   2. Education, Higher—
  Political aspects—United States.   3. Minorities—Education
  (Higher)—United States.   4. Education, Higher—United States—
  Curricula.   I. Thompson, Becky W.   II. Tyagi, Sangeeta.
  LC1099.3.B49   1993
  370.19'6'0973—dc20   93-15603
                                                                    CIP

HARLEM

What happens to a dream deferred?

Does it dry up
like a raisin in the sun?
Or fester like a sore —
And then run?
Does it stink like rotten meat?
Or crust and sugar over —
like a syrupy sweet?

Maybe it just sags
like a heavy load.

Or does it explode?

LANGSTON HUGHES

Contents

Foreword
The Power of Prophets
Derrick Bell

A thousand years from now, anthropologists or their thirty-first-century successors will wonder. Pouring over the recorded remains of what was the United States, they will search for reasons. "How," they will ask, "could so great a nation with so many advantages over its outside adversaries allow itself to be destroyed from within?"

In search of answers, social scientists of that new age will undoubtedly discover that ours was a society that preached inclusiveness and equality while vigorously practicing an ever more pernicious and ultimately destructive discrimination that disadvantaged all those not affiliated closely with mainstream, upper-class whiteness. Predictably, the theories put forth to explain this contradiction will be more complex than accurate — unless, that is, those who offer them discover records like the series of essays compiled here by Becky Thompson and Sangeeta Tyagi.

In these writings, there is ample evidence that the society had been put on notice by those who, often at substantial risk, served as prophets without heavenly credentials. Relying on their experience with what had been, they tried to disseminate the unwelcome truth both about the dangers of racial and ethnic divisiveness and the necessity of a multicultural approach to education at every level. It is important that those who seek to decipher the significance of these writings recognize, as Cornel West does, that the authors are in an inescapable double bind. As progressive scholars, they criticize and advocate for the very structures they are financially dependent upon. In a word, they must bite the hand that feeds them. Simultaneously progressive and co-opted, they know that they must continue, for without pressure, there can be no change.

The wisest among those who in a far-off future ruminate over our ruins will not be surprised that these published warnings and calls for moral redemption through social reform were written by members of subordinated groups. I would hope they would appreciate that these are writings issued against a deeply set grain of conformity. Although the messages of prophecy are aimed at all, they will likely be read mainly by those holding secure positions on campuses of prestige and influence, those least likely to speak out against the ills and injustices that afflict the society. There is in the academy, as in the rest of our modern world, a rather distressing commitment to the unwritten commandment "Thou shalt comply and not confront."

The seeking of comfort, so easily mistaken for security, seems to be a primary priority even though faculty members are tenured, most key staff are equally secure, and students, compared to most of those unable to attend college, are privileged. Paradoxically, in these spheres of intellectual power, there is a perverse reliance on the beatitude "Blessed are the meek, for they shall inherit the earth."

Thus, the prophets in these pages must contend with both academic retaliation in all of its nefarious forms, and that most demeaning mode of rejection: silence. And yet, the authors speak boldly about what should be done. While their messages vary in focus, they are all models of scholarly protest. They urge academic repentance and reform at a time when major change, to put it mildly, is far from likely. They understand that a commitment to change must be combined with a readiness to confront authority—not because their views will always prevail, not because they will always be right, but because faith in what one believes is right must be a living, working faith that draws us away from comfort and security and toward risk through confrontation.

As we learn in James 2:26, "For as the body without the spirit is dead, so faith without works is dead also." In *Beyond a Dream Deferred: Multicultural Education and the Politics of Excellence,* the writers have combined faith and works into prophecies that may not influence current policies, but surely will impress those who at some future time seek evidence that in our era, there were those who tried.

Acknowledgments

Compiling this anthology has been a labor of love, largely made possible by the goodwill and political insights of numerous people. Margaret Andersen and Serina Beauparlant helped us find our way to Lisa Freeman, director of the University of Minnesota Press. Lisa responded to our initial plans with open arms and has sustained her commitment ever since. Elizabeth Higginbotham, Cynthia Enloe, and Henry Giroux quickly reviewed the initial proposal. Their measured and astute suggestions helped us clarify our vision in substantial ways.

Given the recent media parade about the politically correct "thought police," the tenacity of the right wing's assault on progressive change, and the emergence of several widely read conservative tracts bemoaning educational transformation, we hoped to assemble this volume quickly. Knowing that it was almost unconscionable to ask the people we had in mind to contribute original articles quickly—given their commitments to teaching, scholarship, and activism and the overextension the combination often demands—we still asked, fully expecting that most would have to decline. Almost without exception, everyone we initially asked said yes immediately and produced drafts and final versions at lightning speed. In the year during which this anthology was compiled, both of us have been awed by the responsiveness and willingness of the contributors. Their support stands as testimony to their commitment to progressive educational change.

Roanoke College and the Rockefeller Fellowship in African-American Studies at Princeton University afforded us vital time and resources in the final stages of this prjoect. Throughout the process, we have had many animated and compelling conversations with Gloria Anzaldúa, Lisa Hall, Wahneema Lubiano, Evelynn Hammonds, Kim Vaz, Estelle Disch, Charles Nero, Ian Haney López, Earl Jackson, Shulamit Reinharz, and Betty Thompson. Their political, ethical, and sociological insights have sharpened our theoretical focus. Evelyn Hu-DeHart generously shared her networks and political wisdom with us. It has been a joy to work with the many people involved in the book's production at the University of Minnesota Press, including Todd Orjala, Lynn Marasco, Mary Byers, Pamela Johnson, and Kathy Wolter. We also want to extend our appreciation to Atreya Chakraborty, Lynn Davidman, Mandy Devery, Mary Gilfus, Susan Kosoff, and Gayle Pemberton for their emotional and intellectual generosity.

We decided to work together as coeditors of this volume based on the many years of political, intellectual, and emotional companionship we have shared. We have been able to celebrate and draw upon this connection from beginning to end. Ultimately, we thank the visionaries who have made multicultural education both necessary and inevitable as we reach toward the twenty-first century.

Introduction
"A Wider Landscape . . . without the
Mandate for Conquest"

Becky W. Thompson and Sangeeta Tyagi

To say that the past decade has been a tumultuous time in higher education in the United States is to state the obvious. For progressive educators
and those committed to multicultural educational transformation this has
been an invigorating time as well as a period of struggle.[1] Engaged in a
project of reimagining the world and its contours, we have been involved
in examining the historical configurations of power in all their various
expressions and attempting to dismantle those hierarchies in favor of a
more just and equitable society and academy.

This revisioning has been met with entrenched and narrowly defined
notions of an "American" identity. As our college and university campuses have, perforce, begun to reflect the demographic diversity of the
wider society, conservative attempts to retain and further consolidate images of a homogeneous society have gained ground. Clearly, the struggle
over what is to be considered valid knowledge goes much deeper than
issues of educational curricula — this struggle represents the battleground
for the soul and character of American society. As we wrestle with issues
of knowledge production, power, and representation within the academy, we are being told by those fundamentally opposed to the democratization of society and of the academy that multicultural education "di-
lutes the national identity," "weakens the canon," and "fragments a

common Americanness." These attempts to re-create a patriotic nationalism that seeks to rally people around notions of "citizenship" and a "unified nation" come specifically at a time when such images and their underlying ideologies are no longer (if they have ever been) taken for granted by an increasing number of people (family farmers, unemployed working- and middle-class people, black and Latino urban youth, people with AIDS and their care givers, Japanese-Americans, and others).

At this historical moment we are engaged in a profound struggle between those who would like to guard traditional bastions of racial, class, gender, and sexual privileges and those who are clamoring for membership at the center of an expansive and inclusive social fabric. In this context, Troy Duster says that the raging national controversy over multiculturalism and "political correctness" is a storm that is, "at the bottom, about the shifting sands of racial privilege."[2] The very magnitude of the backlash against multicultural education is indicative of the centrality of education in a society charged with reimagining itself in its increasing diversity. It is in this arena that crucial issues of national identity are reshaped and created anew.

The Last Two Decades: A Mean Time in the Academy

During our struggle to make our visions of progressive social change real, we in higher education have witnessed drastic cuts in financial aid and the attendant resources necessary to ensure that education becomes accessible across race and class. We have struggled against a tenuous commitment to affirmative action as many hiring committees continue to consider excellence and diversity inevitable opposites rather than synergistic complements. During the 1980s and 1990s, both administrators and faculty — particularly part-time, non-tenure-track faculty — have felt the burden of lost jobs, benefits, and privileges. This faculty reduction has been coupled with a weakening of unions across the nation, including those within colleges and universities that historically have been the bedrock of job security and benefits for support staff and other key people in the daily operations of campus life. Bias crimes on campuses increased dramatically in the 1980s and early 1990s, making abundantly clear that exposure to psychic and sometimes physical violence may be an unavoidable casualty of simply "being" in the university if you are Jewish, Arab, gay, lesbian, black, Latino, Latina, Asian, or female. These regressive events have been coupled with a dramatic conservative shift on the part of funding institutions that historically have been charged with supporting academic scholarship. A key example was the consolidation of neoconservative power at the National Endowment for the Humanities, the largest source of humanities funding in the country, during the Bush administration. NEH head Lynne Cheney succeeded in urging the Senate to approve eight of her nominees, at least half of them members of the conservative National Association of Scholars.[3]

Particularly in the past few years, conservative perspectives on higher education—exemplified in a renewed commitment to a monocultural version of the Great Books series, establishment of the National Association of Scholars in 1987, and the existence of more than fifty right-wing think tanks—have been buttressed by a remarkable willingness on the part of the mass media to serve as publicists and mouthpieces for the conservative agenda.[4] In 1990 and 1991 a noteworthy array of national magazines ran cover stories denouncing what became euphemistically known as the "politically correct thought police." Scoop-hungry journalists and triumphalists[5] have collectively accused 1960s "radicals" of having taken over the academy as they insinuate doctrinaire policies and political perspectives into the "vulnerable" minds of "innocent" students.

Liberal and progressive faculty have been accused of being hell-bent to eliminate from public memory all of the great works of traditionally recognized scholars. Analytical critique has been confused with censorship, lively debate with fanaticism. Aware that some of these conservative critics (Lynne Cheney and Dinesh D'Souza, to name two obvious examples) used tourism as their main method of collecting data, many faculty watched and worried as speeches and writing of feminists and scholars of color were taken completely out of context, inverted and distorted in the process.

At the height of the media extravaganza, many educators and students have had trouble recognizing their own experiences in descriptions of university classrooms. While the media portrayed the academy as a hotbed of radical classes and sweeping curricular transformation, many students, faculty, and administrators continued on with painfully slow committee work, networking, caucusing, and memo writing. This work often extended over semesters and into years and only sometimes led to the eventual implementation of a single course requirement enabling students to graduate with at least some exposure to scholarship outside of Eurocentric traditions. While the media painted the academy as a place where lesbians, people of color, and people with disabilities soaped the mouths of disrespectful people and leveled discrimination suits at every turn, we on the campuses continued to brainstorm about the efficacy of refusing to hold classes in classrooms that were not accessible to disabled students, often painfully aware that accessible classrooms were few and far between.

Media imagery has suggested that radical faculty are the "new McCarthyites" and that students on racially mixed campuses are "tribalists" who are "Balkanized" to the point of complete racial segregation. In stark contrast to that portrayal, many faculty of color, feminists, and progressive-minded scholars continued to experience both subtle and obvious exclusionary practices, including acts of physical and psychic violence. We witnessed the denial of tenure to faculty dedicated to the dual missions of fine teaching and community-based scholarship and the coalitions across race, gender, and sexuality in student and faculty organizations. We continued to teach, advise students, participate in college service, and support student-based activism while we were frightened by the fragility of our place in the academy. Most college and university faculties in the United States still include less than 5 percent people of color.[6] Only 13 percent of the full professors are women (of any race) compared to 10 percent in 1974, and 2.2 percent of full professors are African-American men or women.[7] And there are still very few "out" gay and lesbian faculty. As the media helped support Roger Kimball's claim that radicals were taking over the academy,[8] Troy Duster's assertion that "finding a leftist on the Berkeley faculty is like searching for a needle in a haystack" aptly applied at countless other colleges and universities as well.[9]

Why the Backlash?

The title of Derrick Bell's newest book, *Faces at the Bottom of the Well: The Permanence of Racism*, is a startling and terrible reminder that many of the gains of the 1960s have been tempered, stymied, and in many cases brutally reversed in the 1980s and 1990s.[10] In part, the regressive assault on democratic change in the academy during the past few years is part of the second great backlash to the civil rights movement. Patricia Williams explains that the first backlash turned urban neighborhoods into the "inner city," as white flight from the city coincided with redlining, unequal distribution of tax dollars to schools, and de facto primary and secondary school segregation. The second backlash, Williams asserts, is being "waged against the hard won principles of equal opportunity in the work place and in the universities as feeders for the work place."[11] At a rally where Bell announced that he would take an unpaid leave from Harvard Law School until the school hired a black female scholar, one of the deans inquired if Bell thought Harvard was a "southern lunch counter." Bell answered in the affirmative. Harvard has yet to make a tenure-track appointment to a black woman legal scholar despite many years of organized student and faculty protest against exclusionary hiring policies and, eventually, the loss of a faculty member of Bell's preeminence and stature (see Ian Haney López, chapter 6). Harvard's intransigence, unfortunately, has been the rule rather than the exception among colleges and universities.

This reality has led scholars to consider the timing of the backlash, understanding that only by putting it in a historical context is it possible to understand its political and social roots. It is certainly not possible to say that the opposition to democratic change is a response to any recent birth announcement about African-American, ethnic, or women's studies. These disciplines and subfields within other disciplines are over twenty years old. Nor are the demographic shifts that underlie changes in the racial and ethnic makeup of college and university student bodies particularly recent. The increase in Asian students can be linked to the 1965 Immigration and Naturalization Act, which went into effect in 1968. The increase in the number of African-American and Latino and Latina students beginning in the 1960s is a direct consequence of gains made in the civil rights movement, whose roots date back to the 1950s. In fact, several theorists have suggested that the timing of the attack by the "mainstream" media, former president Bush, and conservative academics was related to attempts to create a unidimensional national identity in the face of increasing opposition to a single, monocultural vision.[12] The ideology of a unified nation was most vividly exemplified in the Gulf War rhetoric, which sought to generate a seamless patriotic nationalism. This rhetoric was at its zenith during roughly the same months (winter 1990 and spring 1991) that public condemnation of multicultural contributions was also at its height.[13] During this time the Bush administration and the Pentagon policed the press, heading off comprehensive coverage of the war, as many conservative commentators policed progressives in the academy, accusing them of being "thought police" who were denying students their right to free speech. The United States was presented as a free nation with Iraq as its opposite, while the academy was singled out as an institution attempting to undermine domestic freedom. The ideology of nationalism skewed the discourse of multicultural education by treating inclusive curricula as destroyers of "national identity" rather than as attempts to give voice to Americanness in all of its diversity.

There are salient and compelling parallels between the assault on progressive education and the state's unwillingness to confront the underpinnings of the economic recession. In the words of Henry Giroux, "Schools have become the new scapegoat for the increasing failure of the American economy to compete in the world market."[14] Multicultural education has been cast as a superfluous curriculum that has little to do with teaching people the skills they need to survive the imperatives of the marketplace. Within this equation, the skills of cross-cultural and cross-racial communication afforded through African-American and ethnic studies are rendered invisible. At the same time, the portrayal of race-, class-, and gender-conscious education as unnecessary dismisses the value of analytical examinations of domestic and international economic relations. The construction of an analytical engagement with the world—including the realm of economics—as superfluous devalues the tools that can enable students to understand the dramatic changes in domestic and world economic power relations and leaves unexamined the ideology that economic inequality is inevitable and uncontestable.

The construction of a politically powerful group of faculty bent on silencing students has also been the scapegoat to divert attention away from the assault on freedom of speech that occurs by limiting access to education. Freedom of speech and association is predicated upon access to the arenas where the discussion is occurring. Thus it is possible for the state to assert the right to free speech theoretically and yet, by making drastic cutbacks in financial aid while tuition increases, deny free speech by default. In the 1980s and 1990s there has been a steady whittling away of working-class economic security as large corporations have relocated to Third World countries. This corporate profiteering has weakened the ability of working- and middle-class people to finance their own education and their children's. Simultaneously, federal and state funds for education have been severely reduced, making it virtually impossible for many working-class students to attend college and increasingly precarious for middle-class students to finish their degrees. More and more students are forced to juggle their educational dreams with economic demands as they study while they are commuting to campus on the subway, when their children are napping, and during their lunch hours at work. Classist barriers are compounded by racism. As Gerald Jaynes explains, "Despite consistent gains in black high-schoolers' academic achievement relative to that of whites during the period of 1976-1986, relative black college enrollment collapsed during the same period. Indeed, in 1985, the odds that a black high school graduate would enroll in college were lower than the odds in 1976. The government policy that replaced federal grants to college students with federal loans was a key factor in the plummeting Black enrollment."[15] Jaynes remarks that "the very poor students do not borrow what to them are astronomical sums of money to embark on an activity no one in their family or circle of acquaintance has ever experienced."[16] By associating multicultural education with the McCarthyism of the 1940s and 1950s, some conservative commentators have effectively inverted notions of power—presenting those who have had decades of uninterrupted control over the academy and its production of ideas as the "hounded," the "silenced," and the "policed," when in fact working-class students (who disproportionately include single mothers, students of color, and returning students) are among those effectively silenced when budget cuts are made.

Recent attacks on inclusive educational goals may also relate to the larger sociopolitical climate in which the contributions of African-American intellectuals have been marginalized both within and outside the academy. Perhaps the most notable recent instance of this silencing occurred during the 1991 Senate hearings on the nomination of Clarence Thomas to the Supreme Court. Not surprisingly, the testimony of African-American scholars directly contradicted the Senate's construction of Thomas's ascendency as a story of individual success, providing a lens for understanding the racial dynamics involved in his nomination to the Court. The Judiciary Committee refused to consider these scholars' perspectives seriously and simultaneously refused to hear the testimony of experts on sexual harassment who could have elucidated the forces that allow the abuses described by Anita Hill. The statement supported by 1,603 African-American women collectively known as African-American Women in Defense of Ourselves published in the *New York Times* was a highly visible example of the testimony of African-American intellectuals who opposed the confirmation of Clarence Thomas and supported the veracity of Anita Hill's testimony.[17]

The assaults on "political correctness" and multiculturalism are attacks on knowledge and contestations over power. One of the most insidious aspects of the assault on race-conscious scholarship and scholars has been the right's use of people of color like Dinesh D'Souza and Clarence Thomas as fronts for presenting reactionary views on race relations and affirmative action. At the same time, the notion of "reverse discrimination" has been slipped into the social vocabulary. Meanwhile, scholarship by intellectuals who support affirmative action and race-, class-, and gender-consciousness has been excluded from the national debate.[18]

In this sobering time, progressive faculty, students, and administrators have been doing double duty—highlighting the history of progressive accomplishments in education and examining the relation between the assault on curriculum change and the current sociopolitical climate. This work has also involved documenting the promises of multicultural education and offering scholarship that accurately evaluates power inequalities and their influence on the politics of representation and access. Simultaneously, progressive educators tried to hold the line on panic and despair as we bolstered ourselves through a third Republican presidential term and continuing sweeping budgetary cuts. And, as is characteristic of progressive politics, all of this has required a painstaking commitment to understanding our mistakes, shortsightedness, and the limits we place on our own visions.

How Far We Have Come

Many intellectuals who were in the academy during and since the 1960s have offered historical perspectives on changes in education, testifying that as bad as things are now, a quick glimpse back to the 1960s and before is an active reminder of the strides that have been made.[19] Until the late 1960s very few black people were admitted to white graduate schools. Less than twenty-five years ago, women's, ethnic, and African-American studies departments had not yet been established. In the 1960s, the imperialist leanings of many area studies programs had yet to be contested by scholarship made possible by activist-based ethnic and Third World studies programs.

In many ways, the progressive achievements in the academy since the 1960s have been remarkable, enabling scholars to welcome and engage with the increasingly diverse student bodies now in college. Drawing on black studies in its "off-campus incarnation," which began in the eighteenth century, one of the most significant gains of the Black Power and civil rights movements of the 1960s was the establishment of what is now hundreds of Afro-American studies programs.[20] The activism spearheaded by Chicanos and Chicanas, Native Americans, African-Americans, and Asian-Americans in the 1960s also led to the formation of ethnic studies programs, first at San Francisco State, the University of California campuses, and Cornell University and then spreading to 350 campuses across the nation in the following twenty-five years[21] (see chapter 1). This discipline formation has coincided with the establishment of race and ethnicity research centers (the Center for the Study of Race and Ethnicity in America at the University of Colorado at Boulder, the Julian Samora Research Institute in Michigan, and the Center for Research on Women in Memphis, to name three stellar examples) and what can be considered nothing less than a stunning assemblage of race-conscious scholarship and research. Johnnella Butler, one of the pioneers in black studies, has written: "In Black Studies we have set many tasks for ourselves: to correct distortions, to revise the history and other studies of people of African ancestry, and to critique the educational process itself by identifying how the colonization of minds is characteristic of American education."[22]

The emergence of women's studies, like that of black studies, has been a product of activism — which has produced more than six hundred women's studies programs, gender-conscious sections in many of the professional disciplinary organizations, and research institutes dedicated to feminist research.[23] This institutional growth has developed concurrently with a veritable explosion of feminist scholarship and research. In 1989 Catherine R. Stimpson wrote, "Women's Studies has produced a body of thought so big, complex and vital that people who ignore it should be sued for intellectual and academic malpractice."[24] Gay and lesbian studies, the youngest of the disciplines originating in the human rights movements of the second half of the twentieth century, now boasts programs in many colleges and universities. Several major university presses have created gay and lesbian series, and the annual Gay and Lesbian Studies Conference first held in 1987 has ballooned in attendance and gained international recognition. This is no small accomplishment and contribution particularly as conservatives (in Colorado and other states) continue their rampage against granting basic human rights to gay men and lesbians and as the National Endowment for the Humanities and the National Endowment for the Arts have continued to refuse proposals that consider lesbians and gay men and sexuality as appropriate subjects of inquiry.

The new disciplines, set up as oppositional and alternative spaces within largely homogeneous curricula, have fundamentally transformed the "canon" both by including scholarship of those traditionally marginalized and by bringing about basic shifts in theoretical paradigms. Describing these dramatic changes, Edward Said writes, "The ferment in minority, subaltern, feminist and post colonial consciousness has resulted in so many salutary achievements in the curricular and theoretical approach to the study of the humanities as quite literally to have produced a Copernican revolution in all traditional fields of inquiry."[25] As a consequence of this activism and scholarship, the homogeneity of college campuses is no longer accepted as coincidental or even accidental, but has been politicized as the reflection of a larger system of social inequalities. While the establishment of African-American, ethnic, women's, and gay and lesbian studies has not guaranteed that these disciplines have always remained true to their activist roots or offered scholarship that contests hegemonic theory and practice, their existence has, at the least, succeeded in offering a location for possible radical educational change. And, from our perspective, one of the most hopeful signs in this work is the ties that have been created and nurtured between these disciplines.[26] Pioneering efforts of the 1980s—including the women's studies and black studies symposium "An Overdue Partnership" organized by the University of Massachusetts Women's Studies Program and Smith College's Afro-American Studies Department, the founding and growth of the Center for Research on Women at Memphis State University (which, for ten years, has been a powerhouse of race-, class-, and gender-conscious scholarship), and the "Common Differences: Third World Women and Feminist Perspectives" international conference—recognized women of color as being at the heart of the political struggles underlying the formation of these disciplines.

Promises of Multicultural Education

During a regressive historical time, one important task has been to chronicle the visionary potential of multicultural education, to help counter distorted conservative constructions of this movement. In the face of conservative consolidations of power, it is both easy and dangerous to fall into the trap of becoming defensive, trying to hold the line on gains while losing energy to brainstorm about what can and must be done. While there is no one term that captures all that the movement embodies, there is remarkable agreement about the promises and purpose of multicultural educational change across discipline, generation, race, and gender.[27]

Advocates are careful to explain that this educational agenda is not about supplanting Western Eurocentric scholarship with Afrocentric or Islamocentric approaches. Rather, it is based on an intellectual process that seeks to enlarge our vision of exemplary scholarship and reintegrate at the center of human knowledge all of the voices that have been marginalized in Western civilization. As Edward Said explains, "Clamorous dismissals and swooping assertions are in fact caricatural reductions of what the great revisionary gestures of feminism, subaltern or black studies and anti-imperialist resistance originally intended."[28] The work of Toni Morrison stands as a marvelous example of the expansive task of discovery and reinterpretation. Morrison opens *Playing in the Dark: Whiteness and the Literary Imagination* with a description of the task regarding the study of American literature, a description that may be emblematic of the vision now gaining ground in many disciplines. Morrison writes that her wish is to "put forth an argument for extending the study of American literature into what I hope will be a wider landscape. I want to draw a map, so to speak, of a critical geography and use that map to open as much space for discovery, intellectual adventure, and close exploration as did the original charting of the New World—without the mandate for conquest."[29]

Such an exploration not only expands intellectual debate by considering the social commentaries of W. E. B. Du Bois, Frantz Fanon, and James Baldwin alongside those of T. S. Eliot, Matthew Arnold, and Talcott Parsons, for example; it also fundamentally alters our reading of dominant texts, providing us with a fuller sociohistorical context within which to understand their meaning and significance. These expansions and the introduction of different voices are also necessarily accompanied by a transformation of key social concepts. A current example may be seen in the struggles over the definition and scope of reproductive rights for women. While some white middle-class women have framed the issues in terms of abortion rights and an individual woman's right to "choose," women of color in the United States and Third World women around the globe have sought to broaden the debate to include reproductive rights for all women, the right to basic health and sanitation, and the end of forced sterilization of poor women and women of color. New perspectives introduced by feminist historians and historians of color have brought about reevaluations of such taken-for-granted concepts of U.S. history as "equality" and "justice for all."

This expansive and inclusive scholarship also carries within it the promise—indeed, the necessity—of interdisciplinary research, appointments, and perspectives as the bases of theory formation and praxis. The multidimensional nature of social reality requires that our scholarship expand to take account of variations in people's lives instead of attempting to trim reality to fit our narrow theoretical frameworks. Scholars in African-American, ethnic, and women's studies have relied on the links between history, politics, economics, sociology, anthropology, and other fields. Their expansive approaches provide a model for scholars in other fields as they come to appreciate the intellectual rigor of a multidisciplinary scope. Espousing the benefits of an interdisciplinary approach, Patricia Hill Collins writes that while her doctoral training was in sociology, her current academic location in African-American studies has given her "positive and important intellectual space in which to work. . . . Studying African-American women from a holistic perspective has forced me to cross disciplinary boundaries. As a result I find current academic approaches confining and in some cases collaborating in support of systems of oppression."[30] In considering the future of the academy, Collins writes that

> I would like scholars to learn to ask better questions, primarily
> questions that have significance for people's daily lives. To me, a good
> question is one that cannot be answered solely within the boundaries of
> any one discipline. We might retain our training, our specializations, but
> still cooperate across boundaries in creating new knowledge. This is the
> promise of areas such as African-American, American and Women's
> Studies.[31]

It is in these new configurations of voices, ideas, and interdisciplinary ties, then, that the intellectual imperative of multicultural education becomes firmly established: multiple perspectives provide a richer analysis and ultimately a more sophisticated understanding of society and history.

The acceptance of new voices and new perspectives goes hand in hand with vigorous and committed efforts at affirmative-action hiring at all levels within educational institutions. The empowered representation of people of color, white women, people with disabilities, and gay men and lesbians as students, faculty, staff, and administrators is a bedrock priority of multicultural education as colleges and universities proceed to reflect the larger society demographically and culturally. The commitment to representation of traditionally marginalized groups is based on a twofold vision that attempts to dismantle power inequalities by opening faculty, staff, and administrative positions to all people and is predicated upon the inclusion of new "bodies" bringing in new perspectives that challenge traditionally entrenched ways of examining the world and people's place in it.

While multicultural education requires scholarly reinterpretations and reconfigurations, its purpose goes beyond the academic community. Its success rests on its ability to inspire engagement with the world outside of the academy in all of its increasing diversity. In this context, Chandra Mohanty writes that "while discursive categories are clearly central sites of political contestation, they must be grounded in and informed by the material politics of everyday life, especially the daily life struggles for survival of poor people—those written out of history."[32] In the absence of a serious engagement with the lived realities of "those written out of history," a multicultural agenda is reduced to a dangerously empty play of academic rhetoric—reproducing the insulated theorizing that is characteristic of dominant academic trends.[33] Nurturing the activist roots of progressive education thus contributes to a model of human beings as fully engaged with their social environment and committed to a process of just social change. Indeed, it is this visionary potential that we need most urgently as we rally to meet the apocalyptic dangers of the modern world: the threat of nuclear destruction; societies increasingly unequal and polarized on the basis of race, class, and nationality; and the unbridled disregard for democratic principles shown by corporate powers within the United States and around the world.

What Remains to Be Done

General agreements about the overall mission of multicultural education do not preclude continued challenges both from the right wing and from those who generally support its goals and purposes. Part of what is at issue is naming and trying to understand the specific challenges we face as black, Latino, Latina, Asian-American, feminist, gay, and lesbian teachers and scholars as curricular change and representation priorities are undermined, underestimated, co-opted, and sabotaged.

A central issue is the way in which promoting multicultural education often turns out to be a code for advancing white people's interests—white women, white gay men, white ethnic groups—detracting from a fully progressive vision. Strides in affirmative action in the past twenty years have more often benefited white women than either men or women of color. In their 1986 critique of exclusionary practices in women's studies, Maxine Baca Zinn, Lynn Weber Cannon, Elizabeth Higginbotham, and Bonnie Thornton Dill found that those holding the gatekeeping positions at women's studies journals "are as white as are those at any mainstream social science or humanities publication."[34] While exclusionary practices are much more widely recognized in the 1980s and 1990s than they were previously, the steps needed to rectify them are slow in coming. Although there is no argument that black studies and ethnic studies still maintain male biases, scholars working on the cusp of women's studies and black/ethnic studies have often noted that the racism in women's studies cuts deeper than limitations in black and ethnic studies. Based on her twenty years of teaching black and women's studies and ten years of conducting curriculum integration projects, Johnnella Butler wrote, "It may be more difficult for Women's Studies to transform itself than for Ethnic Studies."[35] Ultimately, what is more important than documenting whether black studies is more hospitable to multidimensional analyses than women's studies is sophisticated analyses of the simultaneity of oppressions. These analyses absolutely depend upon accounting for multiple identities and sources of power. Scrutinizing the ways that women's studies has been coded to mean white women's studies can be an enormously useful preventive measure for those who are now at the forefront in developing gay and lesbian studies as a discipline.

At the heart of struggles for representation and inclusion are complicated questions about how the transformative potential of "cultural diversity" and "difference" can be undermined in the face of co-optation and limited understandings of power. Affirmative action can easily be reduced to a tokenistic inclusion of "bodies" regardless of people's commitment to their communities or to understanding oppression in a multidimensional way. This is the Clarence Thomas phenomenon being played out continuously within U.S. society and education, as some people of color (Linda Chavez, Dinesh D'Souza, and others) are carefully chosen and promoted to present reactionary views on race relations and affirmative action. Confronting tokenism requires constant vigilance as we seek to understand the specific ways in which it occurs and effective strategies for challenging it. Tokenism has required us to be very clear that while including people of color and white women is a *necessary* aspect of affirmative action and democratic educational change, it is not *sufficient* to ensure the success of a progressive vision. While there is no denying the importance of people from marginalized groups to serve as role models and mentors within a highly segregated environment, what is also needed is people who have developed a perspective that allows for an analysis of power and privilege. In the absence of such perspectives we will continue to have "bodies" but no fundamental shifts in the balance of power.

This commitment, however, needs to go a step further if there is to be overarching progressive educational change. We must not assume that only those who belong to traditionally marginalized groups and are committed to social justice can or should be the ones wholly responsible for raising issues and developing strategies for just social change. In fact, scholars who have traditionally been at the center of knowledge — white, male, upper class, heterosexual — need to expand their social commitments as they examine their own position within the academy and work toward developing political and personal solidarity with those seeking a place in the center. Only when all people are committed to dismantling the educational power structure and reshaping it into one that is richer and fuller and that mirrors the demographic diversity of the larger society is meaningful change possible. Developing a progressive politics of inclusion within the academy is a mandate that those at the center need to assume as they work toward expanding the center in their academic as well as their personal lives. Without such a commitment, our schools and curriculum will resemble academic ghettos where certain scholars uphold a multicultural imperative based on their own membership in marginalized communities while the traditionally empowered continue to engage in business as usual.

Avoiding the construction of academic ghettos requires developing interdisciplinary research and teaching approaches and at the same time transforming disciplinary boundaries. In her 1989 article assessing the state of women's studies in its twentieth year, Catherine Stimpson describes three groups of opponents to women's studies. First there are the "know-it-all know-nothings" who dismiss women's studies with the rhetoric that with no female Plato, Shakespeare, or Napoleon, there is nothing to study, and therefore no need for a discipline. The "hysterical ideologues" are New Right and neoconservative men and women who are bound and determined to eliminate women's studies because they see it as a breeding ground for the left.[36] A third group is the "anxious neighbors," who "divide up clubhouse rooms according to academic disciplines. The scientists claim that science and the new neighbors on the block have nothing in common. The social scientists and humanists put up one dart board called 'Women's Studies' and another called 'minority studies.' "[37] Division into disciplinary camps weakens the synergistic transformative potential of multicultural education and ultimately constrains its scope and vision.

In addition to nurturing the interdisciplinary roots of progressive undergraduate education, it is also important to increase the availability of women's and ethnic studies in graduate, professional, and high schools as well as support alliances with scholars and research centers internationally.[38] Without this expansion, students who have been exposed to and trained in women's or ethnic studies during their undergraduate schooling are unable to pursue their interests at the graduate level in a sustained and systematic way and important work is lost as students are channeled into different disciplines and specializations. Introducing multicultural programs such as women's and ethnic studies in high school expands the scope of student learning at an earlier age and at the same time sends the message that progressive educational principles are integral parts of what is considered basic education.

Expanding our notion of what constitutes basic education also involves a commitment to the multilingual roots of progressive education. The centrality of language in cultural continuity, identity, and the distribution of power in the United States elucidates why this is a significant priority. It is particularly ironic that as one of the most multicultural groups in the world, the people of the United States are also among the most monolingual. The formation of an American cultural heritage has been built on the enforcement of English as the dominant language despite the fact that, numerically, it was a minority language in the past and may soon become—or already is—a minority language in many states. Acceptance and support of a multilingual society is essential in order to embrace various racial and ethnic identities, since language both reflects and reproduces the soul of a culture. As Gloria Anzaldúa explains:

> Ethnic identity is twin skin to linguistic identity—I am my language. Until I can take pride in my language, I cannot take pride in myself. . . . Until I am free to write bilingually and to switch without having always to translate, while I still have to speak English or Spanish when I would rather speak Spanglish, and as long as I have to accommodate the English speakers rather than having them accommodate me, my tongue will be illegitimate.[39]

Clearly, a sustained commitment to the study of languages, offered in a context that enables people to know how to speak two or more languages as well as to understand how languages reflect intricate cultural patterns is a fundamental challenge of a truly multicultural education.

Finally, in defending the academy and the promise of multicultural education as an important site for critical thinking and active engagement in the outside world, we need to guard against the defensive and ultimately conservative position of saying that the academy is the primary location for radical political change. In *And We Are Not Saved*, Derrick Bell explains the roots of racism in U.S. law through his discussion of what he calls the "Constitutional Contradiction": while the framers of the Constitution espoused the philosophy that all men are created equal, they simultaneously wrote multiple provisions into the document that legalized slavery. These and exclusionary provisions about gender effectively granted equality only to propertied white males.[40] Drawing parallels between the constitutional contradiction and the "academic contradiction" is instructive. While the academy is frequently cited as a haven of free speech and intellectual imagination, who is invited into its halls and allowed to speak has historically been controlled by people of a certain race, class, and gender. Progressive educators face a contradiction as they fight to establish diversity requirements, multiracial academic summer programs, and faculty development seminars within institutions in which the representation of people of color is still marginal and where a Eurocentric curriculum remains the norm. The academic contradiction requires consideration of whether these attempts end up serving as "the master's tools," a question raised by Audre Lorde in her prophetic essay "The Master's Tools Will Never Dismantle the Master's House."[41]

Avoiding co-optation depends upon a commitment to developing and maintaining ties between community organization and activism and the academy while simultaneously acknowledging the academy's need for profound political and structural change. To be effective bearers of this change within the academy, then, we will have to play the dual role of being part of the institution even as we refuse to be implicated in the injustices that occur within its walls.

Organization of This Book

We envisioned a multidisciplinary anthology with chapters by faculty, administrators, and students both activist and intellectual. The volume consolidates progressive moral and political visions of multicultural education, debates within the field, and the institutional changes that have taken place in the past twenty years in the academy. The controversies are situated within larger issues of national identity, the economy, changes in demographics, and conflicts over unequal distributions of power.

Part I, "Moral and Political Visions of Multicultural Education," includes chapters by Evelyn Hu-DeHart, Cornel West, Chandra Mohanty, and Evelynn Hammonds that focus on central moral, political, and cultural issues at the foundation of progressive educational change. This section offers intellectual histories of the disciplinary roots of multicultural education—black, feminist, and ethnic studies—and assessment of its impact on the rest of the curriculum and disciplines. In spelling out the visions and contours of multicultural education, the authors also offer theoretical frameworks to support inclusive educational priorities and establish the historical background of current controversies.

Part II, "Multiple Voices, Ongoing Struggles," spells out key debates—about power, affirmative action, activism, hiring practices, and discipline formation—as they have appeared in dialogue among advocates of multicultural education in the past quarter century. This section contains chapters by Becky Thompson and Sangeeta Tyagi on barriers to affirmative action and curriculum change and strategies for developing politics of inclusion; Ian Haney López on the student diversity movement at Harvard Law School and its evolving strategies regarding hiring practices; and Earl Jackson, Jr., on the centrality of Third World feminism and the contributions of black gay men in the formation of lesbian and gay studies. Lisa Kahaleole Chang Hall considers the relationship between academia and political activism. By identifying impediments to coalitions and political debate among progressives, these authors dispel the notion of a monolithic left wing that supports multicultural education while proposing strategies that will facilitate long-term structural change rather than reformist, Band-Aid measures.

Part III, "New Directions for Critical Engagement," documents the course of educational transformation, highlighting key successes and the alliances that have made them possible. Troy Duster theorizes about the state of multicultural education at the University of California at Berkeley, drawing on the findings of the Diversity Project, the most extensive study to date of the impact of diversity on student life on the campus. The chapter by Estelle Disch and the chapter by Margaret Andersen and Carole Marks document, respectively, the implementation of a diversity requirement at the University of Massachusetts at Boston and the development of a pioneering multiracial summer program in sociology. Barbara Omolade assesses the approaches and priorities of faculty development seminars and grass-roots political organizing at the City University of New York, documenting fundamental contestations between the supporters of the dominant intellectual culture and advocates of radical structural change. Drawing on their authority as educators who have been pioneers in creating institutional change since the 1960s, these authors offer wise and instructive analyses for students and educators who are dedicated to curricular change and affirmation action, highlighting both the strides that have been made and the ways that educational transformation remains a promise but not yet a reality. They also offer a template for change within the academy as we approach the twenty-first century.

We sought out people whose research specializations, teaching, and activism were based on multicultural visions. We reasoned that living and thinking from this expansive perspective was the most vital indicator of their abilities to speak directly, affirmatively, comprehensively, and honestly about the nature and challenges of progressive education. As students, faculty, and administrators who have been at the forefront of creating the "wider landscape" Toni Morrison refers to, they are also among those most articulate about the process and politics involved in establishing an inclusive educational agenda. Many of the authors have been pioneers in African-American studies, women's studies, and ethnic studies since the inception of these disciplines. Since we were seeking the perspectives of public intellectuals — those who understand connections between multicultural pedagogy and political struggles on campus and larger political struggles — we looked for authors who identify themselves as both intellectuals and activists involved in multiracial work within and outside the academy.

In keeping with our commitment to representation of those who have led the way in progressive educational change, most of the chapters are written by people of color — African-American, Latino and Latina, Asian-American, Indian, and native Hawaiian — in addition to chapters by white women and gay and lesbian people. The authors here represent eleven disciplines: African-American studies, religion, ethnic studies, law, history of science, literature, education, sociology, cultural studies, women's studies, and gay and lesbian studies. We hope that the discussions in this book will have multidisciplinary relevance, offering historical perspectives and road maps for the future to students and teachers who are struggling for curricular change and cultural representation on their campuses.[42]

While some recent volumes include conservative and progressive perspectives on political correctness,[43] to the best of our knowledge *Beyond a Dream Deferred* is the first book that assesses multicultural education — its history, conflicts, priorities, successes, and challenges. Through its feminist, race-, and class-conscious analysis, this volume highlights sophisticated frameworks for multicultural education. Progressive education seeks to redefine "legitimate" knowledge as well as who is capable of imparting this knowledge. This vision goes well beyond the scope of separatist constructions within the debate on political correctness. As scholars who must urgently respond to the imperatives of an increasingly diverse and voluble American society, we can no longer be involved in the intellectually bankrupt either/or versions of representation and curricular change. Our project, as Evelyn Hu-DeHart outlines it in chapter 1, is no less than rethinking "America."

Notes

The authors want to thank Cynthia Enloe, Lisa Freeman, Henry Giroux, Elizabeth Higginbotham, and Wahneema Lubiano for their encouragement and their comments on earlier versions of this introduction; we are especially grateful to Wahneema Lubiano for her ideas about education as an arena where "people think themselves into being." The title of our introduction is taken from Toni Morrison, *Playing in the Dark: Whiteness and the Literary Imagination* (Cambridge, Mass.: Harvard University Press, 1992), 3.

1. We use the term "multicultural" cautiously, aware of the myriad ways "multicultural," "pluralism," and "diversity" have been appropriated to co-opt and water down African-American, ethnic, feminist, and gay and lesbian studies. As a product of the civil rights, Black Power, feminist, womanist, anti-imperialist, and gay and lesbian studies movements of the past quarter century, multicultural education rejects a mere listing of cultural differences by grounding cultural analyses in historical and global power relations and countering empty notions of pluralism that overlook critical examination of structural inequalities.

2. Troy Duster, "They Are Taking Over and Other Myths about Race on Campus," *Mother Jones*, September-October 1991: 30.

3. David Segal, "Cheney's Command: A Report from the NEH Trenches," *Lingua Franca*, September-October 1992: 58.

4. For a concise and comprehensive exposé on the influence of the right on higher education, see Ellen Messer-Davidow, "Doing the Right Thing," *Women's Review of Books* 9, no. 5 (February 1992): 19-20.

5. We have borrowed the term "triumphalists" from Evelyn Hu-DeHart, who uses it as an umbrella designation for the convergence of conservatives, neoconservatives (such as Charles Krauthammer, Lynne Cheney, George Will, and William Bennett), and traditionally liberal theorists (such as Arthur Schlesinger, Jr., Eugene Genovese, and C. Vann Woodward) who oppose multicultural educational change. We use this term since the conflicts about education have rendered problematic the traditional split between liberals and conservatives as defined in American political terms as key liberal and neoconservative intellectuals have joined with conservatives in their critique of multicultural education. (See Evelyn Hu-DeHart, chapter 1, and Chandra Mohanty, chapter 3, for discussion of this shift in political and cultural ties.)

6. Black faculty were 2.5 percent of the total in 1975 and now are 3.1 percent. Hispanics were 0.4 percent of the faculty in 1975 and 2.3 percent in 1991. There has been no change in the percentage of Asian-American faculty. See Margaret Andersen, "From the Editor," *Gender & Society*, December 1991: 454.

7. *Women's Review of Books* editors, "Revolution and Reaction," *Women's Review of Books* 9, no. 5 (February 1992): 13.

8. Roger Kimball, *Tenured Radicals: How Politics Has Corrupted Higher Education* (New York: Harper & Row, 1990).

9. A poll conducted by the Higher Education Research Institute at UCLA of 35,478 professors at 392 institutions found that 4.9 percent of professors rank themselves as far left, 36.8 percent as liberal, 40.2 percent as moderate, and 17.8 percent as conservative. See Troy Duster, "They Are Taking Over," 63.

10. Derrick Bell, *Faces at the Bottom of the Well: The Permanence of Racism* (New York: Basic Books, 1992).

11. Patricia J. Williams, "Defending the Gains," in *Beyond PC: Toward a Politics of Understanding*, ed. Patricia Aufderheide (St. Paul, Minn.: Graywolf, 1992), 193.

12. Todd Gitlin, "On the Virtues of a Loose Canon," in *Beyond PC*, ed. Patricia Aufderheide, 185-90.

13. Evan Carton, "The Self Besieged: American Identity on Campus and in the Gulf," *Tikkun* 6, no. 4 (1991): 40-47.

14. Henry Giroux, "Education Reform in the Age of George Bush," *Phi Delta Kappan*, May 1989: 728, 730.

15. Gerald David Jaynes, "Only Blacks Need Apply: African American Studies and Intellectual Diversity in American Colleges," *Reconstruction* 1, no. 3 (1991): 65-67.

16. Ibid., 67.

17. Pam Nadasen, "United We Stand," *Women's Review of Books* 9, no. 5 (February 1992): 31.

18. See, for example, Manning Marable, *The Crisis of Color and Democracy* (Monroe, Maine: Common Courage, 1992); Mari Matsuda, "Affirmative Action and Legal Knowledge: Planting Seeds in Plowed-Up Ground," *Harvard Women's Law Journal* 11 (1988): 1-17; Patricia J. Williams, *The Alchemy of Race and Rights: Diary of a Law Professor* (Cambridge, Mass.: Harvard University Press, 1991).

19. Nellie McKay, Patricia Hill Collins, Mae Henderson, and June Jordan, "The State of the Art," *Women's Review of Books* 8, no. 5 (February 1991): 23-26; Roger Wilkins, "Remembering the Bad Old Days," in *Beyond PC*, ed. Patricia Aufderheide, 161-64; Patricia J. Williams, "Defending the Gains," in *Beyond PC*, ed. Patricia Aufderheide.

20. Nellie McKay et al., "The State of the Art," 25.

21. C. Vann Woodward, "Freedom and the Universities," *New York Review* 38, no. 13 (July 18, 1991): 35.

22. Johnnella E. Butler, "Complicating the Question: Black Studies and Women's Studies," in *Women's Place in the Academy: Transforming the Liberal Arts Curriculum*, ed. Marilyn R. Schuster and Susan R. Van Dyne (Totowa, N.J.: Rowman & Allanheld, 1985), 74.

23. *Women's Review of Books* editors, "Revolution and Reaction," 13.

24. Catherine R. Stimpson, "Setting Agendas, Defining Challenges," *Women's Review of Books* 6, no. 5 (February 1989): 14.

25. Edward Said, "The Politics of Knowledge," in *Debating P.C.*, ed. Paul Berman (New York: Laurel, 1992), 182.

26. For analysis of the ties between women's studies and black/ethnic studies, see Johnnella E. Butler, "The Difficult Dialogue of Curriculum Transformation: Ethnic Studies and Women's Studies," in *Transforming the Curriculum: Ethnic Studies and Women's Studies*, ed. Johnnella E. Butler and John C. Walter (Albany, N.Y.: State University of New York Press, 1991), 1-20; Margaret L. Andersen, "Women's Studies/Black Studies: Learning from Our Common Pasts, Forging a Common Future," in *Women's Place in the Academy*, ed. Marilyn R. Schuster and Susan R. Van Dyne, 72.

27. The terms the authors use in this volume include "multicultural," "democratic," "inclusive," "pluralism," "strong multiculturalism," and "race-, class-, and gender-conscious education," among others.

28. Edward W. Said, "The Politics of Knowledge," in *Debating P.C.*, ed. Paul Berman, 183.

29. Toni Morrison, *Playing in the Dark*, 3.

30. In Nellie McKay et al., "The State of the Art," 26.

31. Ibid.

32. Chandra Talpade Mohanty, "Introduction: Cartographies of Struggle in Third World Women and the Politics of Feminism," in *Third World Women and the Politics of Feminism*, ed. Chandra Talpade Mohanty, Ann Russo, and Lourdes Torres (Indianapolis: Indiana University Press, 1991), 11.

33. In a critique of legal education, Patricia Williams points out the dangers of insulating legal scholarship from struggles for justice and equality. Legal education has lost its important link with such transformative movements as the civil rights movement, as is clearly seen in the fact that "the Rehnquist court can cavalierly undo what took so many lives and years to build: the process of legal education mirrors the social resistance to antidiscrimination law." Patricia Williams, "Defending the Gains," in *Beyond PC*, ed. Patricia Aufderheide, 195.

34. Maxine Baca Zinn, Lynn Weber Cannon, Elizabeth Higginbotham, and Bonnie Thornton Dill, "The Costs of Exclusionary Practices in Women's Studies," *Signs* 11, no. 2 (1986): 293.

35. Johnnella Butler, "Difficult Dialogues," *Women's Review of Books* 6, no. 5 (February 1989): 16.

36. When Stimpson's article was published in 1989, she said of this second group, "The future of this clubhouse is unclear. It may have the money to add a new wing and start up a membership drive. The media may also find this clubhouse a hot new story." How right she was, and frighteningly so.

37. Catherine R. Stimpson, "Setting Agendas, Defining Challenges," 14.

38. Ibid.

39. Gloria Anzaldúa, "How to Tame a Wild Tongue," in *Borderlands/La Frontera: The New Mestiza* (San Francisco: Spinsters/Aunt Lute, 1987), 59.

40. Derrick Bell, *And We Are Not Saved* (New York: Basic Books, 1987): 34.

41. Audre Lorde, "The Master's Tools Will Never Dismantle the Master's House," in *Sister Outsider* (Trumansburg, N.Y.: Crossing, 1984), 110-13.

42. Because we have consolidated progressive debates within such a wide and diverse field as multicultural education, this book has its own gaps and absences. By staying well within the boundaries of higher education in the United States we miss an opportunity for some rich and complex comparative analyses of instituting multicultural changes within different national contexts. The ongoing struggles, strategies, and successes of marginalized groups within British and Canadian society and education are cases in point. In addition, the struggles of people with disabilities to gain representation within the curriculum and academy and the contributions of Jewish studies are inadequately addressed in this volume. See Howard Adelman, "Is Jewish Studies Ethnic Studies?" and Evelyn Torton Beck, "The Politics of Jewish Invisibility in Women's Studies," in *Transforming the Curriculum: Ethnic and Women's Studies*, ed. Johnnella E. Butler and John C. Walter; Lynn Davidman and Shelly Tenenbaum, eds., *Feminist Perspectives on Jewish Studies*, forthcoming from Yale University Press.

43. Patricia Aufderheide, ed., *Beyond PC*; Paul Berman, ed., *Debating PC*.

PART I

Moral and Political Visions of Multicultural Education

Chapter 1

Rethinking America: The Practice and Politics of Multiculturalism in Higher Education

Evelyn Hu-DeHart

Twenty-five years ago, inspired by the civil rights movement and further buoyed by the energies of the antiwar movement, a new generation of students across the nation took to their college campuses, invaded and occupied administration offices, startled and no doubt terrified a few presidents, deans, and professors. Students of color—then called "Third World" students in solidarity with the colonized Third World whence so many of their forebears came as slaves, coolies, or immigrants— demanded some fundamental changes in higher education. Faculties and administrations then were still almost exclusively white and mostly male. The student body, while more women and some minorities were admitted in the sixties, was only somewhat less monolithic than the faculty and administration. The curriculum had been fairly static since probably the first decades of the century and the idea of "multiculturalism" had not yet been invented, but a new vocabulary was emerging to name the many empowerment projects appearing in California and around the country during and immediately after the great civil rights movement.

Negroes became blacks, and Mexican-Americans became Chicanos; American Indians preferred to be called Native Americans, and Americans of Asian provenance and heritage came together to create yet another collective identity, the Asian-Americans. Ethnic pride joined Black

3

Power and Brown Power. Their protests, together with those of feminists, antiwar activists, and gay and lesbian activists, continued the momentum established by the civil rights movement to challenge the status quo and to empower the excluded. These newly awakened, newly enfranchised Americans shared a long common history of exclusion as well as a tortuous, often violent, history of struggle and resistance. During the late sixties, the changes were coming on fast and hard, one on top of another. By no means confined to college campuses, these movements were nevertheless largely spearheaded by young people, who had the most to gain from a redefined American society, who had more time and luxury to think and organize than working people, and who discovered that campuses afforded them a greater measure of freedom of speech and assembly (especially after the Berkeley Free Speech movement of the mid-1960s) than most other locations in American society.

Beginning in 1968 at San Francisco State and the University of California campuses at Berkeley and Santa Barbara, then on campuses across the nation over the next twenty-five years, students of color have been demanding greater access to higher education, recruitment of more faculty of color, and the creation of programs that have come to be known collectively as ethnic studies and separately by a variety of names, including black studies (later also called Afro-American studies and African-American studies), Chicano or Mexican-American studies (later, also Puerto Rican studies or, more generically, Latino studies), American Indian or Native American studies, and Asian-American studies. These various ethnic studies programs are the beginning of multicultural curriculum reform in higher education.

So what is ethnic studies? First of all, it is distinct from area studies programs that arose out of American imperialism in the Third World and bore names such as African studies, Asian studies, and Latin American studies. Their original, founding purpose was to focus on U.S.-Third World relations and to train specialists to uphold U.S. hegemony in regions of the world where the United States had heavy economic and political investments. Although area studies scholars have become far more critical of U.S.-Third World relations since the antiwar movement of the sixties and many have adopted Third World perspectives in their work, they are still predominantly white male scholars entrenched in established departments, subscribing to and benefiting from traditional patterns of distributing power and rewards in the academy and from financial support from private foundations and the U.S. government.[1]

Ethnic studies, on the other hand, having grown out of grass-roots student and community challenges to the prevailing academic power structure and Eurocentric curriculum of our colleges and universities, were insurgent programs with a subversive agenda from the outset, hence suspect and illegitimate even as they were grudgingly allowed into the academy. Program definitions vary from campus to campus and change over time. Chicano scholar Ramón Gutiérrez, founder and chair of the Department of Ethnic Studies at the University of California at San Diego, provides a good general description of ethnic studies as

> the study of the social, cultural, and historical forces that have shaped
> the development of America's diverse ethnic peoples over the last 500
> years and which continue to shape our future. Focusing on immigration,
> slavery, and confinement, those three social processes that combined to
> create in the United States a nation of nations, ethnic studies intensively
> examines the histories, languages, and cultures of America's racial and
> ethnic groups in and of themselves, in their relationships to each other,
> and particularly, *in structural contexts of power.* (emphasis added)[2]

In practice, then, ethnic studies has focused on "marginalized and largely powerless groups" who are racially constructed as distinct from the Europeans who dominated America and defined its identity and are socially constructed as "minorities." African-Americans, Asian-Americans, Latino Americans, and Native Americans have clearly distinct histories in America, but they share a common experience of having been historically denied full access to the benefits and opportunities of American society because of racism and other forms of oppression.

For twenty-five years, despite fits and starts, peaks and valleys, ethnic studies programs have survived and spread from their origins in California to all parts of the country.[3] After some serious cutbacks in the budgetary crisis of the mid-1970s to mid-1980s, they are now back bigger and stronger than ever, revitalized, reorganized, and in some cases reconceptualized, increasingly institutionalized, and definitely here to stay. They have produced a prodigious amount of new scholarship, which, as in all disciplines and fields of learning, includes some that is bad, some that is mediocre, and much that is good and innovative. The new perspectives are intended not only to increase our knowledge base, but also, in time, to transform the whole. Their deep and widespread influence is definitely being felt, as we shall soon see.

Given their history, it is entirely logical that a disproportionate number of ethnic studies programs have been established in public institutions, which are more susceptible to public pressure, and in the western United States, which has a faster growing and more diverse population than other regions. The biggest and most powerful programs—those that incorporate more than one ethnic studies area and have a research emphasis in addition to undergraduate and graduate teaching and community service, with full or near department status—are found in four public research universities in the West: the University of California Berkeley's Department of Ethnic Studies (with some twenty years' history, one of the oldest and the only one that offers a Ph.D. in ethnic studies), the University of California San Diego's Department of Ethnic Studies (created in 1990), the University of Washington's Department of American Ethnic Studies (created in the mid-1980s by consolidating existing small ethnic studies programs), and the University of Colorado at Boulder's Center for Studies of Ethnicity and Race in America (created in 1987 by consolidating existing programs and creating new ones).[4] Most ethnic studies scholars probably subscribe to a progressive political agenda. Not all, but many, are "public intellectuals," that is, scholars who apply theory and knowledge to practice and speak out on critical issues facing U.S. society in order to educate a broad general public and also give leadership and a voice to minority communities.

Concurrent with the establishment of ethnic studies programs, American society has continued to undergo dramatic changes, for better and for worse. The civil rights movement might have removed the last vestiges of legal apartheid in this country, but the rich and powerful and their political surrogates invented other means to continue to segregate, divide, exclude, and in many other ways deny equal opportunity to the historically marginalized communities of color. Two and a half decades after the Kerner Commission Report, which spoke of two Americas — one rich, one poor, one white, one black — the gulf between these two Americas has grown wider than ever, especially during the Reagan-Bush years. To be more specific, by 1992, 1 percent of the American population had gained control of more wealth than 90 percent of the society, a situation that parallels the intolerable reality of much of the Third World.[5] Can it be denied that such gaping economic inequities were a key contributing factor to the Los Angeles uprising of May 1992?

Indeed, we have learned to our dismay that legal reforms brought about by the civil rights movement have not solved the problem of the color line, first identified and named by W. E. B. Du Bois at the beginning of this century. Most American institutions, notably including higher education, still remain largely impenetrable to the vast majority of those on the wrong side of the color line.

Dramatic and very significant demographic changes have also occurred in America during this same quarter century. Since 1965, when U.S. immigration laws eliminated the "national origins" quotas that had clearly favored Europeans, many new immigrants from Asia, Latin America, and the Caribbean (and to a lesser extent Africa) have greatly outnumbered the traditional white European immigrants for the first time in history. Additional impetus for accelerated immigration from Asia and the Latin American/Caribbean region have come as consequences of U.S. economic, political, and military interventions during the post–World War II era. From 1965 to the 1990s, over 80 percent of all new immigrants have been non-Europeans. Almost 9 million came in a great surge in the 1980s. This new wave of immigration accounts for the doubling of the Asian-American population and the 60 percent increase in Hispanic people in the United States.[6]

The upshot of these new immigration patterns is that the American population is fast becoming "colored" and ever more diverse—by race, ethnicity, religion, language, food, music, art, literature, and many other cultural expressions. In fact, with over half of its population already non-European in 1992, California gives us a glimpse of the national future, which is projected to become, by 2050—to use an amusing oxymoron— "majority minority." The relatively higher reproductive rates of minority Americans as well as their lower age distributions mean that people of color will increasingly show up in our classrooms and our work force. In short, there is a demographic imperative at work here: we have no choice but to educate these young Americans of color if America is to remain politically healthy and economically competitive.

A further concern should follow: will Americans of color also integrate our political and economic leadership, not just our classrooms and our work force? Should we not also respond to a moral imperative to bring about a truly pluralistic democracy? To not perpetuate the hypocrisy of the past, when whites ruled while nonwhites toiled in a so-called democracy? If we are not to repeat the sad history of excluding nonwhite Americans from the Jeffersonian pursuit of happiness, then we educators have a crucial role to play, and multicultural education is part of the solution. In short, as we approach the beginning of the third millennium, we must acknowledge our responsibility to educate for citizenship and leadership all members of a vast pluralistic democracy in a world that is, moreover, becoming more interdependent.

Finally, multiculturalists are also heeding the calls of an intellectual imperative to correct the omissions and distortions of the work and perspectives of generations of "triumphalist" scholars and teachers.[7] Triumphalists are conservative, neoconservative, and even liberal historians, writers, high government officials, and opinion makers who champion a traditionalist view of American history as an unbroken string of successes, who willingly ignore inconvenient inconsistencies and readily rationalize the failures. They pronounce the triumphant march toward freedom and democracy true and universal, good and fair for all times and for all Americans. Furthermore, since American triumphs are built on the traditions of Western civilization, American culture is Western culture, thus American national identity is European-derived.

Rather than speaking for others, let me state this thesis in the words of some of its most articulate, impassioned proponents:

—Neoconservative newspaper columnist George Will wishes to "affirm this fact: America is predominantly a product of the Western tradition and is predominantly good because that tradition is good."[8]

—Neoconservative writer and editor Charles Krauthammer, in discussing the triumphalist march of Euro-Americans in the "opening of the American West," otherwise known as Manifest Destiny, rationalized the genocide of millions of Native Americans and the forcing of survivors into "homelands" this way: "The real question is: What eventually grew on this bloodied soil? . . . The great modern civilizations of the Americas—a new world of individual rights, an ever-expanding circle of liberty, and twice in this century, a savior of the world from total barbarism."[9]

—Liberal historian Arthur Schlesinger, Jr., asserts:

> The U.S. escaped the divisiveness of a multiethnic society by a brilliant solution: the creation of a brand new identity. The point of America was not to preserve old cultures but to forge a new, American culture. "By an intermixture with our people," President George Washington told VP John Adams, "immigrants will get assimilated to our customs, measures and laws: in a word, soon become one people."

What these "immigrants" have in common, Schlesinger continues, is "the Western tradition [which] is the source of the ideas of individual freedom and political democracy."[10]

—Yale historian and undergraduate dean Donald Kagan lectured to a recent incoming freshman class:

> Except for the slaves brought from Africa, most came voluntarily, as families and individuals, usually eager to satisfy desires that could not be met in their former homelands. They swiftly became citizens and, within a generation or so, Americans. In our own time finally . . . African-Americans also have achieved freedom, equality before the law, and full citizenship. . . . What they have in common and what brings them together is a system of laws and beliefs that shaped the establishment of the country, a system developed within the context of Western Civilization.[11]

For many Americans educated and socialized in this dominant version of history, which is also the official view, the one usually taught in our schools and universities, it may seem that nothing is wrong with these statements. Indeed, for Americans from European immigrant backgrounds, they probably ring true as accurate renditions of their shared historical experience in America's great melting pot. And they can justifiably take pride in having defined "our national identity" and "our national culture."

But there is also a problem with this version of national history for Americans of non-European heritage, some of whom have been here since before the Europeans arrived. The fact of the matter is that the "our" in "our national identity" and "our national culture" and the "we" in "we the people" historically have been exclusive. Bluntly put, these "other" Americans have lived another history. For one truth that is omitted in all these declarations of Western triumphalism is that the images of the people who built America and benefited from it are overwhelmingly and almost exclusively those of European immigrants and their descendants.

African-Americans, as even Donald Kagan had to concede, were not voluntary immigrants and were not allowed to take part in the formation of the nation. Indeed, in order to sidestep the obvious contradiction between slavery and "all men are created equal," the Founding Fathers — all white male property owners — defined blacks and slaves as less than full human beings. And even if Kagan wishes to suggest that equality before the law has brought them nominal freedom and full citizenship, the reality is fraught with contradictions, as the Los Angeles uprising of May 1992 demonstrated all too clearly. The lingering and still institutionalized legacies of slavery, Jim Crow traditions, and legal apartheid that endure to this day, and that have left most African-Americans still largely excluded or alienated from national life, cannot be blithely brushed aside, as triumphalists like Kagan would wish.[12]

The federal government did not extend universal citizenship to Native Americans, the original inhabitants of this land, until 1924, shamed into doing so only after many had served and died in World War I. By then, most Native American peoples had lost their land and waters; many more had been destroyed by war and disease; still others had been relocated far from their original homelands. Those not wantonly thrown into the streets of the inner cities to sink or swim on their own are still confined to reservations on desolate land in remote places, unemployed and unable to scratch out a decent living, out of sight and therefore out of our conscience and consciousness. Is it any wonder that so many Native Americans protested Columbus quincentenary celebrations, which to them appeared to be celebrating a history of genocide? As peoples whose relationships with the U.S. government were founded on treaties (a Western concept, after all) signed over the course of three centuries —

hundreds of which still remain on the books—they continue to insist on the sovereignty that signing treaties explicitly recognized. Why is it that triumphalists seldom speak of the sovereign rights of Indian peoples in America, not to mention physical and cultural genocide committed against them in the name of Western democracy and freedom?[13]

During the mid-nineteenth century, America won by force or bought at bargain-basement prices huge chunks of land from Mexico, amounting to half of Mexico's national territory, and incorporated wholesale the vast, settled population of mainly Spanish-speaking mestizos (people of mixed Spanish-Indian heritage). Although according to the Treaty of Guadalupe Hidalgo of 1848 the people were promised citizenship and the right to retain their languages and cultures, these commitments have been honored mainly in the breach. Later arrivals from Mexico have often been branded wetbacks and illegal aliens, seldom welcomed as legitimate immigrants. These brown-skinned Mexicans became a disenfranchised, disadvantaged minority group whose ranks would later be swelled by other forcefully incorporated, dark-skinned Spanish speakers on American soil, including Puerto Ricans, collectively known by the government-imposed term "Hispanics."

Their distant connection with Catholic Spain and more recent connection with chaotic, Spanish-speaking Latin America (notably Mexico, Central America, and parts of the Caribbean) render them problematic for purposes of racial classification. Are Hispanics white and European, or are most of them "different" by virtue of their religion (Catholicism), their language (Spanish), and their intermarriage with Indians and blacks?[14]

In this brief and admittedly oversimplified summary of the history of non-European peoples in the United States, Asian/Pacific-Americans remain to be considered. They indeed did migrate to America, but usually not voluntarily, at least not in the nineteenth century when they first came as cheap laborers, lonely men for the most part unaccompanied by families and kin. If European immigrants to America were regarded as potential citizens, Asians unfortunately were not, for it was decided even before their arrival that they would have no access to citizenship. The Naturalization Law enacted in 1790, which remained in effect until 1952, specifically barred nonwhite immigrants from citizenship. Thus, when tens of thousands of Asian workers were brought to the American West during the nineteenth century to build the railroads, work the mines, and clear land for agriculture, they found themselves denied full political participation and integration into U.S. society. From 1882 to World War II, the Chinese were the only people in American history singled out as an undesirable "race" that must be barred from further immigration to this country. During World War II, thousands of Japanese alien residents on the West Coast—also ineligible for citizenship at the time—and their American-born children were interned in camps behind barbed-wire fences, even though not a single one of them had committed any act of disloyalty or sedition against their adopted country.[15] The recent (since the late 1970s) elevation of Asian-Americans to the status of "model minority," deemed superior to other minorities because of their apparent greater ability to assimilate white middle-class virtues, cannot erase this long history of exclusion and unequal treatment.

In summary, from the vantage points of Native Americans, African-Americans, Mexican-Americans, and Asian-Americans, there is an underside to Western triumphalism in America that has not been acknowledged, recorded, and told. The history of individual choice and freedom, and of democracy, unfortunately does not speak to the reality that most of them and their predecessors in America have experienced. These fundamental contradictions—between America's multiracial origins and growing multiracial reality on the one hand and its still dominant self-image as white and European on the other, between ideals of freedom and democracy for all alongside a racialist social order that historically relegated people of color to an inferior status as cheap labor at best and extraneous population at worst, but in any case not equal citizens—are the concern of multicultural scholars.

The noted historian Alexander Saxton, who happens to be white and male, says it well in his book *The Rise and Fall of the White Republic*:

> America's supposed openness to newcomers throughout most of its history has been racially selective. By the time of Jefferson and Jackson the nation had already assumed the form of a *racially exclusive democracy*—democratic in the sense that it sought to provide equal opportunities for the pursuit of happiness by its white citizens through the enslavement of African Americans, extermination of Indians, and territorial expansion at the expense of Indians and Mexicans. If there was an "American orientation" to newcomers, it was not toward giving equal opportunity to all but toward inviting entry by white Europeans and excluding others. It is true that the United States absorbed a variety of cultural patterns among European immigrants at the same time that it was erecting a *white supremacist social structure. Moderately tolerant of European ethnic diversity, the nation remained adamantly intolerant of racial diversity. It is this crucial difference that has been permitted to drop from sight.* (emphasis added)[16]

Ethnic studies scholars and others committed to the multicultural project are determined to bring this "crucial difference" back into focus. For contrary to the Western triumphalists, multicultural scholars assert that there was no national identity or national culture that embraced all Americans, and thus no actual consensus or unity ever existed to be ripped apart by the newborn attention to the histories of the excluded groups. Rather, an official history has been shoved down the throats of those once unable to speak for themselves.

While triumphalists insist that there is really only one historical viewpoint, or at least one true or "best" viewpoint, multiculturalists acknowledge multiple perspectives that depend on status and station in society, which is determined in turn by race, class, gender, and other factors. These multiple perspectives, no one of which speaks the whole truth, can be in conflict with one another, but together they form a more complete picture of our national history, our national identity, our national culture.[17] Accordingly, the New York State Department of Education Curriculum Task Force calls for a "new conceptualization of history, one that recognize[s] multiplicity and contradiction instead of homogeneity and consensus as the basis of our national community."[18] In short, multiculturalists would say that only when the triumphalists confront the past honestly and acknowledge it openly, when the excluded Americans can come forth freely to reclaim their histories, and when institutional barriers to equal opportunity for all Americans have been removed can we speak of seeking common ground, of forging unity and consensus. Until then, liberals like Schlesinger will plead for unity in vain, while rap singers speak greater truths to young blacks in the 'hood and Latinos in the barrio.[19]

Finally, these extreme differences of opinion and interpretation of American history and contemporary reality between the multiculturalists and the triumphalists have given rise to equally sharp national politics. This essay would be incomplete without mention of the battle that is raging on our campuses and even more in the news media. In this battle, which would be amusing were the stakes not so high, triumphalist propagandists have found a handy weapon in charges of "political correctness" leveled against multiculturalists.[20]

Among the sins identified on college campuses are support for curricular changes including multiculturalism, women's and feminist studies, gay and lesbian studies, new cultural and literary studies that challenge the humanities canon, and bilingual education; support for policies such as affirmative action (specifically the recruitment and retention of faculty and students of color) and for so-called race-based scholarships (which account for an insignificant portion of total financial aid monies and are no different in principle from other designated scholarships); and opposition to hate speech and verbal harassment directed primarily at women and minority students. What all these alleged transgressions have in common is that, imperfect though implementation of them may be, they are serious efforts to make the colleges and universities more *inclusive*, in terms of both the knowledge that is produced and imparted, and those who are allowed in as participants.

Upon close examination, charges of overzealous political correctness are but a grab bag of every educational and cultural challenge that dominant Americans find destabilizing, and they have much to do with a growing sense of insecurity about the future. The demise of communism has deprived the United States of a convenient scapegoat for whatever goes wrong domestically and internationally; as the lone superpower, its own economy extremely shaky, the United States has to find new culprits to blame for failures and new ways to flex its muscles. Thus the United States remorselessly beats up poor nations (most recently Panama and Iraq) after first propping up and arming their dictators. Domestically, the triumphalists' reaction to destabilizing changes that challenge the monolithic official view of the past is to curtail discussion just when it has been opened up to previously excluded voices and perspectives. Could it be that these upholders of Western cultural superiority are not really motivated by reverence for the past "but by an aggressive desire to lay hold of the present and future"?[21]

Among those found to be most guilty of political correctness are "tenured sixties radicals" in the professoriate and their misguided allies among campus administrators. The divide is not between liberals and conservatives as defined in American political terms, for many liberal intellectuals (Schlesinger, James David Barber, Eugene Genovese, C. Vann Woodward) seem to be as unsettled as neoconservative stalwarts such as former secretary of education and drug czar William Bennett, National Endowment for the Humanities chair Lynne Cheney, and Irving Kristol, one of the original neoconservative intellectuals.

The campaign builds its case against multiculturalists with alarmist, sensationalist, sometimes hysterical, often ludicrous accounts and tirades supplied by traditionalist academics such as Allan Bloom (*Closing of the American Mind*, 1987), E. D. Hirsch (*Cultural Literacy*, 1987), and Roger Kimball (*Tenured Radicals: How Politics Has Corrupted Our Higher Education*, 1990). But perhaps the best read and most effective among P.C.-busting tracts is the 1991 best-seller by polemical journalist Dinesh D'Souza entitled *Illiberal Education: The Politics of Race and Sex on Campus*. Writing in an easygoing style geared both to entertain and to inflame an uninformed but concerned public, D'Souza, an immigrant from Portuguese India, portrays himself as a person of color and a reasonable moderate who accidentally discovered P.C. horrors on the campuses. Cavalier about facts and often disregarding intellectual honesty and balance, he recounts in sensationalist fashion stories about affirmative action and curricular changes at five of the country's leading public and private institutions: Harvard, Stanford, Duke, Berkeley, and Michigan.[22]

Institutional bases for the anti-P.C. campaign are provided by such conservative think tanks as the Heritage Foundation (which sponsors D'Souza), the Hudson Institute (where Bennett currently hangs his hat), and the Manhattan Institute (where President Reagan's designated Hispanic, Linda Chavez, wrote *Out of the Barrio: Towards a New Politics of Hispanic Assimilation*). The campaign is also waged out of new institutions created specifically for the campus war against student and faculty affirmative action and multicultural curricular changes. Key among the new organizations is the Madison Institute, founded by Bloom and Bennett, which merged with Kristol's older Institute of Educational Affairs. Its many notable activities include the Intercollegiate Network, which sponsors and channels funding to some sixty conservative campus newspapers after the model of the notorious *Dartmouth Review*, whose first editor was none other than the celebrated Mr. D'Souza. Another new organization is the National Association of Scholars (NAS), made up mainly of conservative and neoconservative—and some liberal—white male faculty members disturbed by campus environment and curricular changes.[23] Moreover, the campaign is very significantly aided and abetted by powerful governmental bodies such as the National Endowment for the Humanities (NEH) and its chair, Lynne Cheney (wife of Defense Secretary Dick Cheney), who is touted by admirer George Will as the "secretary of domestic defense," whose multiculturalist foes are more dangerous than the "foreign adversaries" her husband faces.[24]

The anti-P.C. campaign is well financed by several right-wing foundations, notably former treasury secretary William Simon's Olin Foundation, along with the Coors, Scaife, and Sid Richardson foundations.[25] It is important to note that, as in any well-orchestrated campaign, the think tanks, the foundations, the governmental organizations, the faculty associations, and the sixty or so conservative student newspapers who serve as campus watchdogs are all intricately interrelated through interlocking memberships and common sources of financial support, (dis)information, and guidance. In a single round of nominations for the NEH advisory board, four out of eight of Cheney's choices were NAS activists, including founding member and University of Pennsylvania historian Alan Kors, who once crudely branded his multicultural colleagues as "the barbarian in our midst."[26]

Against this well-organized, well-heeled adversary, the decentralized, multidirectional multiculturalists, with enormous diversity within their ranks, are certainly no match in the propaganda war, at least not for the moment.[27] But they have demographics and history on their side, and on the vast majority of U.S. campuses, students, faculty, and staff overwhelmingly support some degree of multiculturalism. This insurmountable barrier explains why triumphalists have chosen to aim their propaganda at the larger American public. Masterful at manipulating media already too willing to sensationalize, they hope that public pressure will eventually silence the multiculturalists.

For our part, scholars and educators must also keep in mind the dynamic nature of intellectual and academic life: there is always change. In the thirteenth century at the University of Paris, the now canonical works of Aristotle were suspect and vigorously resisted by the ecclesiastical authorities then in control.[28] Humanist scholar Bruce Kuklick reminds us that each intellectual era has its "sacred texts and canonical works" and that there are always "disputes about the interpretation of these books and the wisdom of studying them." And the "quest for truth," he writes, always takes place "in a context that is also a quest for preservation of the power of those engaged in developing the higher learning."[29]

America today is not the America of the 1850s or the 1950s, and we can look forward to more changes in the years to come. Education and curricula always adapt to changing values, ideals, concerns, allegiances, and visions. At the crux of the fierce debate between multiculturalists and triumphalists is the meaning of America: who are we, who belongs, who determines, who controls, whose values prevail, in whose image shall the country be made? Are we a civilization in decline because we cannot agree at this point on "national culture," or are we at an exciting crossroads, engaged in lively debate about our national future?

Multiculturalism is about rethinking America.

Notes

1. For a discussion of the historical and historiographical, political, methodological, and other relationships between area studies and ethnic studies (specifically Asian-American studies), see the articles by Shirley Hune, Evelyn Hu-DeHart, Gary Y. Okihiro, and Sucheta Mazumdar in *Asian Americans: Comparative and Global Perspectives*, ed. Shirley Hune et al. (Pullman: Washington State University Press, 1991).

2. [Ramón Gutiérrez], Proposal for the Creation of a Department of Ethnic Studies at the University of California at San Diego, unpublished document, January 25, 1990.

3. There are various accounts of the founding and histories of different ethnic studies programs. See, for example, chapter 12 of Rodolfo Acuña's *Occupied America* (Harper & Row, various editions) for a concise history of Chicano studies; more recently, *Amerasia Journal* devoted a special issue (vol. 12, no. 1, 1989) to the founding of Asian-American studies.

4. These four programs are also quite different in structure and orientation. I cannot elaborate in this brief essay; for details on the programs, write the chairs or directors.

5. Salim Muwakkil, "L.A. Lessons Go Unlearned . . . ," in *In These Times*, May 27–June 9, 1992: 3; also see the *New York Times* cover story of March 5, 1992, headlined "The 1980s: A Very Good Time for the Very Rich. Data Shows the Top 1% Got 60% of Gain in Decade's Boom."

6. The national media have been publishing numerous analyses of the 1990 census data as they are made available. One is a *USA Today* cover story (May 29-31, 1992) by Margaret Usdansky, " 'Diverse' Fits Nation Better Than 'Normal.' "

7. I borrowed the idea of identifying traditionalists as "triumphalists" from Gene Bell-Villada, who used the term to characterize Bloom and Hirsch in "Critical Appraisals of American Education: Dilemmas and Contradictions in the Work of Bloom and Hirsch," *International Journal of Politics, Culture and Society* 3, no. 4 (1990): 484-511.

8. Quoted in Mary Louise Pratt, "Humanities for the Future: Reflections on the Western Culture Debate at Stanford," in *The Politics of Liberal Education*, ed. Darryl J. Gless and Barbara Herrnstein Smith (Durham, N.C.: Duke University Press, 1992), 25.

9. *Time*, May 27, 1991.

10. *Time*, July 8, 1991; *Chronicle of Higher Education*, February 6, 1991.

11. *Yale Alumni Magazine*, November 1990.

12. There are too many good books on the African-American experience to mention here. A good interpretive history is Manning Marable, *How Capitalism Underdeveloped Black America* (Boston: South End, 1982).

13. Little has been written about Native Americans by Native Americans. Probably the best single reader available is M. Annette Jaimes, ed., *The State of Native America* (Boston: South End, 1992).

14. Still probably the single most comprehensive compendium of Chicano history and most widely used is Rodolfo Acuña, *Occupied America* (New York: Harper & Row, periodically updated editions).

15. Good interpretive histories of Asian-Americans include Sucheng Chan, *Asian Americans* (Boston: Twayne, 1991) and Ronald Takaki, *Strangers from a Different Shore: A History of Asian Americans* (New York: Viking Penguin, 1989).

16. Alexander Saxton, *The Rise and Fall of the White Republic* (London: Verso, 1990), 10.

17. Joan Scott, "Liberal Historians: A Unitary Vision," *Chronicle of Higher Education*, September 11, 1991: B1-B2.

18. "One Nation, Many Peoples: A Declaration of Cultural Interdependence," Report of the New York State Social Studies Review and Development Committee, June 1991.

19. One young African-American scholar undertaking serious study of the appeal and significance of rap music is Robin D. G. Kelley, who published a short essay on the subject in *The Nation*, June 8, 1992: 793-96.

20. So much has been written and published on the debate about political correctness, mostly but not exclusively in the popular media, that two anthologies have appeared: Paul Berman, ed., *Debating P.C.: The Controversy over Political Correctness on College Campuses* (New York: Dell, 1992) and Patricia Aufderheide, ed., *Beyond PC: Toward a Politics of Understanding* (St. Paul, Minn.: Graywolf, 1992). In addition, the volume edited by Gless and Smith cited in note 8 contains essays on curricular issues.

21. Pratt, "Humanities for the Future," in *Politics of Liberal Education*, ed. Gless and Smith, 15.

22. The alternative media have been much more aggressive in pursuing D'Souza's personal background and scrutinizing his so-called research. See, for example, Scott Henson, "The Education of Dinesh D'Souza: How an Angry Young Man Parlayed Right-wing

Money into National Attention," *Texas Observer*, September 20, 1991: 6-9. For examples of how responsible critics have rebutted D'Souza, see Bob Byer's article in the *Chronicle of Higher Education*, June 19, 1991: B2; on how D'Souza grossly distorted a Harvard incident involving Professor Stephen Thernstrom, see Professor Jon Wiener's exposé, "What Happened at Harvard?" *The Nation*, September 30, 1991. Unfortunately, while Cheney, Bennett, et al. have repeatedly recycled D'Souza's versions of these incidents, the mainstream media have not picked up the corrected versions, thus letting stand the original damage.

23. The *Chronicle of Higher Education* first focused attention on the National Association of Scholars in its November 23, 1988, issue and has subsequently reported on NAS activities numerous times. Another substantive exposé of the group is Jacob Weisberg's "NAS: Who Are These Guys Anyway?" *Lingua Franca*, April 1991: 34-39.

24. *Newsweek*, April 22, 1991.

25. On funding sources, see Fox Butterfield, "The Right Breeds a College Press Network," *New York Times*, October 24, 1990; Jon Wiener, "The Olin Money Tree: Dollars for Neocon Scholars," *The Nation*, January 1, 1990: 12-14; Liz McMillen, "Olin Fund Gives Millions to Conservative Activities in Higher Education," *Chronicle of Higher Education*, January 22, 1992: A31; and Jacob Weisberg, "Who Are These Guys?"

26. *Chronicle of Higher Education*, July 8, 1992: A15.

27. On the multicultural side, there is nothing comparable to the NAS, the Intercollegiate Network, and funders like Olin, and there is nothing that resembles centralized direction. There are, of course, many professional and academic associations built on issues such as affirmative action, bilingual education, ethnic studies, women's studies, and cultural and literary studies that collectively involve thousands of active members. Specifically organized in opposition to the NAS are two faculty groups, neither of which has the NAS's bountiful funding: Teachers for a Democratic Culture (Professor Gerald Graff, University of Chicago, founder) and the Union of Democratic Intellectuals (Professor Stanley Aronowitz, City University of New York Graduate Center, founder).

28. Francis Oakley, "Against Nostalgia: Reflections on Our Present Discontents in American Higher Education," in *Politics of Liberal Education*, ed. Gless and Smith, 285.

29. Bruce Kuklick, "The Emergence of the Humanities," in *Politics of Liberal Education*, ed. Gless and Smith, 211.

Chapter 2

The New Cultural Politics of Difference

Cornel West

In these last few years of the twentieth century, a significant shift in the sensibilities and outlooks of critics and artists is emerging. In fact, I would go so far as to claim that a new kind of cultural worker, associated with a new politics of difference, is in the making. These new forms of intellectual consciousness advance reconceptions of the vocation of critic and artist, attempting to undermine the prevailing disciplinary divisions of labor in the academy, museum, mass media, and gallery networks while preserving modes of critique within the ubiquitous commodification of culture in the global village. Distinctive features of the new cultural politics of difference are to trash the monolithic and homogeneous in the name of diversity, multiplicity, and heterogeneity; to reject the abstract, general, and universal in light of the concrete, specific, and particular; and to historicize, contextualize, and pluralize by highlighting the contingent, provisional, variable, tentative, shifting, and changing. Needless to say, these gestures are not new in the history of criticism or art, yet what makes them novel—along with the cultural politics they produce—is what constitutes difference and how, the weight and gravity it is given in representation, and the way in which highlighting issues like exterminism, empire, class, race, gender, sexual orientation, age, nation, nature, and region at this historical moment acknowledges some discontinuity and disruption from previous forms of cultural critique.

To put it bluntly, the new cultural politics of difference consists of creative responses to the precise circumstances of our present moment—especially those of marginalized First World agents who shun degraded self-representations, articulating instead their sense of the flow of history in light of the contemporary terrors, anxieties, and fears of highly commercialized North Atlantic capitalist cultures (with their escalating xenophobias against people of color, Jews, women, gays, lesbians, and the elderly). The thawing, yet still rigid, Second World ex-communist cultures (with increasing nationalist revolts against the legacy of hegemonic party henchmen) and the diverse cultures of the majority of inhabitants on the globe smothered by international communication cartels and repressive postcolonial elites (sometimes in the name of communism, as in Ethiopia) or starved by austere World Bank and International Monetary Fund policies that subordinate them to the North (as in free-market capitalism in Chile) also locate vital areas of analysis in this new cultural terrain.

The new cultural politics of difference is neither simply oppositional in contesting the mainstream (or malestream) for inclusion nor transgressive in the avant-gardist sense of shocking conventional bourgeois audiences. Rather, it is distinct articulations of talented (and usually privileged) contributors to culture who wish to align themselves with demoralized, demobilized, depoliticized, and disorganized people in order to empower and enable social action and, if possible, to enlist collective insurgency for the expansion of freedom, democracy, and individuality. This perspective impels these cultural critics and artists to reveal, as an integral component of their production, the very operations of power within their immediate work contexts (i.e., academy, museum, gallery, mass media). This strategy, however, also puts them in an inescapable double bind—while linking their activities to the fundamental, structural overhaul of these institutions, they often remain financially dependent on them (so much for "independent" creation). For these critics of culture, the gesture is simultaneously progressive and co-opted. Yet without social movement or political pressure from outside these institutions (extraparliamentary and extracurricular actions like the social movements of the recent past), transformation degenerates into mere accommodation or sheer stagnation, and the role of the "co-opted progressive"—no matter how fervent one's subversive rhetoric—is rendered more difficult. There can be no artistic breakthrough or social progress without some form of crisis in civilization—a crisis usually generated by organizations or collectivities that convince ordinary people to put their bodies and their lives on the line. There is, of course, no guarantee that such pressure will yield the result one wants, but there is a guarantee that the status quo will remain or regress if no pressure is applied at all.

The new cultural politics of difference faces three basic challenges—intellectual, existential, and political. The intellectual challenge—usually cast as methodological debate in these days in which academicist forms of expression have a monopoly on intellectual life—is how to think about representational practices in terms of history, culture, and society. How does one understand, analyze, and enact such practices today? An adequate answer to this question can be attempted only after one comes to terms with the insights and blindnesses of earlier attempts to grapple with the question in light of the evolving crisis in different histories, cultures, and societies. I shall sketch a brief genealogy—a history that highlights the contingent originals and often ignoble outcomes—of exemplary critical responses to the question. This genealogy sets forth a historical framework that characterizes the right yet deeply flawed Eurocentric traditions that the new cultural politics of difference build upon yet go beyond.

The Intellectual Challenge

An appropriate starting point is the ambiguous legacy of the Age of Europe. Between 1492 and 1945, European breakthroughs in oceanic transportation, agricultural production, state consolidation, bureaucratization, industrialization, urbanization, and imperial dominion shaped the modern world. Precious ideals like the dignity of persons (individuality) and the popular accountability of institutions (democracy) were unleashed around the world. Powerful critiques of illegitimate authorities—of the Protestant Reformation against the Roman Catholic Church, the Enlightenment against state churches, liberal movements against absolutist states and feudal guild constraints, workers against managerial subordination, people of color and Jews against white and gentile supremacist decrees, gays and lesbians against homophobic sanctions—were fanned and fueled by these precious ideals refined within the crucible of the Age of Europe. Yet the discrepancy between sterling rhetoric and lived reality, glowing principles and actual practices, loomed large.

By the last European century—the last epoch in which European domination of most of the globe was uncontested and unchallenged in a substantive way—a new world seemed to be stirring. At the height of England's reign as the major imperial European power, its exemplary cultural critic, Matthew Arnold, painfully observed in his "Stanzas from the Grande Chartreuse" that he felt some sense of "wandering between two worlds, one dead / The other powerless to be born." Following his Burkean sensibilities of cautious reform and fear of anarchy, Arnold acknowledged that the old glue—religion—that had tenuously and often unsuccessfully held together the ailing European regimes could not do so in the mid-nineteenth century. Like Alexis de Tocqueville in France, Arnold saw that the democratic temper was the wave of the future. So he proposed a new conception of culture—a secular, humanistic one—that could play an integrative role in cementing and stabilizing an emerging bourgeois civil society and imperial state. His famous castigation of the immobilizing materialism of the declining aristocracy, the vulgar philistinism of the emerging middle classes, and the latent explosiveness of the working-class majority was motivated by a desire to create new forms of cultural legitimacy, authority, and order in a rapidly changing moment in nineteenth-century Europe.

Arnold's new conception of culture

> seeks to do away with classes; to make the best that has been thought and known in the world current everywhere; to make all men live in an atmosphere of sweetness and light. . . .
>
> This is the social idea and the men of culture are the true apostles of equality. The great men of culture are those who have had a passion for diffusing, for making prevail, for carrying from one end of society to the other, the best knowledge, the best ideas of their time, who have laboured to divest knowledge of all that was harsh, uncouth, difficult, abstract, professional, exclusive; to humanize it, to make it efficient outside the clique of the cultivated and learned, yet still remaining the best knowledge and thought of the time, and a true source, therefore, of sweetness and light. (*Culture and Anarchy*, 1869)

As an organic intellectual of an emergent middle class—as the inspector of schools in an expanding educational bureaucracy, professor of poetry at Oxford (the first noncleric and the first to lecture in English rather than Latin), and an active participant in the thriving magazine network—Arnold defined and defended a new secular culture of critical discourse. For him, this discursive strategy would be lodged in the educational and periodical apparatuses of modern societies as they contained and incorporated the frightening threats of an arrogant aristocracy and especially of an "anarchic" working-class majority. His ideals of disinterested, dispassionate, and objective inquiry would regulate this new secular cultural production, and his justifications for the use of state power to quell any threats to the survival and security of this culture were widely accepted.

He aptly noted, "Through culture seems to lie our way, not only to perfection, but even to safety."

This sentence is revealing in two ways. First, it refers to "our way" without explicitly acknowledging who constitutes the "we." This is characteristic of bourgeois, male Eurocentric critics whose universalizing gestures exclude (by guarding a silence around) or explicitly degrade women and peoples of color. Second, the sentence links culture to safety—presumably the safety of the "we" against the barbaric threats of the "them," that is, those viewed as different in some debased manner. Needless to say, Arnold's negative attitudes toward British working-class people, women, and especially Indians and Jamaicans in the Empire clarify why he conceives of culture as, in part, a weapon for bourgeois male European "safety."

For Arnold the best of the Age of Europe—modeled on a mythological mélange of Periclean Athens, late Republican/early Imperial Rome, and Elizabethan England—could be promoted only if there was an interlocking affiliation among the emerging middle classes, a homogenizing of cultural discourse in the educational and university networks, and a state advanced enough in its policing techniques to safeguard it. The candidates for participation and legitimation in this grand endeavor of cultural renewal and revision would be detached intellectuals willing to shed their parochialism, provincialism, and class-bound identities for Arnold's middle-class-skewed project: "aliens, if we may so call them—persons who are mainly led, not by their class spirit, but by a general humane spirit, by the love of human perfection." Needless to say, this Arnoldian perspective still informs many of the academic practices and secular cultural attitudes today—dominant views about the canon, university admission procedures, and collective self-definitions of intellectuals, for example. Yet Arnold's project was disrupted by the collapse of nineteenth-century Europe into World War I. This unprecedented war brought to the surface the crucial role and violent potential not of the masses Arnold feared but of the state he heralded. Out of the ashes of this wasteland of human carnage—some of it the civilian European population—T. S. Eliot emerged as the grand cultural spokesman.

Eliot's project of reconstituting and reconceiving European highbrow culture—and thereby regulating critical and artistic practices—after the internal collapse of imperial Europe can be seen as a response to the probing question posed by Paul Valéry in "The Crisis of the Spirit" after World War I: "This Europe, will it become what it is in reality, i.e., a little cape of the Asiatic continent? or will this Europe remain rather what it seems, i.e., the priceless part of the whole earth, the pearl of the globe, the brain of a vast body?"

Eliot's image of Europe as a wasteland, a culture of fragments with no cementing center, predominated in postwar Europe. And though his early poetic practices were more radical, open, and international than his Eurocentric criticism, Eliot posed a return to and revision of tradition as the only way of regaining European cultural order and political stability. For Eliot, contemporary history had become, as James Joyce's Stephen declared in *Ulysses* (1922), "a nightmare from which he was trying to awake"—"an immense panorama of futility and anarchy," as Eliot put it in his renowned review of Joyce's modernist masterpiece. In his influential essay "Tradition and the Individual Talent" (1919), Eliot stated that

> if the only form of tradition, of handing down, consisted in following
> the ways of the immediate generation before us in a blind or timid
> adherence to its successes, "tradition" should positively be discouraged.
> We have seen many such simple currents soon lost in the sand; and
> novelty is better than repetition. Tradition is a matter of much wider
> significance. It cannot be inherited, and if you want it you must attain it
> by great labour.

Eliot's fecund notion of tradition is significant in that it promotes a historicist sensibility in artistic practice and cultural reflection. This historicist sensibility—regulated in Eliot's case by a reactionary politics— produced a powerful assault on existing literary canons (in which, for example, romantic poets were displaced by the metaphysical and symbolist ones) and unrelenting attacks on modern Western civilization (on the liberal ideas of democracy, equality, and freedom, for example). Like Arnold's notion of culture, Eliot's idea of tradition was part of his intellectual arsenal, to be used in the battles raging in European cultures and societies.

Eliot found this tradition in the Church of England, to which he converted in 1927. Here was a tradition that left room for his Catholic cast of mind, Calvinistic heritage, puritanical temperament, and ebullient patriotism for the old American South (where he was brought up). Like Arnold, Eliot was obsessed with the idea of civilization and the horror of barbarism (echoes of Joseph Conrad's Kurtz in *Heart of Darkness*) or more pointedly, the notion of the decline and decay of European civilization. With the advent of World War II, Eliot's obsession became a reality. Again-unprecedented human carnage (50 million dead)—including an indescribable genocidal attack on Jewish people—throughout Europe as well as around the globe put the last nail in the coffin of the Age of Europe. After 1945, Europe consisted of a devastated and divided continent, crippled by humiliating dependency on and deference to the United States and the Soviet Union.

The second historical coordinate of my genealogy is the emergence of the United States as a world power. The United States was unprepared for world-power status. With the recovery of Stalin's Russia (after losing 20 million dead), however, the United States felt compelled to make its presence felt around the globe. Then with the Marshall Plan to strengthen Europe against Russian influence (and provide new markets for U.S. products), the 1948 Russian takeover of Czechoslovakia, the 1948 Berlin blockade, the 1950 beginning of the Korean War, and the 1952 establishment of NATO forces in Europe, it seemed clear that there was no escape from world power obligations.

The post-World War II era in the United States, or the first decades of what Henry Luce envisioned as "the American century," was not only a period of incredible economic expansion but also of active cultural ferment. In the classical Fordist formula, mass production required mass consumption. With unchallenged hegemony in the capitalist world, the United States took economic growth for granted. Next to exercising its crude anticommunist, McCarthyist obsessions, buying commodities became the primary act of civic virtue for many American citizens at this time. The creation of a mass middle class—a prosperous working class with a bourgeois identity—was countered by the first major emergence of subcultures of American non-WASP intellectuals: the so-called New York intellectuals in criticism, the abstract expressionists in painting, and the bebop artists in jazz music. This emergence signaled a vital challenge to an American male WASP elite loyal to an older and eroding European culture.

The first significant blow was dealt when assimilated Jewish Americans entered the higher echelons of the cultural apparatuses (academy, museums, galleries, mass media). Lionel Trilling is an emblematic figure. This Jewish entrée into the anti-Semitic and patriarchal critical discourse of the exclusivistic institutions of American culture initiated the slow but sure undoing of the male WASP cultural hegemony and homogeneity. Lionel Trilling's project was to appropriate Matthew Arnold for his own political and cultural purposes—thereby unraveling the old male WASP consensus while erecting a new post-World War II liberal academic consensus around cold war, anticommunist renditions of the values of complexity, difficulty, variousness, and modulation. In addition, the postwar boom laid the basis for intense professionalization and specialization in expanding institutions of higher education—especially in the natural sciences, which were compelled to somehow respond to Russia's successful ventures in space. Humanistic scholars found themselves searching for new methodologies that could buttress self-images of rigor and scientific seriousness. For example, the close reading techniques of New Criticism (severed from their conservative, organicist, anti-industrialist ideological roots), the logical precision of reasoning in analytic philosophy, and the jargon of Parsonian structural functionalism in sociology helped create such self-images. Yet towering cultural critics like C. Wright Mills, W. E. B. Du Bois, Richard Hofstadter, Margaret Mead, and Dwight Macdonald bucked the tide. This suspicion of the academicization of knowledge is expressed in Trilling's well-known essay "On the Teaching of Modern Literature":

> Can we not say that, when modern literature is brought into the classroom, the subject being taught is betrayed by the pedagogy of the subject? We have to ask ourselves whether in our day too much does not come within the purview of the academy. More and more, as the universities liberalize themselves, turn their beneficent imperialistic gaze upon what is called life itself, the feeling grows among our educated classes that little can be experienced unless it is validated by some established intellectual discipline.

Trilling laments the fact that university instruction often quiets and domesticates radical and subversive works of art, turning them into objects "of merely habitual regard." This process of "the socialization of the anti-social, or the acculturation of the anti-cultural, or the legitimization of the subversive" leads Trilling to "question whether in our culture the study of literature is any longer a suitable means for developing and refining the intelligence." Trilling asks this question not in the spirit of denigrating and devaluing the academy but rather in the spirit of highlighting the possible failure of an Arnoldian conception of culture to contain what he perceives as the philistine and anarchic alternatives becoming more and more available to students of the 1960s—namely, mass culture and radical politics.

This threat is partly associated with the third historical coordinate of my genealogy—the decolonization of the Third World. It is crucial to recognize the importance of this world-historical process if one wants to grasp the significance of the end of the Age of Europe and the emergence of the United States as a world power. With the first defeats of Western nations by non-Western nations—in Japan's victory over Russia (1905), revolutions in Persia (1905), Turkey (1908), China (1912), Mexico (1911-12), and much later the independence of India (1947) and China (1948) and the triumph of Ghana (1957)—the actuality of a decolonized globe loomed large. Born of violent struggle, consciousness-raising, and the reconstruction of identities, decolonization simultaneously brings with it new perspectives on that long-festering underside of the Age of Europe (of which colonial domination represents the *costs* of "progress," "order," and "culture") and requires new readings of the economic boom in the United States (wherein the black, brown, yellow, red, female, elderly, gay, lesbian, and white working class lives the same *costs* as cheap labor at home as well as in U.S.-dominated Latin American and Pacific rim markets).

The impetuous ferocity and moral outrage that motors the decolonization process is best captured by Frantz Fanon in *The Wretched of the Earth* (1961):

> Decolonization, which sets out to change the order of the world, is obviously, a program of complete disorder. . . . Decolonization is the meeting of two forces, opposed to each other by their very nature, which in fact owe their originality to that sort of substantification which results from and is nourished by the situation in the colonies. Their first encounter was marked by violence and their existence together—that is to say the exploitation of the native by the settler—was carried on by dint of a great array of bayonets and cannons. . . . In decolonization, there is therefore the need of a complete calling in question of the colonial situation. If we wish to describe it precisely, we might find it in the well-known words: "The last shall be first and the first last." Decolonization is the putting into practice of this sentence.
>
> The naked truth of decolonization evokes for us the searing bullets and bloodstained knives which emanate from it. For if the last shall be first, this will only come to pass after a murderous and decisive struggle between the two protagonists.

Fanon's strong words, though excessively Manichaean, still describe the feelings and thoughts between the occupying British army and colonized Irish in Northern Ireland, the occupying Israeli army and subjugated Palestinians on the West Bank and Gaza Strip, the South African army and oppressed black South Africans in the townships, the Japanese police and Koreans living in Japan, the Russian army and subordinated Armenians and others in the southern and eastern USSR. His words also invoke a feeling many black Americans have toward police departments in urban centers. In other words, Fanon is articulating a century of heartfelt human responses to being degraded and despised, hated and hunted, oppressed and exploited, marginalized and dehumanized at the hands of powerful xenophobic European, American, Russian, and Japanese imperial countries.

During the late 1950s, 1960s, and early 1970s in the United States, these decolonized sensibilities fanned and fueled the civil rights and Black Power movements, as well as the student antiwar, feminist, gray, brown, gay, and lesbian movements. In this period we witnessed the shattering of male WASP cultural homogeneity and the collapse of the short-lived liberal consensus. The inclusion of African-Americans, Latino and Latina Americans, Asian-Americans, Native Americans, and American women into the culture of critical discourse yielded intense intellectual polemics and inescapable ideological polarization that focused principally on the exclusions, silences, and blindnesses of male WASP cultural homogeneity and its concomitant Arnoldian notions of the canon.

In addition, these critiques promoted three crucial processes that affected intellectual life in the country. First is the appropriation of the theories of postwar Europe—especially the work of the Frankfurt school (Marcuse, Adorno, Horkheimer), French and Italian Marxisms (Sartre, Althusser, Lefebvre, Gramsci), structuralisms (Lévi-Strauss, Todorov), and poststructuralisms (Deleuze, Derrida, Foucault). These diverse and disparate theories—all preoccupied with keeping alive radical projects after the end of the Age of Europe—tend to fuse versions of transgressive European modernisms with Marxist or post-Marxist left politics and unanimously shun the term "postmodernism." Second, there is the recovery and revisioning of American history in light of the struggles of white male workers, women, African-Americans, Native Americans, Latino and Latina Americans, gays, and lesbians. Third is the impact of forms of popular culture such as television, film, music videos, and even sports on highbrow literate culture. The black-based hip-hop culture of youth around the world is one grand example.

After 1973, with the crisis in the international world economy, America's slump in productivity, the challenge of OPEC nations to the North Atlantic monopoly of oil production, the increasing competition in high-tech sectors of the economy from Japan and West Germany, and the growing fragility of the international debt structure, the United States entered a period of waning self-confidence (compounded by Watergate) and a nearly contracting economy. As the standard of living for the middle classes declined as a result of runaway inflation and the quality of life fell for most as a result of escalating unemployment, underemployment, and crime, religious and secular neoconservatism emerged with power and potency. This fusion of fervent neonationalism, traditional cultural values, and "free market" policies served as the groundwork for the Reagan-Bush era.

The ambiguous legacies of the European Age, American preeminence, and decolonization continue to haunt our postmodern moment as we come to terms with the European, American, Japanese, Soviet, and Third World *crimes against* and *contributions to* humanity. The plight of Africans in the New World can be instructive in this regard.

By 1914 European maritime empires had dominion over more than half of the land and a third of the peoples in the world—almost 72 million square kilometers of territory and more than 560 million people were under colonial rule. Needless to say, this European control included brutal enslavement, institutional terrorism, and cultural degradation of black diaspora people. The death of roughly 75 million Africans during the centuries-long transatlantic slave trade is but one reminder of the assault on black humanity. The black diaspora condition of New World servitude—in which people were viewed as mere commodities with production value and had no proper legal status, social standing, or public worth—can be characterized as, following Orlando Patterson, natal alienation. This state of perpetual and inheritable domination that diaspora Africans had at birth produced the *modern black diaspora problematic of invisibility and namelessness*. White supremacist practices—enacted under the auspices of the prestigious cultural authorities of the churches, print media, and scientific academics—promoted black inferiority and constituted the European background against which black diaspora struggles for identity, dignity (self-confidence, self-respect, self-esteem), and material resources took place.

An inescapable aspect of this struggle was that the black diaspora peoples' quest for validation and recognition occurred on the ideological, social, and cultural terrains of other, nonblack peoples. White supremacist assaults on black intelligence, ability, beauty, and character required persistent black efforts to hold self-doubt, self-contempt, and even self-hatred at bay. Some of the strategies employed were selective appropriation, incorporation, and rearticulation of European ideologies, cultures, and institutions alongside an African heritage—a heritage more or less confined to linguistic innovation in theoretical practices, stylizations of the body in forms of occupying an alien social space (hairstyles, ways of walking and standing, hand expressions, talking), and means of constituting and sustaining camaraderie and community (e.g., antiphonal, call-and-response styles, rhythmic repetition, risk-ridden syncopation in spectacular modes in musical and rhetorical expressions).

The modern black diaspora problematic of invisibility and namelessness can be understood as the condition of relative lack of *black people's power to represent themselves to themselves and others as complex human beings, and thereby to contest the bombardment of negative, degrading stereotypes put forward by white supremacist ideologies*. The initial black response to being caught in this whirlwind of Europeanization was to resist the misrepresentation and caricature of the terms set by uncontested nonblack norms and models and fight for self-representation and recognition. All modern black people, especially cultural disseminators, encounter this problematic of invisibility and namelessness. The initial black diaspora response was a mode of resistance that was *moralistic in content and communal in char-*

acter. That is, the fight for representation and recognition highlighted moral judgments regarding black "positive" images over and against white supremacist stereotypes. These images "re-presented" monolithic and homogeneous black communities in a way that could displace past misrepresentations of these communities. Stuart Hall has talked about these responses as attempts to change "the relations of representation."

These courageous yet limited black efforts to combat racist cultural practices uncritically accepted nonblack conventions and standards in two ways. First, they proceeded in an assimilationist manner that set out to show that black people were really like white people — thereby eliding differences (in history and culture) between whites and blacks. Black specificity and particularity was thus banished in order to gain white acceptance and approval. Second, these black responses rested upon a homogenizing impulse that assumed that all black people were really alike — hence obliterating differences (class, gender, region, sexual orientation) among black peoples. I submit that there are elements of truth in both claims, yet the conclusions are unwarranted owing to the basic fact that nonblack paradigms set the terms of the replies.

The insight in the first claim is that blacks and whites are in some important sense alike — that is, in their positive capacities for human sympathy, moral sacrifice, service to others, intelligence, and beauty, and negatively, in their capacity for cruelty. Yet the common humanity they share is jettisoned when the claim is cast in an assimilationist manner that subordinates black particularity to a false universalism, that is, nonblack rubrics or prototypes. Similarly, the insight in the second claim is that all blacks are in some significant sense "in the same boat" — that is, subject to white supremacist abuse. Yet this common condition is stretched too far when it is viewed in a homogenizing way that overlooks how racist treatment vastly differs owing to class, gender, sexual orientation, nation, region, hue, and age.

The moralistic and communal aspects of the initial black diaspora responses to social and psychic erasure were not simply cast into simplistic binary oppositions of positive/negative, good/bad images that privileged the first term in light of a white norm so that black efforts remained inscribed within the very logic that dehumanized them. They were further complicated by the fact that these responses were also advanced principally by anxiety-ridden, middle-class black intellectuals (predominantly male and heterosexual) grappling with their sense of double consciousness — namely, their own crisis of identity, agency, and audience — and caught between a quest for white approval and acceptance and an attempt to overcome the internalized association of blackness with inferiority. And I suggest that these complex anxieties of modern Black diaspora intellectuals partly motivate the two major arguments that ground the assimilationist moralism and homogeneous communalism just outlined.

Kobena Mercer has talked about these two arguments as the reflectionist and the social engineering arguments. The reflectionist argument holds that the fight for black representation and recognition must reflect the real black community, not simply the negative and depressing representations of it. The social engineering argument claims that since any form of representation is constructed—that is, selective in light of broader aims—black representation (especially given the difficulty of blacks gaining access to positions of power to produce a black imagery) should offer positive images in order to inspire achievement among young black people, thereby countering racist stereotypes. The hidden assumption of both arguments is that we have unmediated access to what the "real black community" is and what "positive images" are. In short, these arguments presuppose the very phenomena to be interrogated, and thereby foreclose the very issues that should serve as the subject matter to be investigated.

Any notions of "the real black community" and "positive images" are value-laden, socially loaded, and ideologically charged. To pursue this discussion is to call into question the possibility of such an uncontested consensus regarding them. Stuart Hall has rightly called this encounter "the end of innocence or the end of the innocent notion of the essential Black subject . . . the recognition that 'Black' is essentially a politically and culturally constructed category." This recognition—more and more pervasive among the postmodern black diaspora intelligentsia—is facilitated in part by the slow but sure dissolution of the European Age's maritime empires, the unleashing of new political possibilities and cultural articulations among ex-colonialized peoples around the globe.

One crucial lesson of this decolonization process remains the manner in which most Third World authoritarian bureaucratic elites deploy essentialist rhetorics about "homogeneous national communities" and "positive images" in order to repress and regiment their diverse and heterogeneous populations. Yet in the diaspora, especially among First World countries, this critique has emerged not so much from the black male component of the left but more from the black women's movement. The decisive push of postmodern black intellectuals toward a new cultural politics of difference has been made by the powerful critiques and constructive explorations of black diaspora women (Toni Morrison, for example). The coffin used to bury the innocent notion of the essential black subject was nailed shut with the termination of the black male monopoly on the construction of the black subject. In this regard, the black diaspora womanist critique has had a greater impact than the critiques that highlight exclusively class, empire, age, sexual orientation, or nature.

This decisive push toward the end of black innocence—though prefigured in various degrees in the best moments of W. E. B. Du Bois, Anna Cooper, C. L. R. James, James Baldwin, Claudia Jones, Malcolm X, Frantz Fanon, Amiri Baraka, and others—forces black diaspora cultural workers to encounter what Hall has called the "politics of representation." The main aim now is not simply access to representation in order to produce positive images of homogeneous communities—though broader access remains a practical and political problem. Nor is the primary goal here that of contesting stereotypes—though contestation remains a significant but limited venture. Following the model of the black diaspora traditions of music, athletics, and rhetoric, black cultural workers must constitute and sustain discursive and institutional networks that deconstruct earlier modern black strategies for identity formation; demystify power relations that incorporate class, patriarchal, and homophobic biases; and construct more multivalent and multidimensional responses that articulate the complexity and diversity of black practices in the modern and postmodern world.

Furthermore, black cultural workers must investigate and interrogate the other of blackness—whiteness. One cannot deconstruct the binary oppositional logic of images of blackness without extending it to the contrary condition of blackness/whiteness itself. A mere dismantling will not do, however, for the very notion of a deconstructive social theory is oxymoronic. Yet social theory is what is needed to examine and explain the historically specific ways in which "whiteness" is a politically constructed category parasitic on "blackness," and thereby to conceive of the profoundly hybrid character of what we mean by "race," "ethnicity," and "nationality." For instance, European immigrants arrived on American shores perceiving themselves as "Irish," "Sicilian," "Lithuanian," and so forth. They had to learn that they were "white" principally by adopting an American discourse of positively valued whiteness and negatively charged blackness. This process by which people define themselves physically, socially, sexually, and even politically in terms of whiteness or blackness has much bearing not only on constructed notions of race and ethnicity but also on how we understand the changing character of U.S. nationalities. And given the Americanization of the world, especially in the sphere of mass culture, such inquiries—encouraged by the new cultural politics of difference—raise critical issues of "hybridity," "exile," and "identity" on an international scale. Needless to say, these inquiries must also traverse those of male/female, colonizer/ colonized, heterosexual/homosexual, and so forth.

In light of this brief sketch of the emergence of our present crisis — and the turn toward history and difference in cultural work — four major historicist forms of theoretical activity provide resources for how we understand, analyze, and enact our representational practices: Heideggerian *destruction* of the Western metaphysical tradition; Derridean *deconstruction* of the Western philosophical tradition; Rortian *demythologization* of the Western intellectual tradition; and Marxist, Foucauldian, feminist, antiracist, or antihomophobic *demystification* of Western cultural and artistic conventions.

Despite Martin Heidegger's abominable association with the Nazis, his project is useful in that it discloses the suppression of temporality and historicity in the dominant metaphysical systems of the West from Plato to Rudolf Carnap. This is noteworthy in that it forces one to understand philosophy's representational discourses as thoroughly historical phenomena. Hence, they should be viewed with skepticism, as they are often flights from the specific, concrete, practical, and particular. The major problem with Heidegger's project — as noted by his neo-Marxist student Herbert Marcuse — is that he views history in terms of fate, heritage, and destiny. He dramatizes the past and present as if it were a Greek tragedy with no tools of social analysis to relate cultural work to institutions and structures or antecedent forms and styles.

Jacques Derrida's version of deconstruction is one of the most influential schools of thought among young academic critics. It is salutary in that it focuses on the political power of rhetorical operations — of tropes and metaphors in binary oppositions like white/black, good/bad, male/ female, machine/nature, ruler/ruled, reality/appearance — showing how these operations sustain hierarchal worldviews by devaluing the second terms as elements subsumed under the first. Most of the controversy about Derrida's project revolves around this austere epistemic doubt that unsettles binary oppositions while undermining any determinate meaning of a text such as a book, an art object, a performance, a building. Yet his views about skepticism are no more alarming than those of David Hume, Ludwig Wittgenstein, or Stanley Cavell. He simply revels in it for transgressive purposes, whereas others provide us with ways to dissolve, sidestep, or cope with skepticism. None, however, slides down the slippery, crypto-Nietzschean slope of sophomoric relativism as alleged by old-style humanists, be they Platonists, Kantians, or Arnoldians.

The major shortcoming of Derrida's deconstructive project is that it puts a premium on a sophisticated ironic consciousness that tends to preclude and foreclose analyses that guide action with purpose. And given Derrida's own status as an Algerian-born Jewish leftist marginalized by a hostile French academic establishment (quite different from his reception by the youth in the American academic establishment), the sense of political impotence and hesitation regarding the efficacy of moral action is understandable — but not justifiable. His works and those of his followers too often become rather monotonous, Johnny-one-note rhetorical readings that disassemble texts with little attention to the effects and consequences these dismantlings have in relation to the operations of military, economic, and social powers.

Richard Rorty's neopragmatic project of demythologization is insightful in that it provides descriptive mappings of the transient metaphors — especially the ocular and specular ones — that regulate some of the fundamental dynamics in the construction of self-descriptions dominant in highbrow European and American philosophy. His perspective is instructive because it discloses the crucial role of narrative as the background for rational exchange and critical conversation. To put it crudely, Rorty shows why we should speak not of History, but of histories, not of Reason, but of historically constituted forms of rationality, not of Criticism or Art, but of socially constructed notions of criticism and art — all linked but not reducible to political purposes, material interests, and cultural prejudices.

Rorty's project nonetheless leaves one wanting as a result of its distrust of social analytical explanation. Similar to the dazzling new historicism of Stephen Greenblatt, Louis Montrose, and Catherine Gallagher — inspired by the subtle symbolic cum textual anthropology of Clifford Geertz and the powerful discursive materialism of Michel Foucault — Rorty's mappings and descriptions are given with no explanatory accounts for change and conflict. In this way, we get an aestheticized version of historicism in which the provisional and variable are celebrated at the expense of highlighting who gains, loses, or bears what costs.

Demystification is the most illuminating mode of theoretical inquiry for those who promote the new cultural politics of difference. Social structural analyses of empire, exterminism, class, race, gender, nature, age, sexual orientation, nation, and region are the springboards — though not landing grounds — for the most desirable forms of critical practice that take history (and herstory) seriously. Demystification tries to keep track of the complex dynamics of institutional and other related power structures in order to disclose options and alternatives for transformative praxis; it also attempts to grasp the way in which representational strategies are creative responses to novel circumstances and conditions. In this way, the central role of human agency (always enacted under circumstances not of one's choosing)—be it in the critic, artist, or constituency and audience—is accented.

I call demystificatory criticism "prophetic criticism"—the approach appropriate for the new cultural politics of difference—because while it begins with social structural analyses it also makes explicit its moral and political aims. It is partisan, partial, engaged, and crisis-centered, yet always keeps open a skeptical eye to avoid dogmatic traps, premature closures, formulaic formulations, and rigid conclusions. In addition to social structural analyses, moral and political judgments, and sheer critical consciousness, there indeed is evaluation. Yet the aim of this evaluation is neither to pit art objects against one another like racehorses nor to create eternal canons that dull, discourage, or even dwarf contemporary achievements. We listen to Ludwig van Beethoven, Charlie Parker, Luciano Pavarotti, Laurie Anderson, Sarah Vaughan, Stevie Wonder, or Kathleen Battle, read William Shakespeare, Anton Chekhov, Ralph Ellison, Doris Lessing, Thomas Pynchon, Toni Morrison, or Gabriel García Márquez, see works of Pablo Picasso, Ingmar Bergman, Le Corbusier, Martin Puryear, Barbara Kruger, Spike Lee, Frank Gehry or Howardena Pindell not in order to undergird bureaucratic assents or enliven cocktail party conversations, but rather to be summoned by the styles they deploy for their profound insight, pleasures, and challenges. Yet all evaluation—including a delight in Eliot's poetry despite his reactionary politics, or a love of Zora Neale Hurston's novels despite her Republican party affiliations—is inseparable from, though not identical or reducible to, social structural analyses, and moral and political judgments and the workings of a curious critical consciousness.

The deadly traps of demystification—and any form of prophetic criticism—are those of reductionism, be it of the sociological, psychological, or historical sort. By reductionism I mean either one-factor analyses (crude Marxisms, feminisms, racialisms, etc.) that yield a one-dimensional functionalism or a hypersubtle analytical perspective that loses touch with the specificity of an art work's form and the context of its reception. Few cultural workers of whatever stripe can walk the tightrope between the Scylla of reductionism and the Charybdis of aestheticism—yet demystificatory (or prophetic) critics must.

The Existential Challenge

The existential challenge to the new cultural politics of difference can be stated simply: how does one acquire the resources to survive and the cultural capital to thrive as a critic or artist? By cultural capital (Pierre Bourdieu's term), I mean not only the high-order skills required to engage in critical practices but also, and more important, the self-confidence, discipline, and perseverance necessary for success without an undue reliance on the mainstream for approval and acceptance. This challenge holds for all prophetic critics, yet it is especially difficult for people of color. The widespread modern European denial of the intelligence, ability, beauty, and character of people of color puts a tremendous burden on critics and artists of color to "prove" themselves in light of norms and models set by white elites whose own heritage devalued and dehumanized them. In short, in the court of criticism and art—or any matters regarding the life of the mind—people of color are guilty, that is, not expected to meet standards of intellectual achievement, until "proven" innocent, that is, acceptable to "us."

This is more a structural dilemma than a matter of personal attitudes. The profoundly racist and sexist heritage of the European Age has bequeathed to us a set of deeply ingrained perceptions about people of color, including, of course, the self-perceptions of people of color. It is not surprising that most intellectuals of color in the past directed much of their energy and many of their efforts toward gaining acceptance and approval by white "normative" gazes. The new cultural politics of difference advises critics and artists of color to put aside this mode of mental bondage, thereby freeing themselves both to interrogate the ways in which they are bound by certain conventions and to learn from and build on these very norms and models. One hallmark of wisdom in the context of any struggle is to avoid knee-jerk rejection and uncritical acceptance.

Self-confidence, discipline, and perseverance are not ends in themselves. Rather they are the necessary stuff of which enabling criticism and self-criticism are made. Notwithstanding inescapable jealousies, insecurities, and anxieties, one telling characteristic of critics and artists of color linked to the new prophetic criticism should be their capacity for and promotion of relentless criticism and self-criticism—be it the normative paradigms of their white colleagues that tend to leave out considerations of empire, race, gender, and sexual orientation or the damaging dogmas about the homogeneous character of communities of color.

There are four basic options for people of color interested in representation who wish to survive and thrive as serious practitioners of their craft. First, there is the Booker T. Temptation, namely, the individual preoccupation with the mainstream and its legitimizing power. Most critics and artists of color take this bait. It is nearly unavoidable, yet few succeed in a substantive manner. It is no accident that the most creative and profound among them—especially those with staying power beyond mere flashes in the pan to satisfy faddish tokenism—are usually marginal to the mainstream. Even the pervasive professionalization of cultural practitioners of color in the past few decades has not produced towering figures who reside within the established white patronage system that bestows the rewards and prestige for chosen contributions to American society.

It certainly helps to have some trustworthy allies within this system, yet most of those who enter and remain tend to lose much of their creativity, diffuse their prophetic energy, and dilute their critiques. Still, it is unrealistic for creative people of color to think they can sidestep the white patronage system. And though there are indeed some white allies conscious of the tremendous need to rethink identity politics, it is naive to think that being comfortably nested within this very same system — even if one can be a patron to others — does not affect one's work, one's outlook, and, most important, one's soul.

The second option is the Talented Tenth Seduction, namely, a move toward arrogant group insularity. This alternative has a limited function — to preserve one's sanity and sense of self as one copes with the mainstream. It is, at best, a transitional and transient activity. If it becomes a permanent option it is self-defeating in that it usually reinforces the very inferiority complexes promoted by the subtly racist mainstream. Hence it tends to revel in a parochialism and encourage a narrow racialist and chauvinistic outlook.

The third strategy is the Go-It-Alone option. This is an extreme rejectionist perspective that shuns the mainstream and group insularity. Almost all critics and artists of color contemplate or enact this option at some time in their pilgrimage. It is healthy in that it reflects the presence of independent, critical, and skeptical sensibilities toward perceived constraints on one's creativity. Yet it is, in the end, difficult if not impossible to sustain if one is to grow, develop, and mature intellectually, as some semblance of dialogue with a community is necessary for almost any creative practice.

The most desirable option for a person of color who promotes the new cultural politics of difference is to be a critical organic catalyst. By this I mean a person who stays attuned to the best of what the mainstream has to offer — its paradigms, viewpoints, and methods — yet maintains a grounding in affirming and enabling subcultures of criticism. Prophetic critics and artists of color should be exemplars of what it means to be intellectual freedom fighters, that is, cultural workers who simultaneously position themselves within (or alongside) the mainstream while they are clearly aligned with groups who vow to keep alive potent traditions of critique and resistance. In this regard, one can take clues from the great musicians and preachers of color who are open to the best of what other traditions offer yet are rooted in nourishing subcultures that

build on the grand achievements of a vital heritage. Openness to others—
including the mainstream—does not entail wholesale co-optation, and
group autonomy is not group insularity. Louis Armstrong, W. E. B.
Du Bois, Ella Baker, Jose Carlos Mariatequi, M. M. Thomas, Wynton
Marsalis, Martin Luther King, Jr., and Ronald Takaki have understood
this well.

The new cultural politics of difference can thrive only if there are communities, groups, organizations, institutions, subcultures, and networks
of people of color who cultivate critical sensibilities and personal accountability without inhibiting individual expressions, curiosities, and
idiosyncrasies. This is especially needed given the escalating racial hostility, violence, and polarization in the United States. Yet this critical coming together must not be a narrow closing of ranks. Rather, it must be a
strengthening and nurturing endeavor that can forge more solid alliances
and coalitions. In this way, prophetic criticism—with its stress on historical specificity and artistic complexity—directly addresses the intellectual
challenge. The cultural capital of people of color—with its emphasis on
self-confidence, discipline, perseverance, and subcultures of criticism—
also tries to meet the existential requirement. They are mutually reinforcing. Both are motivated by a deep commitment to individuality and democracy, the moral and political ideals that guide the creative response to
the political challenge.

The Political Challenge

Adequate rejoinders to intellectual and existential challenges equip the
practitioners of the new cultural politics of difference to meet the political
ones. The political challenge principally consists of forging solid and re-
liable alliances of people of color and white progressives guided by a
moral and political vision of greater democracy and individual freedom
in communities, states, and transnational enterprises such as corporations
and information and communications conglomerates.

Jesse Jackson's Rainbow Coalition is a gallant yet flawed effort in this
regard: gallant as a result of the tremendous energy, vision, and courage
of its leader and followers, yet flawed because of its failure to take critical
and democratic sensibilities seriously within its own operations. In fact,
Jackson's attempt to gain power at the national level is a symptom of the
weakness of U.S. progressive politics and a sign that the capacity to generate extraparliamentary social motion or movements has waned. Yet
given the present organizational weakness and intellectual timidity of left
politics in the United States, the best option is multiracial grass-roots citizens' participation in credible projects in which people see that their ef-

forts can make a difference. The salutary revolutionary developments in Eastern Europe are encouraging and inspiring in this regard. Ordinary people, organized, can change societies.

The most significant theme of the new cultural politics of difference is the agency, capacity, and ability of human beings who have been culturally degraded, politically oppressed, and economically exploited by bourgeois liberal and communist illiberal status quos. This theme neither romanticizes nor idealizes marginalized peoples. Rather, it accentuates their humanity and tries to attenuate the institutional constraints on their chances for surviving and thriving. In this way, the new cultural politics of difference shuns narrow particularisms, parochialisms, and separatisms, just as it rejects false universalisms and homogeneous totalisms. Instead, the new cultural politics of difference affirms the perennial quest for the precious ideals of individuality and democracy by digging deep in the depths of human particularities and social specificities in order to construct new kinds of connections, affinities, and communities across empire, nation, region, race, gender, age, and sexual orientation.

The major impediments to the radical libertarian and democratic projects of the new cultural politics are threefold: the pervasive processes of objectification, rationalization, and commodification throughout the world. Objectification—best highlighted in Georg Simmel's *The Philosophy of Money* (1900)—consists of transforming human beings into manipulable objects. It promotes the notion that people's actions have no impact on the world, that we are but spectators, not participants in making and remaking ourselves and the larger society. Rationalization—initially examined in the seminal works of Max Weber—expands bureaucratic hierarchies that impose impersonal rules and regulations in order to increase efficiency, be it defined in terms of better service or better surveillance. This process leads to disenchantment with past mythologies of deadening, flat, banal ways of life. The third and most important process, commodification—best examined in the works of Karl Marx, Georg Lukács, and Walter Benjamin—augments market forces in the form of oligopolies and monopolies that centralize resources and powers and promote cultures of consumption that view people as mere spectatorial consumers and passive citizens.

These processes cannot be eliminated, but their pernicious effects can be substantially alleviated. The audacious attempt to lessen their impact—to preserve people's agency, increase the scope of their freedom, and expand the operations of democracy—is the fundamental aim of the new cultural politics of difference. This is why the crucial questions become, What is the moral content of one's cultural identity? and What are the political consequences of this moral content and cultural identity?

In the recent past, the dominant cultural identities have been circumscribed by immoral patriarchal, imperial, jingoistic, and xenophobic constraints. The political consequences have been principally a public sphere regulated by and for well-to-do white males in the name of freedom and democracy. The new cultural criticism exposes and explodes the exclusions, blindnesses, and silences of the past, calling from it radical libertarian and democratic projects that will create a better present and future. The new cultural politics of difference is neither an ahistorical Jacobin program that discards tradition and ushers in new self-righteous authoritarianisms nor a guilt-ridden, leveling anti-imperialist liberalism that celebrates token pluralism for smooth inclusion. Rather, it acknowledges the uphill struggle of fundamentally transforming highly objectified, rationalized, and commodified societies and cultures in the name of individuality and democracy. This means locating the structural causes of unnecessary forms of social misery (without reducing all such human suffering to historical causes), depicting the plight and predicaments of demoralized and depoliticized citizens caught in market-driven cycles of therapeutic release—drugs, alcoholism, consumerism—and projecting alternative visions, analyses, and actions that proceed from particularities and arrive at moral and political connectedness. This connectedness does not signal a homogeneous unity or monolithic totality but rather a contingent, fragile building of coalitions in an effort to pursue common, overlapping radical libertarian and democratic goals.

In a world in which most of the resources, wealth, and power are centered in huge corporations and mutually supportive political elites, the new cultural politics of difference may appear to be solely visionary, utopian, and fanciful. Recent cutbacks in social service programs, business takebacks from workers at the negotiation tables, speedups at the workplace, and buildups of military budgets reinforce this perception. And surely the growing disintegration and decomposition of civil society—of shattered families, neighborhoods, and schools—adds to this perception. Can a civilization that evolves more and more around market activity, more and more around the buying and selling of commodities, expand the scope of freedom and democracy? Can we simply bear witness to its slow decay and doom—a painful denouement prefigured already in many poor black and brown communities and rapidly embracing all of us? These haunting questions remain unanswered, yet the challenge they pose must not remain unmet. The new cultural politics of difference tries to confront these enormous and urgent challenges. It will require all the imagination, intelligence, courage, sacrifice, care, and laughter we can muster.

The time has come for critics and artists of the new cultural politics of difference to cast their nets widely, flex their muscles broadly, and thereby refuse to limit their visions, analyses, and praxis to their particular terrains. The aim is to dare to recast, redefine, and revise the very notions of "modernity," "mainstream," "margins," "difference," "otherness." We have now reached a new stage in the perennial struggle for freedom and dignity. And while much of the First World intelligentsia adopts retrospective and conservative outlooks that defend the crisis-ridden present, we promote a prospective and prophetic vision with a sense of possibility and potential, especially for those who bear the social costs of the present. We look to the past for strength, not solace; we look at the present and see people perishing, not profits mounting; we look toward the future and vow to make it different and better.

To put it boldly, the new kind of critic and artist associated with the new cultural politics of difference consists of an energetic breed of New World *bricoleurs* with improvisational and flexible sensibilities who sidestep mere opportunism and mindless eclecticism; persons from all countries, cultures, genders, sexual orientations, ages, and regions with protean identities who avoid ethnic chauvinism and faceless universalism; intellectual and political freedom fighters with partisan passion, international perspectives, and, thank God, a sense of humor that combats the ever-present absurdity that threatens our democratic and libertarian projects and dampens the fire that fuels our will to struggle. We will struggle and stay, as those brothers and sisters on the block say, "out there" — with intellectual rigor, existential dignity, moral vision, political courage, and soulful style.

Chapter 3

On Race and Voice: Challenges for Liberal Education in the 1990s
Chandra Talpade Mohanty

Feminism and the Language of Difference

"Isn't the whole point to have a voice?" This is the last sentence of a recent essay by Marnia Lazreg on writing as a woman on women in Algeria.[1] Lazreg examines academic feminist scholarship on women in the Middle East and North Africa in the context of what she calls a "Western gynocentric" notion of the difference between First and Third World women. Arguing for an understanding of "intersubjectivity" as the basis for comparison across cultures and histories, Lazreg formulates the problem of ethnocentrism and the related question of voice in this way:

> To take intersubjectivity into consideration when studying Algerian women or other Third World women means seeing their lives as meaningful, coherent, and understandable instead of being infused "by us" with doom and sorrow. It means that their lives like "ours" are structured by economic, political, and cultural factors. It means that these women, like "us," are engaged in the process of adjusting, often shaping, at times resisting and even transforming their environment. It means they have their own individuality; they are "for themselves" instead of being "for us." An appropriation of their singular

individuality to fit the generalizing categories of "our" analyses is an assault on their integrity and on their identity.[2]

In my own work I have argued in a similar way against the use of analytic categories and political positionings in feminist studies that discursively present Third World women as a homogeneous, undifferentiated group leading truncated lives, victimized by the combined weight of "their" traditions, cultures, and beliefs, and "our" (Eurocentric) history.[3] In examining particular assumptions of feminist scholarship that are uncritically grounded in Western humanism and its modes of "disinterested scholarship," I have tried to demonstrate that this scholarship inadvertently produces Western women as the only legitimate subjects of struggle, while Third World women are heard as fragmented, inarticulate voices in (and from) the dark. Arguing against a hastily derived notion of "universal sisterhood" that assumes a commonality of gender experience across race and national lines, I have suggested the complexity of our historical (and positional) differences and the need for creating an analytical space for understanding Third World women as the "subjects" of our various struggles "in history." Other scholars have made similar arguments, and the question of what we might provisionally call "Third World women's 'voices' " has begun to be addressed seriously in feminist scholarship.

In the last decade there has been a blossoming of feminist discourse around questions of "racial difference" and "pluralism." While this work is often an important corrective to earlier middle-class (white) characterizations of sexual difference, the goal of the analysis of difference and the challenge of race was not pluralism as the proliferation of discourse on ethnicities as discrete and separate cultures. The challenge of race resides in a fundamental reconceptualization of our categories of analysis so that differences can be historically specified and understood as part of larger political processes and systems.[4] The central issue, then, is not one of merely "acknowledging" difference; rather, the most difficult question concerns the kind of difference that is acknowledged and engaged. Difference seen as benign variation (diversity), for instance, rather than as conflict, struggle, or the threat of disruption, bypasses power as well as history to suggest a harmonious, empty pluralism.[5] On the other hand, difference defined as asymmetrical and incommensurate cultural spheres situated within hierarchies of domination and resistance cannot be accommodated within a discourse of "harmony in diversity." A strategic critique of the contemporary language of difference, diversity, and power thus would be crucial to a feminist project concerned with revolutionary social change.

In the best, self-reflexive traditions of feminist inquiry, the production of knowledge about cultural and geographical Others is no longer seen as apolitical and disinterested. But while feminist activists and progressive scholars have made a significant dent in the colonialist and colonizing feminist scholarship of the late seventies and early eighties, this does not mean that questions of what Lazreg calls "intersubjectivity," or of history vis-à-vis Third World peoples, have been successfully articulated.[6]

In any case, "scholarship"—feminist, Marxist, or Third World—is not the only site for the production of knowledge about Third World women/peoples.[7] The very same questions (as those suggested in relation to scholarship) can be raised in relation to our teaching and learning practices in the classroom, as well as the discursive and managerial practices of American colleges and universities. Feminists writing about race and racism have had a lot to say about scholarship, but perhaps our pedagogical and institutional practices and their relation to scholarship have not been examined with quite the same care and attention. Radical educators have long argued that the academy and the classroom itself are not mere sites of instruction. They are also political and cultural sites that represent accommodations and contestations over knowledge by differently empowered social constituencies.[8] Thus teachers and students produce, reinforce, re-create, resist, and transform ideas about race, gender, and difference in the classroom. Also, the academic institutions in which we are located create similar paradigms, canons, and voices that embody and transcribe race and gender.

It is this frame of institutional and pedagogical practice that I examine in this essay. Specifically, I analyze the operation and management of discourses of race and difference in two educational sites: the women's studies classroom and the workshops on "diversity" for upper level (largely white) administrators. The links between these two educational sites lie in the (often active) *creation* of discourses of "difference." In other words, I suggest that educational practices as they are shaped and reshaped at these sites cannot be analyzed as merely transmitting already codified ideas of difference. These practices often produce, codify, and even rewrite histories of race and colonialism in the name of difference. But let me begin the analysis with a brief discussion of the academy as the site of political struggle and transformation.

Knowledge and Location in the U.S. Academy

A number of educators, Paulo Freire among them, have argued that education represents both a struggle for meaning and a struggle over power relations. Thus, education becomes a central terrain where power and politics operate out of the lived culture of individuals and groups situated in asymmetrical social and political positions. This way of understanding the academy entails a critique of education as the mere accumulation of disciplinary knowledges that can be exchanged on the world market for upward mobility. There are much larger questions at stake in the academy these days, not the least of which are questions of self and collective knowledge of marginal peoples and the recovery of alternative, oppositional histories of domination and struggle. Here, disciplinary parameters matter less than questions of power, history, and self-identity. For knowledge, the very act of knowing, is related to the power of self-definition. This definition of knowledge is central to the pedagogical projects of fields such as women's studies, black studies, and ethnic studies. By their very location in the academy, fields such as women's studies are grounded in definitions of difference, difference that attempts to resist incorporation and appropriation by providing a space for historically silenced peoples to construct knowledge. These knowledges have always been fundamentally oppositional, while running the risk of accommodation and assimilation and the consequent depoliticization in the academy. It is only in the late twentieth century, on the heels of domestic and global oppositional political movements, that the boundaries dividing knowledge into its traditional disciplines have been shaken loose, and new, often heretical, knowledges have emerged, modifying the structures of knowledge and power as we have inherited them. In other words, new analytic spaces have been opened up in the academy, spaces that make possible thinking of knowledge as praxis, of knowledge as embodying the very seeds of transformation and change. The appropriation of these analytic spaces and the challenge of radical educational practice are thus to involve the development of critical knowledges (what women's, black, and ethnic studies attempt), and simultaneously, to critique knowledge itself.

Education for critical consciousness or critical pedagogy, as it is sometimes called, requires a reformulation of the knowledge-as-accumulated-capital model of education and focuses instead on the link between the historical configuration of social forms and the way they work subjectively. This issue of subjectivity represents a realization of the fact that who we are, how we act, what we think, and what stories we tell become more intelligible within an epistemological framework that begins by recognizing existing hegemonic histories. The issue of subjectivity and voice thus concerns the effort to understand our specific locations in the educational process and in the institutions through which we are constituted. Resistance lies in self-conscious engagement with dominant, normative discourses and representations and in the active creation of oppositional analytic and cultural spaces. Resistance that is random and isolated is clearly not as effective as that which is mobilized through systematic politicized practices of teaching and learning. Uncovering and reclaiming subjugated knowledges is one way to lay claim to alternative histories. But these knowledges need to be understood and defined "pedagogically," as questions of strategy and practice as well as of scholarship, in order to transform educational institutions radically. And this, in turn, requires taking the questions of experience seriously.

To this effect, I draw on scholarship on and by Third World educators in higher education, on an analysis of the effects of my own pedagogical practices, on documents about "affirmative action" and "diversity in the curriculum" published by the administration of the college where I worked, and on my own observations and conversations over the past three years.[9] I do so in order to suggest that the effect of the proliferation of ideologies of pluralism in the 1960s and 1970s, in the context of the (limited) implementation of affirmative action in institutions of higher education, has been to create what might be called the Race Industry, an industry that is responsible for the management, commodification, and domestication of race on American campuses. This commodification of race determines the politics of voice for Third World peoples, whether they/we happen to be faculty, students, administrators, or service staff. This, in turn, has long-term effects on the definitions of the identity and agency of nonwhite people in the academy.

There are a number of urgent reasons for undertaking such an analysis: the need to assess the material and ideological effects of affirmative action policies within liberal (rather than conservative—Bloom or Hirsch style) discourses and institutions that profess a commitment to pluralism and social change, the need to understand this management of race in the liberal academy in relation to a larger discourse on race and discrimination within the neoconservatism of the United States, and the need for Third World feminists to move outside the arena of (sometimes) exclusive engagement with racism in white women's movements and scholarship and to broaden the scope of our struggles to the academy as a whole.

The management of gender, race, class, and sexuality are inextricably linked in the public arena. The New Right agenda since the mid 1970s makes this explicit: busing, gun rights, and welfare are clearly linked to the issues of reproductive and sexual rights.[10] And the links between abortion rights (gender-based struggles) and affirmative action (struggles over race and racism) are becoming clearer in the 1990s. While the most challenging critiques of hegemonic feminism were launched in the late 1970s and the 1980s, the present historical moment necessitates taking on board institutional discourses that actively construct and maintain a discourse of difference and pluralism. This in turn calls for assuming responsibility for the politics of voice as it is institutionalized in the academy's "liberal" response to the very questions feminism and other oppositional discourses have raised.[11]

Black/Ethnic Studies and Women's Studies: Intersections and Confluences

> *For us, there is nothing optional about "black experience" and/or "black studies": we must know ourselves.*
>
> —June Jordan

The origins of black, ethnic, and women's studies programs, unlike those of most academic disciplines, can be traced to oppositional social movements. In particular, the civil rights movement, the women's movement, and other Third World liberation struggles fueled the demand for a knowledge and history "of our own." June Jordan's claim that "we must know ourselves" suggests the urgency embedded in the formation of black studies in the late 1960s. Between 1966 and 1970 most American colleges and universities added courses on Afro-American experience and history to their curricula. This was the direct outcome of a number of sociohistorical factors, not the least of which was an increase in black student enrollment in higher education and the broad-based call for a fundamental transformation of a racist, Eurocentric curriculum. Among the earliest programs were the black and African-American studies programs at San Francisco State and Cornell, both of which came into being in 1968, on the heels of militant political organizing on the part of students and faculty at these institutions.[12] A symposium on black studies in early 1968 at Yale University not only inaugurated African-American studies at Yale, but also marked a watershed in the national development of black studies programs.[13] In spring 1969, the University of California at Berkeley instituted a department of ethnic studies, divided into Afro-American, Chicano, contemporary Asian-American, and Native American studies divisions.

A number of women's studies programs also came into being around this time. The first women's studies program was formed in 1969 at San Diego State University. Today 520 such programs exist across the United States.[14] Women's studies programs often drew on the institutional frameworks and structures of existing interdisciplinary programs such as black and ethnic studies. In addition, besides sharing political origins, an interdisciplinary project, and foregrounding questions of social and political inequality in their knowledge base, women's, black, and ethnic studies programs increasingly share pedagogical and research methods. Such programs thus create the possibility of a counterhegemonic discourse and oppositional analytic spaces within the institution. Of course, since these programs are most often located within the boundaries of conservative or liberal white-male-dominated institutions, they face questions of co-optation and accommodation.

In an essay examining the relations among ethnicity, ideology, and the academy, Rosaura Sanchez maintains that new academic programs arise out of specific interests in bodies of knowledge.[15] Sanchez traces the origins of ethnic and women's studies programs, however, to a defensive political move, the state's institutionalization of a discourse of reform in response to the civil rights movement:

> Ethnic studies programs were instituted at a moment when the
> university had to speak a particular language to quell student protests
> and to ensure that university research and business could be conducted
> as usual. The university was able to create and integrate these programs
> administratively under its umbrella, allowing on the one hand, for a
> potential firecracker to diffuse itself and, on the other, moving on to
> prepare the ground for future assimilation of the few surviving faculty
> into existing departments.[16]

Sanchez identifies the pressures (assimilation and co-optation versus isolation and marginalization) that ethnic studies programs have inherited in the 1990s. In fact, it is precisely in the face of the pressure to assimilate that questions of political strategy and of pedagogical and institutional practice assume paramount importance.

For such programs, progress (measured by institutional power, number of people of color in faculty and administrations, effect on the general curricula, etc.) has been slow. Since the 1970s, there have also been numerous conflicts between ethnic, black, and women's studies programs. One example of these tensions is provided by Niara Sudarkasa. Writing in 1986 about the effect of affirmative action on black faculty and administrators in higher education, she argues: "As a matter of record, however, both in the corporate world and in higher education, the progress of white females as a result of affirmative action has far outstripped that for blacks and other minorities."[17] Here Sudarkasa is pointing to a persistent presence of racism in the differential access and mobility of white women and people of color in higher education. She goes on to argue that charges of "reverse discrimination" against white people are unfounded because affirmative action has had the effect of privileging white women above men and women of color. Thus, for Sudarkasa, charges of reverse discrimination leveled at minorities "amount to a sanction of continued

discrimination by insisting that inequalities resulting from privileges historically reserved for whites as a *group* must now be perpetuated in the
name of 'justice' for the *individual*."[18] This process of individualization of
histories of dominance is also characteristic of educational institutions
and processes in general, where the experiences of different constituencies are defined according to the logic of cultural pluralism.

In fact, this individualization of power hierarchies and of structures of
discrimination suggests the convergence of liberal and neoconservative
ideas about gender and race in the academy. Individualization, in this
context, is accomplished through the fundamentally class-based process
of professionalization. In any case, the post-Reagan years (characterized
by financial cutbacks in education, the consolidation of the New Right
and the right-to-life lobby, the increasing legal challenges to affirmative
action regulations, etc.) suggest that it is alliances among women's,
black, and ethnic studies programs that will ensure the survival of such
programs. This is not to imply that these alliances do not already exist,
but, in the face of the active corrosion of the collective basis of affirmative action by the federal government in the name of "reverse discrimination," it is all the more urgent that our institutional self-examinations
lead to concrete alliances. Those of us who teach in some of these programs know that, in this context, questions of voice—indeed, the very
fact of claiming a voice and wanting to be heard—are very complicated
indeed.

To proceed with the first location or site, I attempt an analysis of the
effect of my own pedagogical practices on students when I am teaching
about Third World peoples in a largely white institution. I suggest that a
partial (and problematic) effect of my pedagogy, the location of my
courses in the curriculum and the liberal nature of the institution as a
whole, is the sort of attitudinal engagement with diversity that encourages an empty cultural pluralism and domesticates the historical agency
of Third World people.

Classroom Pedagogies of Gender and Race

How do we construct oppositional pedagogies of gender and race?
Teaching about histories of sexism, racism, imperialism, and homophobia potentially poses very fundamental challenges to the academy and its
traditional production of knowledge, since it has often situated Third
World peoples as populations whose histories and experiences are deviant, marginal, or inessential to the acquisition of knowledge. And this
has happened systematically in our disciplines as well as in our pedagogies. Thus the task at hand is to decolonize our disciplinary and pedagog-

ical practices. The crucial question is how we teach about the West and its Others so that education becomes the practice of liberation. This question becomes all the more important in the context of the significance of education as a means of liberation and advancement for Third World and postcolonial peoples and their/our historical belief in education as a crucial form of resistance to the colonization of hearts and minds.

As a number of educators have argued, however, decolonizing educational practices requires transformations at a number of levels, both within and outside the academy. Curricular and pedagogical transformation has to be accompanied by a broad-based transformation of the culture of the academy, as well as by radical shifts in the relation of the academy to other state and civil institutions. In addition, decolonizing pedagogical practices requires taking seriously the relation between knowledge and learning, on the one hand, and student and teacher experience, on the other. In fact, the theorization and politicization of experience is imperative if pedagogical practices are to focus on more than the mere management, systematization, and consumption of disciplinary knowledge.

I teach courses on gender, race, and education, on international development, on feminist theory, and on Third World feminisms, as well as core women's studies courses such as "Introduction to Women's Studies" and a senior seminar. All of the courses are fundamentally interdisciplinary and cross-cultural. At its most ambitious, this pedagogy is an attempt to get students to think critically about their place in relation to the knowledge they gain and to transform their worldview fundamentally by taking the politics of knowledge seriously. It is a pedagogy that attempts to link knowledge, social responsibility, and collective struggle. And it does so by emphasizing the risks that education involves, the struggles for institutional change, and the strategies for challenging forms of domination and by creating more equitable and just public spheres within and outside educational institutions.

Thus, pedagogy from the point of view of a radical teacher does not entail merely processing received knowledges (however critically one does this) but also actively transforming knowledges. In addition, it involves taking responsibility for the material effects of these very pedagogical practices on students. Teaching about "difference" in relation to power is thus extremely complicated and involves not only rethinking questions of learning and authority but also questions of center and margin. In writing about her own pedagogical practices in teaching African-American women's history, Elsa Barkley Brown[19] formulates her intentions and method in this way:

How do our students overcome years of notions of what is normative? While trying to think about these issues in my teaching, I have come to understand that this is not merely an intellectual process. It is not merely a question of whether or not we have learned to analyze in particular kinds of ways, or whether people are able to intellectualize about a variety of experiences. It is also about coming to believe in the possibility of a variety of experiences, a variety of ways of understanding the world, a variety of frameworks of operation, without imposing consciously or unconsciously a notion of the norm. What I have tried to do in my own teaching is to address both the conscious level through the material, and the unconscious level through the structure of the course, thus, perhaps, allowing my students, in Bettina Apthekar's words, to "pivot the center: to center in another experience."[20]

Clearly, this process is very complicated pedagogically, for such teaching must address questions of audience, voice, power, and evaluation, while retaining a focus on the material being taught. Teaching practices must also combat the pressures of professionalization, normalization, and standardization, the very pressures or expectations that implicitly aim to manage and discipline pedagogies so that teacher behaviors are predictable (and perhaps controllable) across the board.

Barkley Brown draws attention to the centrality of experience in the classroom. While this is an issue that merits much more consideration than I can give here, a particular aspect of it ties into my general argument. Feminist pedagogy has always recognized the importance of experience in the classroom. Since women's and ethnic studies programs are fundamentally grounded in political and collective questions of power and inequality, questions of the politicization of individuals along race, gender, class, and sexual parameters are at the very center of knowledges produced in the classroom. This politicization often involves the "authorization" of marginal experiences and the creation of spaces for multiple, dissenting voices in the classroom. The authorization of experience is thus a crucial form of empowerment for students—a way for them to enter the classroom as speaking subjects. However, this focus on the centrality of experience can also lead to exclusions: it often silences those whose "experience" is seen to be that of the ruling-class groups. This more-authentic-than-thou attitude to experience also applies to the teacher. For instance, in speaking about Third World peoples, I have to watch constantly the tendency to speak "for" Third World peoples. For I often come to embody the "authentic" authority and experience for many of my students; indeed, they construct me as a native informant in the same way that left-liberal white students sometimes construct all people of color as the authentic voices of their people. This is evident in the classroom when the specific "differences" (of personality, posture, behavior, etc.) of one woman of color stand in for the difference of the whole collective, and a collective voice is assumed in place of an individual voice. In effect, this results in the reduction or averaging of Third World peoples in terms of individual personality characteristics: complex ethical and political issues are glossed over, and an ambiguous and more easily manageable ethos of the "personal" and the "interpersonal" takes their place.

Thus, a particularly problematic effect of certain pedagogical codifications of difference is the conceptualization of race and gender in terms of personal or individual experience. Students often end up determining that they have to "be more sensitive" to Third World peoples. The formulation of knowledge and politics through these individualistic, attitudinal parameters indicates an erasure of the very politics of knowledge involved in teaching and learning about difference. It also suggests an erasure of the structural and institutional parameters of what it means to understand difference in historical terms. If all conflict in the classroom is seen and understood in personal terms, it leads to a comfortable set of oppositions: people of color as the central voices and the bearers of all knowledge in class, and white people as "observers" with no responsibility to contribute and/or nothing valuable to contribute. In other words, white students are constructed as marginal observers and students of color as the real "knowers" in such a liberal or left classroom. While it may seem like people of color are thus granted voice and agency in the classroom, it is necessary to consider what particular kind of voice it is that is allowed them/us. It is a voice located in a different and separate space from the agency of white students.[21] Thus, while it appears that in such a class the histories and cultures of marginalized peoples are now "legitimate" objects of study and discussion, the fact is that this legitimation takes place purely at an attitudinal, interpersonal level rather than in terms of a fundamental challenge to hegemonic knowledge and history. Often the culture in such a class vacillates between a high level of tension and an overwhelming desire to create harmony, acceptance of "difference," and cordial relations in the classroom. Potentially this implicitly binary construction (Third World students versus white students) undermines the understanding of co-implication that students must take seriously in order to understand "difference" as historical and relational. Co-implication refers to the idea that all of us (First and Third World) share certain histories as well as certain responsibilities: ideologies of race define both white and black peoples, just as gender ideologies define both women and men. Thus, while "experience" is an enabling focus in the classroom, unless it is explicitly understood as historical, contingent, and the result of interpretation, it can coagulate into frozen, binary, psychologistic positions.

To summarize, this effective separation of white students from Third World students in such an explicitly politicized women's studies classroom is problematic because it leads to an attitudinal engagement that bypasses the complexly situated politics of knowledge and potentially shores up a particular individual-oriented codification and commodification of race. It implicitly draws on and sustains a discourse of cultural pluralism, or what Henry Giroux calls "the pedagogy of normative pluralism,"[22] a pedagogy in which we all occupy separate, different, and equally valuable places and where experience is defined not in terms of individual qua individual, but in terms of an individual as representative of a cultural group. This results in a depoliticization and dehistoricization of the idea of culture and makes possible the implicit management of race in the name of cooperation and harmony.

Cultural pluralism is an inadequate response, however, because the academy as well as the larger social arena are constituted through hierarchical knowledges and power relations. In this context, the creation of oppositional knowledges always involves both fundamental challenges and the risk of co-optation. Creating counterhegemonic pedagogies and combating attitudinal, pluralistic appropriations of race and difference thus involves a delicate and ever-shifting balance between the analysis of experience as lived culture and as textual and historical representations of experience. But most of all, it calls for a critical analysis of the contradictions and incommensurability of social interests as individuals experience, understand, and transform them. Decolonizing pedagogical practices requires taking seriously the different logics of cultures as they are located within asymmetrical power relations. It involves understanding that culture, especially academic culture, is a terrain of struggle (rather than an amalgam of discrete consumable entities). And finally, within the classroom, it requires that teachers and students develop a critical analysis of how experience itself is named, constructed, and legitimated in the academy. Without this analysis of culture and of experience in the classroom, there is no way to develop and nurture oppositional practices. After all, critical education concerns the production of subjectivities *in relation* to discourses of knowledge and power.

The Race Industry and Prejudice-Reduction Workshops

In his incisive critique of current attempts at minority canon formation, Cornel West locates the following cultural crises as circumscribing the present historical moment: the decolonization of the Third World that signaled the end of the European Age; the repoliticization of literary studies in the 1960s; the emergence of alternative, oppositional, subaltern histories; and the transformation of everyday life through the rise of a predominantly visual, technological culture. West locates contests over Afro-American canon formation in the proliferation of discourses of pluralism in the American academy, thus launching a critique of the class interests of Afro-American critics who "become the academic superintendents of a segment of an expanded canon or a separate canon."[23] A similar critique, on the basis of class interests and "professionalization," can be leveled against feminist scholars (First or Third World) who specialize in "reading" the lives/experiences of Third World women. What concerns me here, however, is the predominately white upper-level administrators at our institutions and their "reading" of the issues of racial diversity and pluralism. I agree with West's internal critique of a black managerial class, but I think it is important not to ignore the power of a predominantly white managerial class (men and women) who, in fact, frame and hence determine our voices, livelihoods, and sometimes even our political alliances. Exploring a small piece of the creation and institutionalization of this Race Industry, prejudice-reduction workshops involving upper-level administrators, counselors, and students in numerous institutions of higher education—including the college where I used to teach—shed light on a particular aspect of this industry. Interestingly, the faculty often do not figure in these workshops at all; they are directed either at students and resident counselors or at administrators.

To make this argument, I draw upon the institution I used to teach at, a college that has an impressive history of progressive and liberal policies. But my critique applies to liberal/humanistic institutions of higher education in general. While what follows is a critique of certain practices at the college, I undertake it out of a commitment to and engagement with the academy. The efforts of the college to take questions of difference and diversity on board should not be minimized. However, these efforts should also be subject to rigorous examination because they have far-reaching implications for the institutionalization of multiculturalism in the academy. While multiculturalism itself is not necessarily problematic, its definition in terms of an apolitical, ahistorical cultural pluralism needs to be challenged.

In the last few years there has been an increase in this kind of activity—often as a response to antiracist student organization and demands, or in relation to the demand for and institutionalization of "non-Western" requirements at prestigious institutions—in a number of academic institutions nationally. More precisely, however, these issues of multiculturalism arise as a response to the recognition of changing demographics in the United States. For instance, the fact that by the year 2000 almost 42 percent of all public school students will be minority children or other impoverished children and the fact that by the year 2000 women and people of color will account for nearly 75 percent of the labor force are crucial in understanding institutional imperatives concerning "diversity."[24] As Rosaura Sanchez suggests, for the university to conduct "research and business as usual" in the face of the overwhelming challenges posed by even the very presence of people of color, it has to enact policies and programs aimed at accommodation rather than transformation.

In response to certain racist and homophobic incidents in the spring of 1988, this college instituted a series of "prejudice-reduction" workshops aimed at students and upper- and middle-level administrative staff. These sometimes took the form of "unlearning racism" workshops conducted by residential counselors and psychologists in dorms. Workshops such as these are valuable in "sensitizing" students to racial conflict, behavior, and attitudes, but an analysis of their historical and ideological bases indicates their limitations.

Briefly, prejudice-reduction workshops draw on the psychologically based "race relations" analysis and focus on "prejudice" rather than on institutional or historical domination. The workshops draw on co-counseling and reevaluation counseling techniques and theory and often aim for emotional release rather than political action. The name of this approach is itself somewhat problematic, since it suggests that "prejudice" (rather than domination, exploitation, or structural inequality) is the core problem and that we have to "reduce" it. The language determines and shapes the ideological and political content to a large extent. In focusing on "the healing of past wounds" this approach also equates the positions of dominant and subordinate groups, erasing all power inequities and hierarchies. And finally, the location of the source of "oppression" and "change" in individuals suggests an elision between ideological and structural understandings of power and domination and individual, psychological understandings of power.

Here again, the implicit definition of experience is important. Experience is defined as fundamentally individual and atomistic, subject to behavioral and attitudinal change. Questions of history, collective memory, and social and structural inequality as constitutive of the category of experience are inadmissible within this framework. Individuals speak as representatives of majority or minority groups whose experience is predetermined within an oppressor/victim paradigm. These questions are addressed in A. Sivanandan's incisive critique of the roots of racism awareness training in the United States (associated with the work of Judy Katz et al.) and its embodiment in multiculturalism in Britain.

Sivanandan draws attention to the dangers of the actual degradation and refiguration of antiracist, black political struggles as a result of the racism awareness training focus on psychological attitudes. Thus, while these workshops can indeed be useful in addressing deep-seated psychological attitudes and thus creating a context for change, the danger resides in remaining at the level of personal support and evaluation, and thus often undermining the necessity for broad-based political organization and action.[25]

Prejudice-reduction workshops have also made their way into the upper echelons of the administration at the college. At this level, however, they take a very different form: presidents and their male colleagues do not go to workshops; they "consult" about issues of diversity. Thus, this version of "prejudice reduction" takes the form of "managing diversity" (another semantic gem that suggests that "diversity" [a euphemism for people of color] will be out of control unless it is managed). Consider the following passage from the publicity brochure of a recent consultant:

> Program in Conflict Management Alternatives: A team of applied
> scholars is creating alternative theoretical and practical approaches to the
> peaceful resolution of social conflicts. A concern for maximizing social
> justice, and redressing major social inequities that underlie much social
> conflict, is a central organizing principle of this work. Another concern
> is to facilitate the implementation of negotiated settlements, and
> therefore contribute to long-term change in organizational and
> community relations. Research theory development, organizational and
> community change efforts, networking, consultations, curricula,
> workshops and training programs are all part of the Program.[26]

This passage foregrounds the primary focus on conflict resolution, negotiated settlement, and organizational relations—all framed in a language of research, consultancy, and training. All three strategies—conflict resolution, settlement negotiation, and long-term organizational relations—can be carried out between individuals and between groups. The point is to understand the moments of friction and to resolve the conflicts "peacefully"; in other words, domesticate race and difference by formulating the problems in narrow, interpersonal terms and by rewriting historical contexts as manageable psychological ones.

As in the example of the classroom discussed earlier, the assumption here is that individuals and groups, as individual atomistic units in a social whole composed essentially of an aggregate of such units, embody difference. Thus, conflict resolution is best attempted by negotiating between individuals who are dissatisfied as individuals. One very important ideological effect of this is the standardization of behaviors and responses so as to make them predictable (and thus manageable) across a wide variety of situations and circumstances. If complex structural experiences of domination and resistance can be ideologically reformulated as individual behaviors and attitudes, they can be managed while carrying on business as usual.

Another example of this kind of program is the approach of a company called Diversity Consultants: "Diversity Consultants believe one of the most effective ways to manage multicultural and race awareness issues is through assessment of individual environments, planned educational programs, and management strategy sessions which assist professionals in understanding themselves, diversity, and their options in the workplace."[27]

The key ideas in this statement involve an awareness of race issues (the problem is assumed to be cultural misunderstanding or lack of information about other cultures), understanding yourself and people unlike you (diversity — we must respect and learn from each other; this may not address economic exploitation, but it will teach us to treat each other civilly), negotiating conflicts, altering organizational sexism and racism, and devising strategies to assess and manage the challenges of diversity (which results in an additive approach: recruiting "diverse" people, introducing "different" curriculum units while engaging in teaching as usual — that is, not shifting the normative culture versus subcultures paradigm). This is, then, the "professionalization" of prejudice reduction, where culture is a supreme commodity. Culture is seen as noncontradictory, as isolated from questions of history, and as a storehouse of nonchanging facts, behaviors, and practices. This particular definition of culture and of cultural difference is what sustains the individualized discourse of harmony and civility that is the hallmark of cultural pluralism. Prejudice-reduction workshops eventually aim for the creation of this discourse of civility. Again, this is not to suggest that there are no positive effects of this practice — for instance, the introduction of new cultural models can cause a deeper evaluation of existing structures, and clearly such consultancies could set a positive tone for social change. However, the baseline is still maintaining the status quo; diversity is always and can only be added on.

So what does all this mean? Diversity consultants are not new. Private industry has been using these highly paid management consulting firms since the civil rights movement. When upper-level administrators in higher education inflect discourses of education and "academic freedom" with discourses of the management of race, however, the effects are significant enough to warrant close examination. There is a long history of the institutionalization of the discourse of management and control in American education, but the management of race requires a somewhat different inflection at this historical moment. As a result of historical, demographic, and educational shifts in the racial makeup of students and faculty in the last twenty years, some of us even have public voices that have to be "managed" for the greater harmony of all. The hiring of consultants to "sensitize educators to issues of diversity" is part of the post-1960s proliferation of discourses of pluralism. But it is also a specific and containing response to the changing social contours of the U.S. polity and to the challenges posed by Third World and feminist studies in the academy. By using the language of the corporation and the language of cognitive and affectional psychology (and thereby professionalizing questions of sexism, racism, and class conflict), new alliances are consolidated. Educators who are part of the ruling administrative class are now managers of conflict, but they are also agents in the construction of "race"—a word that is significantly redefined through the technical language that is used.

Race, Voice, and Academic Culture

The effects of this relatively new discourse in the higher levels of liberal arts colleges and universities are quite real. Affirmative action hires are now highly visible and selective; now every English department is looking for a black woman scholar to teach Toni Morrison's writings. What happens to such scholars after they are hired, and particularly when they come up for review or tenure, is another matter altogether. A number of scholars have documented the debilitating effects of affirmative action hiring policies that seek out and hire only those Third World scholars who are at the top of their fields—hence the pattern of musical chairs in which selected people of color are bartered at very high prices. Our voices are carefully placed and domesticated: one in history, one in English, perhaps one in the sociology department. Clearly these hiring practices do not guarantee the retention and tenure of Third World faculty. In fact, while the highly visible bartering for Third World "stars" serves to suggest that institutions of higher education are finally becoming responsive to feminist and Third World concerns, this particular commodification and personalization of race suggests there has been very little change since the 1970s—in terms of either a numerical increase of Third World faculty or our treatment in white institutions.

In a recent article on racism faced by Chicano faculty in institutions of

higher education, Maria de la Luz Reyes and John J. Halcon[28] characterize the effects of the 1970s policies of affirmative action:

> In the mid-1970s, when minority quota systems were being
> implemented in many nonacademic agencies, the general public was left
> with the impression that Chicano or minority presence in professional or
> academic positions was due to affirmative action, rather than to
> individual qualifications or merit. But that impression was inaccurate.
> Generally [institutions of higher education] responded to the affirmative
> action guidelines with token positions for only a handful of minority
> scholars in nonacademic and/or "soft" money programs. For example,
> many Blacks and Hispanics were hired as directors for programs such as
> Upward Bound, Talent Search, and Equal Opportunity Programs.
> Other minority faculty were hired for bilingual programs and ethnic
> studies programs, but affirmative action hires did not commonly extend
> to tenure-track faculty positions. The new presence of minorities on
> college campuses, however, which occurred during the period when
> attention to affirmative action regulations reached its peak, left all
> minority professionals and academics with a legacy of tokenism—a
> stigma that has been difficult to dispel.[29]

De la Luz Reyes and Halcon go on to argue that we are still living with
the effects of the implementation of these policies in the 1980s. They examine the problems associated with tokenism and the ghettoization of
Third World people in the academy, detailing the complex forms of racism that minority faculty face today. To this characterization, I would
add that one of the results of the Reagan-Bush years has been that black,
women's, and ethnic studies programs are often further marginalized,
since one of the effects of the management of race is that individuals
come to embody difference and diversity, while programs that have been
historically constituted on the basis of collective oppositional knowledges are labeled "political," "biased," "shrill," and "unrigorous."[30]
Any inroads made by such programs and departments in the seventies are
being slowly undermined in the eighties and the nineties by the management of race through attitudinal and behavioral strategies, with their logical dependence on individuals seen as appropriate representatives of
"their race" or some other equivalent political constituency. Race and
gender are reformulated as individual characteristics and attitudes, and
thus an individualized, ostensibly "unmarked" discourse of difference is
being put into place. This shift in the academic discourse on gender and
race actually rolls back any progress that has been made in carving out
institutional spaces for women's and black studies programs and departments.

Earlier, it was these institutional spaces that determined our collective voices. Our programs and departments were by definition alternative and oppositional. Now they are often merely alternative—one among many. Without being nostalgic about the good old days (and they were problematic in their own ways), I am suggesting that there has been an erosion of the politics of collectivity through the reformulation of race and difference in individualistic terms. By no means is this a conspiratorial scenario. The discussion of the effects of my own classroom practices indicates my complicity in this context over definitions of gender and race in discursive and representational as well as personal terms. The 1960s and 1970s slogan "The personal is political" was recrafted in the 1980s as "The political is personal." In other words, all politics is collapsed into the personal, and questions of individual behaviors, attitudes, and lifestyles stand in for the political analysis of the social. Individual political struggles are seen as the only relevant and legitimate form of political struggle.

There is, however, another, more crucial reason to be concerned about (and to challenge) this management of race in the liberal academy: this process of the individualization of race and its effects dovetail rather neatly with the neoconservative politics and agenda of the Reagan-Bush years—an agenda that is constitutively recasting the fabric of American life in the pre-1960s mold. The recent Supreme Court decisions on "reverse discrimination" are based on precisely similar definitions of "prejudice," "discrimination," and "race." In an essay that argues that the U.S. Supreme Court's rulings on reverse discrimination are fundamentally tied to the rollback of reproductive freedom, Zillah Eisenstein discusses the individualist framework on which these decisions are based:

> The court's recent decisions pertaining to affirmative action make quite clear that existing civil rights legislation is being newly reinterpreted. Race, or sex (gender) as a collective category is being denied and racism, and/or sexism, defined as a structural and historical reality has been erased. Statistical evidence of racial and/or sexual discrimination is no longer acceptable as proof of unfair treatment of "black women as a group or class." Discrimination is proved by an individual only in terms of their specific case. The assault is blatant: equality doctrine is dismantled.[31]

Eisenstein goes on to analyze how the government's attempts to redress racism and sexism are at the core of the struggle for equality and how, in gutting the meaning of discrimination and applying it only to individual cases and not statistical categories, it has become almost impossible to prove discrimination because there are always "other" criteria to excuse discriminatory practices. Thus, the Supreme Court decisions on reverse discrimination are clearly based on a particular individualist politics that domesticates race and gender. This is an example of the convergence of neoconservative and liberal agendas concerning race and gender inequalities.

Those of us who are in the academy also potentially collude in this domestication of race by allowing ourselves to be positioned in ways that contribute to the construction of these images of pure and innocent diversity, to the construction of these managerial discourses. For instance, since the category of race is not static but a fluid social and historical formation, Third World peoples are often located in antagonistic relationships with each other. Those of us who are from Third World countries are often played off against Third World peoples native to the United States. As an Indian immigrant woman in the United States, for instance, in most contexts I am not as potentially threatening as an African-American woman. Yes, we are both nonwhite and Other, subject to various forms of overt or disguised racism, but I do not bring with me a history of slavery—a direct and constant reminder of the racist past and present of the United States. Of course my location in the British academy would be fundamentally different because of the history of British colonization, because of patterns of immigration and labor force participation, and because of the existence of working-class, trade union, and antiracist politics—all of which define the position of Indians in Britain. An interesting parallel in the British context is the recent focus on and celebration of African-American women as the "true" radical black feminists who have something to say, while black British feminists ("black" in contemporary Britain refers to British citizens of African, Asian, or Caribbean origin) are marginalized and rendered voiceless by the publishing industry and the academy. These locations and potential collusions thus have an impact on how our voices and agencies are constituted.

Critical Pedagogy and Cultures of Dissent

If my argument in this essay is convincing, it suggests why we need to take on questions of race and gender as they are being managed and commodified in the liberal U.S. academy. One mode of doing this is actively creating public cultures of dissent where these issues can be debated in terms of our pedagogies and institutional practices.[32] Creating such cultures in the liberal academy is a challenge in itself, because liberalism allows and even welcomes "plural" or even "alternative" perspectives. However, a public culture of dissent entails creating spaces for epistemological standpoints that are grounded in the interests of people and that recognize the materiality of conflict, of privilege, and of domination. Thus, creating such cultures is fundamentally about making the axes of power transparent in the context of academic, disciplinary, and institutional structures as well as in the interpersonal relationships (rather than individual relations) in the academy. It is about taking the politics of everyday life seriously as teachers, students, administrators, and members of hegemonic academic cultures. Culture itself is thus redefined to incorporate individual and collective memories, dreams, and history that are contested and transformed through the political praxis of day-to-day living.

Cultures of dissent are also about seeing the academy as part of a larger sociopolitical arena that itself domesticates and manages Third World people in the name of liberal capitalist democracy. The struggle to transform our institutional practices fundamentally also involves the grounding of the analysis of exploitation and oppression in accurate history and theory, seeing ourselves as activists in the academy—drawing links between movements for social justice and our pedagogical and scholarly endeavors and expecting and demanding action from ourselves, our colleagues, and our students at numerous levels. This requires working hard to understand and to theorize questions of knowledge, power, and experience in the academy so that one effects both pedagogical empowerment and transformation. Racism, sexism, and homophobia are very real, day-to-day practices in which we all engage. They are not reducible to mere curricular or policy decisions—that is, to management practices.

I said earlier that what is at stake is not the mere recognition of difference. The sort of difference that is acknowledged and engaged has fundamental significance for the decolonization of educational practices. Similarly, the point is not simply that one should have a voice; the more crucial question concerns the sort of voice one comes to have as the result of one's location—both as an individual and as part of collectives.[33] The important point is that it be an active, oppositional, and collective voice that takes seriously the current commodification and domestication of Third World people in the academy. And this is a task open to all—to people of color as well as progressive white people—in the academy.

Notes

This paper was originally written for a conference, "Feminisms and Cultural Imperialism: The Politics of Difference," held at Cornell University April 22-24, 1989. I would like to thank Gloria Watkins (bell hooks), Satya Mohanty, and Jacqui Alexander for numerous passionate discussions on these issues. All three have helped sharpen the arguments in this essay; all faults, however, are mine.

1. Marnia Lazreg, "Feminism and Difference: The Perils of Writing as a Woman on Women in Algeria," *Feminist Studies* 14, no. 1 (Spring 1988): 81-107.

2. Ibid., 98.

3. See especially my "Under Western Eyes: Feminist Scholarship and Colonial Discourses," *Feminist Review* 30 (Autumn 1988): 61-88, and "Feminist Encounters: Locating the Politics of Experience," in the special issue "Fin de Siècle 2000," of *Copyright* 1 (Fall 1987): 30-44. The present essay continues the discussion of the politics of location that I began in "Feminist Encounters" and can, in fact, be seen as a companion text to it.

4. I am referring here to a particular trajectory of feminist scholarship in the last two decades. While scholarship in the 1970s foregrounded gender as *the* fundamental category of analysis and thus enabled the transformation of numerous disciplinary and canonical boundaries, on the basis of the recognition of sexual difference as hierarchy and inequality, scholarship in the 1980s introduced the categories of race and sexuality in the form of internal challenges to the earlier scholarship. These challenges were introduced on both political and methodological grounds by feminists who often considered themselves disenfranchised by the 1970s' feminism: lesbian and heterosexual women of color, postcolonial, Third World women, poor women, etc. While the recent feminist turn to postmodernism suggests the fragmentation of unitary assumptions of gender and enables a more differentiated analysis of inequality, this critique was prefigured in the earlier political analyses of Third World feminists. This particular historical trajectory of the political and conceptual categories of feminist analysis can be traced by analyzing developments in feminist journals such as *Signs* and *Feminist Studies*, feminist publishing houses, and curriculum "integration" projects through the 1970s and 1980s.

5. For instance, Jessie Bernard's *The Female World from a Global Perspective* (Bloomington: Indiana University Press, 1987) codifies difference as the exclusive relation of men to women, and women to women: difference as variation *among* women and as conflict *between* men and women.

6. It is clear from Lazreg's reliance on a notion like intersubjectivity that her understanding of the issue I am addressing in this essay is far from simple. Claiming a voice is for her, as well as for me, a complex historical and political act that involves understanding the interrelationships of voices. The term "intersubjectivity," however, drawing as it does on a phenomenological humanism, brings with it difficult political programs. For a nonhumanist, alternative account of the question of "historical agencies" and their "imbrication," see S. P. Mohanty's recent essay "Us and Them: On the Philosophical Bases of Political Criticism," *Yale Journal of Criticism* 2, no. 2 (Spring 1989): 1-31, and his forthcoming *Literary Theory and the Claims of History* (Cornell University Press, 1994), especially the introduction and chapter 6. Mohanty discusses the question of agency and its historical imbrication (rather than "intersubjectivity") as constituting the fundamental theoretical basis for comparison across cultures.

7. In spite of problems of definition, I use the term "Third World," and in this particular context (the U.S. academy), I identify myself as a "Third World" scholar. I use the term here to designate peoples from formerly colonized countries, as well as people of color in the United States. Using the designation "Third World" to identify colonized peoples in the domestic as well as the international arena may appear reductive because it suggests a commonality and perhaps even an equation among peoples with very diverse cultures and histories and appears to reinforce implicitly existing economic and cultural hierarchies between the "First" and the "Third" World. This is not my intention. I use the term with full awareness of these difficulties and because these are the terms available to us at the moment. In addition, in the particular discursive context of Western feminist scholarship and of the U.S. academy, "Third World" is an oppositional designation that can be empowering even

while it necessitates a continuous questioning. For an elaboration of these questions of definition, see my "Cartographies of Struggle: Third World Women and the Politics of Feminism" in the volume I have edited with Lourdes Torres and Ann Russo (*Third World Women and the Politics of Feminism* [Bloomington: Indiana University Press, 1991]).

8. See especially the work of Paulo Freire, Michael Apple, Basil Bernstein, Pierre Bourdieu, and Henry Giroux. While a number of these educational theorists offer radical critiques of education on the basis of class hierarchies, very few do so on the basis of gender or race. However, the theoretical suggestions in this literature are provocative and can be used to advantage in feminist analysis. The special issue "On Racism and American Education," *Harvard Educational Review* 58, no. 3 (1988) is also an excellent resource. See also Paulo Freire, *Pedagogy of the Oppressed*, trans. Myra Bergman Ramos (New York: Seabury, 1973); Paulo Freire and Donaldo Macedo, *Literacy: Reading the Word and the World* (South Hadley, Mass.: Bergin and Garvey, 1985); Michael Apple, *Ideology and the Curriculum* (London: Routledge and Kegan Paul, 1979); Basil Bernstein, *Class, Codes, and Control*, vol. 3 (London: Routledge and Kegan Paul, 1975); Henry Giroux, *Theory and Resistance in Education: A Pedagogy for the Opposition* (South Hadley, Mass.: Bergin and Garvey, 1983); Henry Giroux, *Teachers As Intellectuals: Toward a Critical Pedagogy of Learning* (South Hadley, Mass.: Bergin and Garvey, 1988); and Pierre Bourdieu and J. C. Passeron, *Reproduction in Education, Society and Culture*, trans. Richard Nice (Beverly Hills, Calif.: Sage, 1977). For feminist analyses of education and the academy, see Charlotte Bunch and Sandra Pollack, eds., *Learning Our Way: Essays in Feminist Education* (Trumansburg, N.Y.: Crossing, 1983); Elizabeth Minnich et al., eds. *Reconstructing the Academy: Women's Education and Women's Studies* (Chicago: University of Chicago Press, 1988); Marilyn Schuster and Susan Van Dyne, *Women's Place in the Academy: Transforming the Liberal Arts Curriculum* (Totowa, N.J.: Rowman and Allanheld, 1985); and Elizabeth Minnich, *Transforming Knowledge* (Philadelphia: Temple University Press, 1990). See also back issues of the journals *Women's Studies Quarterly*, *Women's Studies International Forum*, and *Frontiers: A Journal of Women's Studies*.

9. I am fully aware that I am drawing on an extremely limited (and some might say atypical) sample for this analysis. Clearly, in the bulk of American colleges and universities, the very introduction of questions of pluralism and difference is itself a radical and oppositional gesture. However, in the more liberal institutions of higher learning, questions of pluralism have had a particular institutional history, and I draw on the example of the college I currently teach at to investigate the implications of this specific institutionalization of discourses of pluralism. I am concerned with raising some political and intellectual questions that have urgent implications for the discourses of race and racism in the academy, not with providing statistically significant data on U.S. institutions of higher learning, nor with claiming "representativeness" for the liberal arts college I draw on to raise these questions.

10. For analyses of the intersection of the race and sex agendas of the New Right, see essays in the special double issue of *Radical America* 15, nos. 1 and 2 (1981). I have utilized Zillah Eisenstein's "Feminism v. Neoconservative Jurisprudence: The Spring '89 Supreme Court" (unpublished manuscript, 1990). I am indebted to her for sharing this essay with me and for our discussions on this subject.

11. Some of the most poignant and incisive critiques of the inscription of race and difference in scholarly institutional discourses have been raised by Third World scholars working outside women's studies. See Cornel West, "Minority Discourse and the Pitfalls of Canon Formation," *Yale Journal of Criticism* 1, no. 1 (Fall 1987): 193-202; A. Sivanandan, "RAT and the Degradation of Black Struggle," *Race and Class* 26, no. 4 (Spring 1985): 1-34; and S. P. Mohanty, "Us and Them."

12. Information about the origins of black studies is drawn from Nathan I. Huggins, *Afro-American Studies, A Report to the Ford Foundation*, July 1985. For provocative analyses

64 Chandra Talpade Mohanty

and historic essays on black studies in the 1960s and 1970s, see John W. Blassingame, ed., *New Perspectives on Black Studies* (Urbana: University of Illinois Press, 1973).

13. For documentation of this conference, see Armstead I. Robinson, Craig C. Foster, and Donald H. Ogilvie, eds., *Black Studies in the University, A Symposium* (New York: Bantam, 1969).

14. This information is culled from the National Women's Studies Association Task Force Report on *The Women's Studies Major*, 1990. See also essays in Minnich et al., eds., *Reconstructing the Academy*.

15. Rosaura Sanchez, "Ethnicity, Ideology and Academia," *The Americas Review* 15, no. 1 (Spring 1987): 80–88.

16. Ibid., 86.

17. Niara Sudarkasa, "Affirmative Action or Affirmation of Status Quo? Black Faculty and Administrators in Higher Education," *American Association of Higher Education Bulletin*, February 1987: 3–6.

18. Ibid., 4.

19. Elsa Barkley Brown, "African-American Women's Quilting: A Framework for Conceptualizing and Teaching African-American Women's History," *Signs* 14, no. 4 (Summer 1989): 921-29.

20. Ibid., 921.

21. As a contrast, and for an interesting analysis of similar issues in the pedagogical context of a white woman teaching multicultural women's studies, see Peggy Pascoe's "At the Crossroad of Culture," *Women's Review of Books* 7, no. 5 (February 1990): 22-23.

22. Giroux, *Teachers As Intellectuals*, 95.

23. West, "Minority Discourse," 197.

24. See the American Council on Education, Education Commission of the States, "One-Third of a Nation: A Report of the Commission on Minority Participation in Education and American Life" (Washington, D.C.: American Council on Education, 1988). See also articles on "America's Changing Colors" in *Time*, April 9, 1990, especially William H. Henry III, "Beyond the Melting Pot," for statistics on changing demographics in U.S. economic and educational spheres.

25. This discussion of the ideological assumptions of "prejudice reduction" is based on Patti DeRosa's presentation at the Society for International Education, Training, and Research Conference in May 1987.

26. From "Towards Prejudice Reduction: A Resource Document of Consultants, Audio/Visual Aids, and Providers of Workshops, Training and Seminars," a document prepared by Sue E. Prindle, associate director of personnel and affirmative action officer at Oberlin (Ohio) College, 1988: I.

27. Ibid., 8.

28. Maria de la Luz Reyes and John J. Halcon, "Racism in Academia: The Old Wolf Revisited," *Harvard Educational Review* 58, no. 3 (1988): 299-314.

29. Ibid., 303.

30. This marginalization is evident in the financial cutbacks that such programs have experienced in recent years. The depoliticization is evident in, for instance, the current shift from "women's" to "gender" studies—by all measures, a controversial reconstitution of feminist agendas.

31. Eisenstein, "Feminism v. Neoconservative Jurisprudence," 5.

32. Gloria Watkins (bell hooks) and I have attempted to do this in a collegewide faculty colloquium called "Pedagogies of Gender, Race, and Empire" that focuses on our practices in teaching and learning about Third World people in the academy. While the effects of this colloquium have yet to be thoroughly examined, at the very least it has created a public

culture of dialogue and dissent where questions of race, gender, and identity are no longer totally dismissed as "political" and thus extraneous to academic endeavor, nor are they automatically ghettoized in women's studies and black studies. These questions are seen (by a substantial segment of the faculty) as important, constitutive questions in revising a Eurocentric liberal arts curriculum.

33. See my "Feminist Encounters" for an elaboration of these issues.

Chapter 4

Clarence Thomas, Affirmative Action, and the Academy

Evelynn Hammonds

It is perhaps stating the obvious to note that the Senate confirmation hearings of Clarence Thomas, who was named an associate justice of the United States Supreme Court in the fall of 1991, were a historic event. The testimony of former Thomas employee and current University of Oklahoma law professor Anita Hill that she was sexually harassed by Thomas was for many the most startling event of the confirmation proceedings. Startling indeed were her accusations, as was his response. Nearly a century of racial and sexual tension within African-American communities and in the larger U.S. society crystallized before our very eyes during these proceedings. Yet, coming as they did at the end of the hearings, Hill's accusations only highlighted tensions that were present from the very moment Thomas was nominated to the Court. Many analyses of the hearings focused on the Hill allegations, with less attention to the debates over Thomas's record on affirmative action.

In the summer of 1991, President George Bush nominated Judge Clarence Thomas to fill the Supreme Court position left vacant by the retirement of Justice Thurgood Marshall. In what was clearly a politically motivated appointment, Bush declared Thomas to be the "best man for the job." Political pundits and commentators rushed to point out that Bush's choice of this nominee revealed his recognition of the need to shore up his image in the black community by replacing Marshall with another black man, albeit one who espoused a conservative ideology. For a president tainted by his use of racial stereotypes in his 1988 Willie Horton campaign ads, surely this was a shrewd political move. The Thomas nomination and confirmation hearings revealed the racial tensions and the disputes over affirmative action that had been simmering outside of public view since the end of the civil rights era and throughout the period of the Republican domination of the presidency.

While these issues received scant analysis in the daily press and national news magazines during the past twenty years, in-depth analysis has occurred in the academy. As higher education has become more democratic, debates over affirmative action in admission and hiring and over the inclusion in college curricula of African-American literature, culture, and history, of ethnic studies, and of women's studies have increasingly occupied center stage. These debates intensified in 1990, when scholars, writers, and other self-described conservative commentators began to attack the trend toward democratization occurring in the universities across the country. This recent conflict in the academy has been shaped by the reaction to the presence of larger numbers of students of color; the use of new methodologies in scholarship on race, ethnicity, and gender; and the presence of more faculty women and people of color with tenure, especially at elite universities. It seems that few outside the academy realized the scope of the debates or the impact of the demographic and curriculum changes on U.S. higher education until media attention focused on the publication of Dinesh D'Souza's *Illiberal Education* and other conservative books warning that the barbarians were at the gates.

Against this conservative backdrop, Bush moved ahead with his nomination of Thomas to the Supreme Court. During the confirmation hearings, the testimony of African-American scholars and intellectuals holding views contrary to that of the nominee was discounted by the Senate committee and by the news media. The sophisticated analyses of race, affirmative action, legal issues, and the need to support civil rights legislation were largely incomprehensible to the committee members, and they were distorted by reporters more concerned with the "authentic" voice of people in barber shops and shopping malls.

In this essay I want to discuss the ways in which the testimony of African-American intellectuals and scholars in the Thomas confirmation hearings was juxtaposed with the position taken by Thomas and his Republican supporters to ultimately undermine both liberal left political views on affirmative action and African-American scholars whose research supports those views. I realize that the Thomas confirmation hearings were a highly politicized event. The behind-the-scenes machinations can be known now only through press accounts, though more detailed and scholarly accounts of the hearings will certainly appear in the future. As an African-American woman doctoral student and teacher in the academy, I watched the proceedings with a great deal of skepticism, cynicism, and, ultimately, despair. The gavel-to-gavel television coverage showed so starkly that we live in a country governed by and for white men. But most importantly, the hearings confirmed my own view that little of the recent scholarship documenting the history of African-Americans and women, few of the sophisticated analyses of race and ethnicity, and few of the sociological studies of institutional discrimination based on race, class, and gender have filtered into public discussion of these issues. The senators and the media alike seemed largely uninformed about and unaware of this work, though the familiar rhetoric of those engaged in the ideological attack on the academy—and their deployment of buzzwords like "political correctness" to denigrate study of race, class, and gender—was fully evident in the hearings.

The Thomas confirmation hearings served as one more public forum for the backlash against the hard-won principles of equal opportunity in the workplace and in the university. The hearings made it clear that affirmative action, like "political correctness," will be subjected to distortions by the right and their mouthpieces in the media. We in the academy have to be prepared when those who oppose affirmative action and multicultural education use these distortions in discussions of faculty searches and promotions.

The Thomas Testimony

On September 10, 1991, Clarence Thomas made his opening remarks to the Senate Judiciary Committee. He began with a vivid and moving story of growing up in the small town of Pin Point, Georgia. His father had abandoned the family, and his mother, struggling to make ends meet on a salary of ten dollars a week, eventually gave Clarence and his brother over to be raised by their grandfather. "Imagine if you will," he said, "two little boys with all their belongings in two grocery bags. Our grandparents were two great and wonderful people who loved us dearly. I wish they were sitting here today, sitting here so that they could see that all their efforts, their hard work were not in vain, and so that they could see that hard work and strong values can make for a better life."[1] Those in the hall and many watching on television wiped tears from their eyes as Thomas spoke. After paying homage to the leaders of the civil rights movement and to Justice Marshall, Thomas concluded by asking that the committee view him as "an honest, decent and fair person. I believe that the obligations and responsibilities of a judge in essence involve just such basic values. A judge must be fair and impartial. A judge must not bring to his job, to the Court, the baggage of preconceived notions, of ideology, and certainly not an agenda."[2]

The evening news repeatedly showed the teary-eyed Thomas making his statement, which evoked for many whites and for some African-Americans the quintessential American myth of Horatio Alger pulling himself up from humble beginnings against tremendous odds to reach the pinnacle of his profession. Thomas's opening speech skillfully set the tone for the strategy he and his Republican supporters had mapped out. Thomas pictured himself as a black man with humble beginnings in the segregated South who had by the sheer force of his own persistence and the support of his stalwart grandparents lifted himself up to make a successful life. It was a story of individual achievement made possible more by his own strong values than by government programs or social change. He was careful not to discount the fact that the civil rights movement and the work of Justice Marshall had to some extent cleared the way for him, but he clearly presented the influence of his grandparents and his Catholic-school teachers as the primary factors in his success.

The subtext of this speech was ripe for use by the conservative right-wingers who argued that affirmative action programs were no longer needed, and soothed the many white Americans who wanted to be relieved of responsibility for individual and institutional racism and the plight of poor, uneducated African-Americans in the inner cities. The speech also undermined the leadership of the traditional civil rights organizations by putting them in the position of having to disagree with an African-American man in the glare of the white-controlled media.

Thomas's record as head of the Equal Employment Opportunity Commission (EEOC) during two Republican administrations quickly became the focus of questions from the members of the Senate Judiciary Committee, and his views on affirmative action received a great deal of attention. Since affirmative action loomed so large in the hearings, I want to state here my own views. I am not a legal scholar, so I have had to rely on others' interpretations of the statutes and court cases that define affirmative action policies. Rather than focus solely on legal interpretations, which though they figured prominently in the hearings were difficult for the average person to follow, I have relied on more general discussions of the issue. I define affirmative action in the broadest way as active measures—not merely passive nondiscrimination—to increase significantly the recruitment and promotion of minorities in the workplace and in educational institutions.[3] The as yet unrealized goal of such policies is, as Gertrude Ezorsky notes, to reduce institutional racism and increase occupational and educational integration. As the Senate debate indicates, one of the most controversial aspects of affirmative action programs is the question of preferences. Affirmative action programs do not require that employers hire unqualified women or blacks at the expense of qualified white males. Unfortunately, it is widely perceived that African-Americans hired under affirmative action programs are unqualified—as evidenced by the campaign advertisement used by Senator Jesse Helms showing an unemployed white male worker who ostensibly lost his job because of affirmative action. Conservatives have been particularly adept at suggesting that the issue of preferences in affirmative action programs undermines the entire premise of such programs.

Like most aspects of the Thomas hearings, the tone and slant of the questions split along party lines. Senator Orrin Hatch, a Republican from Utah, acknowledged that there is no consensus on what affirmative action means: "It can mean reviewing one's employment practices to eliminate discriminatory practices. It can mean increasing an employer's outreach and recruitment activities aimed at increasing the numbers of minorities and women in the applicant pool, from which all applicants will then be considered fairly, without regard to race or gender."[4] Hatch claimed that most Americans do not object to these kinds of affirmative action programs. The controversial and deeply divisive programs were those that, in his view, "call for preference on the basis of race, ethnicity, and gender," those in which "lesser qualified persons are preferred over better qualified persons in jobs, educational admissions, and contract awards on the basis of race, ethnicity, and gender."[5]

Thomas, in his response to questions from Hatch, agreed that no preference should be given to unqualified persons on the basis of race, ethnicity, or gender. He advocated vigorous training programs and employee recruitment programs to broaden the applicant pools, yet he maintained that promotions, for example, should be based solely on qualifications, thus reinforcing the conservative view that under affirmative action programs this was not the case.

Questioned by Senator Edward Kennedy on the issue of affirmative action, Thomas reiterated that statutes that require only neutrality—without regard to race, sex, or national origin, even in the face of discriminatory employment practices—should be upheld. Overall, Thomas held fast to the view that "with respect to affirmative action programs, I tried to explain . . . the tensions between the notion of fairness to everyone and this desire to help people who are left out. There is a tension. And how far do you go in trying to include people who are left out and not be unfair to other individuals? I have initiated affirmative action programs. I have supported affirmative action programs. Whether or not I agree with all of them, I think, is a matter of record. But the fact that I don't agree with all of them does not mean that I am not a supporter of the underlying effort. I am and have been my entire adult life."[6]

The questioning of Thomas by the Senate on the issue of affirmative action illuminated many problems evident in debates on this subject in the academy. No one offered a clear, concise, or complete description of what constitutes affirmative action either in the workplace or in educational institutions, and no one presented data on the effectiveness of laws governing affirmative action programs. The questions implied that the "real" issue in this debate was that at some point such programs had begun to depart from their original purpose of supporting equal opportunity and were instead promoting inequality. The ugly specter of reverse discrimination was thus raised, though no evidence was presented to show that reverse discrimination was either widespread or a direct result of affirmative action policies.

Many white male commentators, especially conservative Republicans, have argued that affirmative action programs now promote inequality rather than equality. The assumption underlying this argument is that we now live in a color-blind society where the racist policies of the past have been redressed, and that therefore we have no need of policies that address past inequities. This point of view is buttressed by prominent African-American male writers like Shelby Steele and Stephen Carter who argue that affirmative action programs stigmatize their beneficiaries.[7] Thomas himself had a history of speaking out against affirmative action programs prior to his confirmation hearings. He is quoted as referring to such programs as "a narcotic of dependency" on which black people were hooked. They had come to expect help rather than earn their way upward, he argued.[8]

The fact that Thomas's and other black conservatives' views on affirmative action were at odds with those of many leading civil rights organizations and some prominent African-American scholars formed the backdrop to the questioning of Thomas on this issue but was never articulated during the confirmation hearings. No one in the media brought to the fore the divergent views on affirmative action. Thus, the public was left less than fully informed about the complexity of the issue of affirmative action and had little basis for evaluating the testimony in support of and opposition to Thomas. I suggest, however, that this testimony is crucial for those of us in the academy who support affirmative action programs in the face of increasing criticism.

Testimony of Public Witnesses

A number of prominent African-American scholars and activists testified for and against Thomas's nomination to the Supreme Court, including law professors Drew Days of Yale, Charles Lawrence of Stanford, and Christopher Edley of Harvard, all of whom testified on September 17. Days argued that he was concerned that Thomas's speeches and his articles indicated a "detachment from history."[9] In particular, Days said, Thomas tended to speak of affirmative action issues as if "they arose only yesterday . . . in some cases, the day before he began to speak about the issues, rather than as a consequence of very long and difficult, and hard and painful efforts by a number of people including civil rights groups to deal with the problems of discrimination and exclusion."[10]

The problem with Thomas's focus on individual perspectives rather than the history of African-Americans as a group was pointed out by Edley, who argued that Thomas asked to be judged on the basis of his individual character in order to obscure his record on affirmative action. Edley noted that "the heart of the administration's affirmative case is Judge Thomas's personal story and character, in hopes perhaps that this strategy will undergird his credibility and present an image strikingly more attractive than piles of speeches and abstractions."[11]

Days suggested that Thomas wanted the Court to "think only in terms of the individual and not see the institutional context," and he noted that Yale Law School had an affirmative action program that Thomas had benefited from. Yale had instituted the program, Days argued, precisely because "in this country there has been a systematic exclusion of minorities and women from legal education and other types of higher education, [so that] it was necessary for institutions to reach out and find qualified individuals and bring them in because doing it by the numbers, putting them through a computer, would not produce that result [including women and minorities]."[12] Lawrence added that it was important to remember that "we are not so far away from *Brown v. Board of Education* that we have reached a place where these institutions are meaningfully integrated, certainly not at the levels of faculty and administration, and not even at the levels of our students."

In the ensuing questioning, Senator Arlen Specter, a Republican from Pennsylvania, asked the law professors whether Thomas held "reasonable" views on the issue of affirmative action. They replied that Thomas's views could be seen as somewhat reasonable, though all three disagreed with them. Specter took their answers to suggest that there was simply a matter of difference of opinion rather than a substantive and serious disagreement on the issue.

As the questioning continued, the Republican senators often said to the witnesses that Thomas supported the notion of race neutrality in promotions and the protection of, as Senator Hatch put it, "innocent persons

who are discriminated against in what is called reverse discrimination."
Days responded that including race and sex as hiring or promotion criteria is not de facto reverse discrimination and noted that many types of
preferences are used in our society—those for veterans, for example. The
questioning focused on the differences between Thomas's view of how to
apply affirmative action programs in a race-neutral way versus these law
professors' assertions of the faults with Thomas's perspective. Discussions of the particulars of various contemporary and past cases before the
Court did little to make these differences clearer. Hatch pointedly said
that "all . . . of us . . . —the three of you and myself and, I think, Clarence Thomas[—]would like the same type of results. . . . Where we
differ is what is mainstream in America, and what isn't? And I submit
that the vast majority of American people would agree with Clarence
Thomas on the issue of preference."[13]

As I watched this exchange on television and later, as I was reading the
transcript, it was clear that the Republicans' strategy was to highlight the
most troubling aspect of affirmative action programs, the issue of preferences, and to cast Thomas as a supporter of fairness. They simultaneously disallowed any argument suggesting that the fact of past and
present discrimination could undermine such an eminently fair position.
Finally, Specter's questions made it apparent that he felt the important
point was to determine whether Thomas's views were in step with mainstream views on affirmative action. While never clarifying what he meant
by the term, other Republicans on the committee seemed to suggest that
ordinary citizens—not scholars or representatives of civil rights, wom-
en's, or labor groups—were the "mainstream." Specter's question—"Is
Judge Thomas's view a reasonable one?"—would be asked again and
again of witnesses for and against Thomas.

The positions taken by the law professors indicated that there was
some dissension in the black community on the issue of affirmative action in general and on Thomas's position in particular. Niara Sudarkasa,
an anthropologist and the first black female president of Lincoln University, appeared in support of Thomas, but to some extent she disagreed
with him on the question of affirmative action. She declared her support
for him based on the fact that he was an "open-minded and independent
thinker" and thus could be "persuaded to see and indeed, has been persuaded to see, that in order to redress past discrimination, the concept of
equity rather than strict equality has to be applied." Furthermore, she
said, she understood where Thomas's view came from. Thomas was a
product of his times, himself a beneficiary of affirmative action programs. Many in his generation had problems coming to terms with
whites' perception of these programs. "When I was a professor of an-

thropology and associate vice president at the University of Michigan,"
she said, "many students came to me with grave concerns about the way
they were being treated by their peers as well as by faculty members because of the perception that they came to the university on something
other than their own merit."[14] While she did not dispute that affirmative
action was the cause of such views, she noted that "affirmative action is
little more than two decades old. . . . There is nothing sacrosanct about
this as the only means by which we can attain equity and justice for those
who have been discriminated against. . . . If we listen carefully to . . .
the critics of some aspects of affirmative action practice, we may be able
to improve upon that particular means of access. It is not simply that one
is either for affirmative action or against it. One can be for affirmative
action and still seek out ways to improve it."[15]

Sudarkasa expressed her belief that Thomas's criticisms of affirmative
action were in the mainstream and, perhaps anticipating the questions she
would be asked, noted that leaders of the African-American community
have often expressed divergent views, citing differences between Martin
Delany and Frederick Douglass, between W. E. B. Du Bois and Booker
T. Washington, and between Martin Luther King, Jr., and Malcolm X.
Her point was that these leaders had "brought us thus far on our way. We
see in [Thomas] a leader with a different voice for a different time."
Other witnesses supported Sudarkasa's views. A black lawyer from At-
lanta testified that "black Americans need not and should not all think
alike, and this diversity of opinion within the black community on how
black Americans should advance is deeply rooted in our history and has
served black Americans and this nation well over the years." Members of
the Congressional Black Caucus, however, took exception to this view.
Rep. Washington said the issue was not simply a difference of opinion
among the black leadership. "Judge Thomas's view," Washington argued, "is that whatever happened to him, good or bad, happened to him
as an individual. . . . Nothing could be further from the truth. Prejudice
is prejudgment because of group identification."[16]

Though the witnesses were correct in their assertion that there is a history of dissent within the African-American community as to how best
to advance the cause of the race, it is the content of those debates that is
important. Furthermore, while dissent in itself is certainly laudable, it is
far from reasonable to ignore the profound and not always positive consequences that the differences among African-American leaders has had
on the status of African-Americans in this country. These witnesses were
arguing, to some extent, the question of whether self-help as espoused by
Thomas could possibly erase the barriers that African-Americans experience as a group because of racial prejudice. In her testimony, law pro-

fessor Pat Williams said, "While self-help and strong personal values are marvelous virtues, they are no stand-in for zealous protection of civil and human rights. . . . The problem with Thomas's espousal of self-help values is that he positions them in direct either/or tension with any other value. Self-help is presented as bitterly competitive rather than in complete concert with those social remedies and measures that would help ever more rather than ever fewer people."[17]

The response of the members of the judiciary committee to these witnesses indicated that they—and probably the majority of white Americans—were largely unaware that such differences on the issue of affirmative action and other means to advance the race existed within the African-American community. The historical references to other debates on this question were largely ignored and had little impact on the discussion in the confirmation hearings. The fact that this history was unknown contributed to the depiction by the senators and in the media of the discussion as a mere difference of opinion among reasonable people in the African-American community. Self-help was portrayed by the Republicans as a more reasonable option for African-Americans than continued reliance on government programs to address the concerns of African-Americans—an approach that, it was claimed, had largely failed. The Democrats on the committee appeared to be unable to bring to the fore how this notion of self-help was being used by the Republicans to support their political agenda of restricting current affirmative action programs.

Not only was there little consensus on the definition of affirmative action, the committee largely dismissed the analysis offered by legal scholars and activists. The testimony of Thomas supporters appeared to be more acceptable. The Reverend Soires, pastor of the First Baptist Church of Somerset, New Jersey, testifying in favor of Thomas, described his views of affirmative action thus:

> Affirmative action for me and for those persons I grew up with meant . . . that there was an inside crowd and an outside crowd. The inside crowd had been protected by laws and by traditions which virtually excluded the outside crowd irrespective of qualifications. Affirmative action meant that the inside crowd would use creative ideas and meaningful efforts to include the outside crowd based on the fact that they had been excluded without regard to qualifications. And so affirmative action meant that the government would protect the outsiders from being excluded simply by virtue of the color of their skin. Government intervention has never been the question that we debate. . . . We are against using affirmative action as a means of denying other people opportunities in the name of helping the outsiders

so that the outsiders are now discriminating against the insiders, and then become victims themselves.[18]

Soires's comments were startling. While he recognized that government intervention was necessary to redress past discriminatory practices, he seemed to be suggesting that black people now practiced discrimination against whites. Most importantly, he was simply presenting his personal opinion about affirmative action. Meanwhile, Yale Law School Dean Guido Calabresi's testimony reflected his awareness of the various legal debates on the issue, and he knew where Thomas's position fell within those debates:

> Affirmative action is a very complicated issue. . . . One of the key things for me . . . is, is affirmative action really something that is benefiting a disadvantaged group where the bulk of the burdens are being borne by people who have all the advantages, and then I am for it, and it is in that respect that I disagree with Judge Thomas. . . . On the other hand, it is often the case that what is described as affirmative action is not those who have put a burden on themselves for the benefit of the have nots, which is admirable and should be supported. But is those who have put a burden on one group of have nots in order to help another group of have nots and that is much more of a problem. . . . Judge Thomas has been too sensitive to this second part and thinks that it always is this way. I think some of the people on the other side have been too insensitive to the existence of that.[19]

Neither the senators nor the media pundits made an attempt to make clear the substantive differences between the testimony of witnesses like Calabresi and Soires. Calabresi was speaking to the fact that though a well-off white male might lose a place at Yale because of affirmative action programs, he would mostly likely have other equally favorable chances to attend a good law school, though in the workplace, affirmative action programs could potentially harm persons who had few opportunities for a job elsewhere.

The issue was to what extent some white men might have been deprived of benefits as a result of affirmative action programs. Calabresi and Soires both had opinions but little data, and no sustained discussion revealed to what extent this was really a problem in the workplace or anywhere else in American society. Most importantly, in these hearings the witnesses most engaged in the legal, employment, and educational aspects of affirmative action programs, those with the most expertise on the subject, were seen as ideologues rather than as bearers of the most informed commentary.

The Vote

At the end of the first set of Thomas hearings, the committee members cast their votes. The vote was clearly split along party lines, yet the reasons given by the senators for their votes shows how the presentations of the various public witnesses had been received. In general, the Republicans were impressed by those who knew Thomas personally. Several commented on the love and affection displayed toward him by the people who knew him best. Others agreed with those who said Thomas's views on affirmative action represented the mainstream, though two senators commented that they were puzzled by the opposition to Thomas from leaders of civil rights organizations. Overall, it was Thomas's personal character and his support of race-neutral affirmative action policies that carried the day.

The Democratic senators who voted against Thomas emphasized the problems they found in his record, particularly during his tenure as head of the EEOC. One of the senators noted that he was voting against Thomas because of the opposition of the civil rights organizations that came out against him. None acknowledged the points raised by witnesses who either supported or opposed Thomas's views on affirmative action.

There was nothing surprising in the vote. The senators' responses reflected the political nature of the hearings and the motivations of the Bush administration. There was little clarity about what affirmative action programs have accomplished in the past or about how they might be improved. The debate in this first round of Thomas confirmation hearings underscored the Bush administration and Republican party agenda of defining affirmative action programs as responsible for instituting quotas and preferential treatment for undeserving women and people of color. In effect, it promoted the notion that deserving white men have been victims of the reverse discrimination ascribed to affirmative action programs. The complex nature of affirmative action programs was simply lost in the political maneuvers.

Conclusion

It is useful for academics to look at the parallels between the Thomas confirmation hearings and the so-called debate on "political correctness" on our campuses. We should not forget that in the months preceding the hearings, the Bush administration had challenged the right of universities to set aside monies for minority scholarships. The Department of Education had questioned the authority of accrediting agencies to require diversity on college campuses.[20] The unfounded accusations made by conservative writers from groups such as the National Association of Scholars consistently claim that white men are being silenced in the classroom by feminists and by African-American and ethnic studies scholars. Many have pointed out the fallacy of such views, arguing that the new courses encourage honest and open debate about some of the most complex and emotional issues faced by our society[21] — and cover areas of our history and culture that traditionally have been left out of college curricula. These rebuttals have largely failed to gain the upper hand in public discourse, which continues to focus on the so-called harm being done to white men rather than the continuing discrimination against women and people of color.

The hearings also revealed the abysmal ignorance of African-American history among the U.S. citizenry. The senators from both parties and the media commentators often seemed puzzled by or simply ignored the historical references made by the witnesses. Informed, sustained, and substantive debate about affirmative action will not be possible without broader knowledge of the history of race relations in this country. The same is true of women's issues, as was shown by the second round of hearings that followed the allegations of sexual harassment made by Professor Anita Hill. The potential for distortion and demagoguery that ignorance of history can breed was painfully evident throughout the hearings.

Rather than feeling disheartened by the events that led to the appointment of Clarence Thomas to the Supreme Court, I have slowly regained a sense of hope. These events revealed the vital need for scholarship on race, ethnicity, gender, and class. We must make it clear that the critical analyses of these subjects produced in the academy are necessary — not peripheral — to governmental and public debate. Those of us committed to this work must make alliances with the media in order to make it accessible to wider audiences. There is no guarantee that the work we have done in the academy on race and gender relations could have made a difference in the outcome of the Thomas confirmation, yet I deeply believe it is critical to the struggle for an egalitarian, truly democratic society that includes all of the people who live in this country.

Notes

1. Testimony of Clarence Thomas as quoted in Timothy Phelps and Helen Winternitz, *Capitol Games: Clarence Thomas, Anita Hill, and the Story of a Supreme Court Nomination* (New York: Hyperion, 1992), 173.

2. Ibid., 174.

3. One of the most cogent analyses of affirmative action that I am familiar with is Gertrude Ezorsky's *Racism and Justice: The Case for Affirmative Action* (Ithaca, N.Y.: Cornell

University Press, 1991), 31. Ezorsky documents the development of affirmative action programs and policies and explicates the moral questions that they have raised.

4. Transcript of the hearings of the Senate Judiciary Committee on the nomination of Clarence Thomas to the United States Supreme Court, September 12, 1991.

5. Ibid.

6. Ibid.

7. See Shelby Steele, "A Negative Vote on Affirmative Action," *New York Times Magazine*, May 13, 1990, and Stephen Carter, *Reflections of an Affirmative Action Baby* (New York: Basic Books, 1991).

8. Phelps and Winternitz, *Capitol Games*, 95.

9. Transcript, September 17, 1991.

10. Ibid.

11. Ibid.

12. Ibid.

13. Ibid.

14. Ibid.

15. Ibid.

16. Transcript, September 19, 1991.

17. Transcript, September 20, 1991.

18. Transcript, September 19, 1991.

19. Transcript, September 17, 1991.

20. See comments by Senator Paul Simon at the Thomas confirmation hearings, September 17, 1991.

21. See, for example, the essay by Ian Haney López in this volume.

PART II

Multiple Voices, Ongoing Struggles

Chapter 5

The Politics of Inclusion: Reskilling the Academy
Becky W. Thompson and Sangeeta Tyagi

> *Decolonizing educational practices requires transformations at a number of levels,*
> *both within and outside of the academy. . . . Decolonizing pedagogical practices*
> *requires taking seriously the relation between knowledge and learning, on the one*
> *hand, and student and teacher experience, on the other. In fact, the theorization and*
> *politicization of experience is imperative if pedagogical practices are to focus on*
> *more than the mere management, systemization, and consumption of disciplinary*
> *knowledge.*
>
> —Chandra Talpade Mohanty[1]

During the past quarter century there has been an unprecedented progressive movement in the United States charged with fundamentally transforming higher education.[2] This movement has pushed to increase the representation of people of color, working-class people, gay men and lesbians, and white women at all levels of the academy. It has also helped to foreground issues of power and resistance, examining the consequences that differential access to power has for student and teacher experiences and for the politics of learning. Incorporation of scholarship that has traditionally been excluded from academic inquiry has begun to transform the curriculum, a process that has been coupled with an examination and restructuring of the ways in which knowledge is organized and produced.

With the consolidation of conservative power during the Reagan and Bush administrations, we witnessed a backlash against more inclusive curricula in the academy;[3] a whittling away of affirmative action policies; and an extreme contraction of federal and state support for affordable higher education. These regressive practices have left those who are dedicated to establishing multicultural education and the coalitions it requires spending much of our time justifying the validity of progressive education rather than effecting change.

As teachers of sociology and women's studies, we are among many whose teaching and activism have been shaped and largely made possible by this movement. In our years of teaching, we have been troubled by how educational transformation is undermined not only by conservatives and neoconservatives who unapologetically oppose it but also by those who generally support it. There are at least two ways in which new forms of knowledge and involvement of new people can be sabotaged. One is to simply not invite this knowledge or these people in. Another is to make the invitation but then trivialize, ignore, or marginalize them. Specifically, we are concerned with how new people and ideas are encouraged to participate but then are not granted legitimacy. We are interested in how this process of dismissal occurs and are seeking strategies through which faculty, students, and administrators can critically engage with the complexities of representation and curriculum transformation. We offer this framework as a complement to scholarship on integrating multicultural perspectives into the curriculum and feminist, race-conscious pedagogy.[4]

Insider/Outsider Relations

At the heart of the struggle for power within the academy lie complicated questions about authority and representation. Theorists in ethnic studies, women's studies, and gay and lesbian studies have articulated the empowered representation of people of color, gay men and lesbians, and working-class people as the bedrock of educational transformation. Identity politics is one important aspect of this agenda.[5] Ian Haney López (see chapter 6) explains two key arguments for hiring people from traditionally marginalized communities: the role model theory and the perspective theory. According to the role model theory, outsiders contribute to academic environments as symbols, exemplars, and mentors. The perspective theory sees outsider groups as a source of insights—based on their ties to historically subordinated communities—that suggest distinct methodologies, a revisioning of established debates, formulations of new theories, and implementation of new pedagogical styles. Underlying both the role model and the perspective theories is the assertion that the realities lived by "outsiders" and their communities shape how and what they think, which, in turn, inform their decisions about teaching methods and priorities. Thus, one's community ties provide at least a partial basis for claiming authority to teach a particular subject.[6] Explaining the way many African-American women intellectuals have made positive use of their marginality, sociologist Patricia Hill Collins writes that "this 'outsider within' status has provided a special standpoint on self, family and society for African-American women. . . . Many Black intellectuals, especially those in touch with their marginality in academic settings, tap this standpoint in producing distinctive analyses of race, class and gender."[7]

We—the authors of this chapter—use our ties to "outsider" communities (one of us is a lesbian, the other an Indian woman living in the United States) to inform our teaching and research interests. Our experience of subordination and resistance gives our work clarity and urgency as we teach from the perspective of those who have been denied access to power. At the same time, our multiple identities require that we acknowledge the power afforded to us as members of dominant groups (as a white woman and a heterosexual, middle-class woman). Historically, white owning-class men made up the majority of those in power, in the academy and elsewhere. The increasing number of people with ties to both subordinated and dominant communities requires a more nuanced understanding of power. In other words, "insider" and "outsider" can no longer be interpreted as simple, mutually exclusive categories.

The role model and perspective theories take us halfway in explaining the unequal distribution of power in the academy and what we must do to change it: they effectively explain that redistribution of power depends upon a critical mass of "outsiders" within the academy. What we still need to grapple with, however, is what people who traditionally have been the "insiders" (white, straight, owning-class men) can do to expand their scholarship and confront the unequal distribution of power. In addition, we still need to address the responsibility that people who are both "outsiders" and "insiders" have to this same agenda since these people sometimes fail to take seriously the power they *do* have to interrupt exclusionary practices. Patterns of segregation and dismissal occur when people fail to see themselves in relation to their multiple identities and when they make essentialist links between identity and perspective, assuming that one's identity automatically determines what one can teach.

Academic Segregation

One example of the essentialism that assumes that people's social location determines their perspectives occurs when people of color and other groups are segregated to particular courses and research interests based on the notion that, as "outsiders," they have greater access to certain subject matter and are the only ones who can effectively teach certain courses. This notion of "privileged access" views access to certain knowledge and ideas not as an acquired skill that is the result of commitment to a community and its issues but rather as "biological" or "natural."

This essentialist understanding conceals political judgments about which scholars and scholarship are considered valuable. For example, institutions are often more supportive of affirmative action hiring in fields directly related to race than in other substantive areas. A department seeking a person to teach Chicano literature may assume that any Latino or Latina can teach it, regardless of the person's scholarly background, areas of interest, and expertise. The same scholar, deemed an expert on Chicano literature on the basis of his or her skin color, may not be thought of as qualified for a position not having to do directly with race. A female social theorist whose training includes feminist theory may not be considered for a social theory position since what she does is feminist (i.e., not social) theory. Similarly, a department that seeks a person to teach courses on the family may assume that any female scholar, regardless of her interests, can teach the course. Thus, when women and people of color are recruited, it is only in certain capacities—to teach gender courses in sociology, the Third World economic development course in economics, or the course on women's art.

Selective Responsibility Syndrome

A second example of essentialism follows from the logic that supports academic segregation. Within this framework, faculty maintain that unless a teacher was raised with ties to a particular subordinated community, he or she does not have the authority to teach about it. This logic also is based on an essentialism that draws boundaries around certain scholarship and disciplines that are then considered out of range for those who are not, for example, African-American, Latino, or female. One consequence of this reasoning is the mistaken notion that those who are not outsiders in terms of race, class, or gender do not need to diversify their curricula. For example, if a person of color is teaching courses on race and ethnicity, white faculty in the department may continue to ignore issues of race and racism in their own courses. Clearly, such assumptions limit the range of topics any one person can investigate, preventing a serious engagement with anything outside of one's own social location.

Knowledge may be rendered invisible not merely by excluding it from one's curricula and classroom but also by distorting it. When teachers have not done the necessary academic, personal, and political work to understand scholarship by and about people of color or gay men and lesbians, for example, they may perpetuate stereotypes that distort these groups' experiences. For example, in an upper level sociology course on social movements, a professor dramatically explained an empty chair at a panel discussion on lesbian politics as the seat of the "missing lesbian of color." Instead of acknowledging that she knew no lesbian women of color and had no academic or political networks with lesbians, she put the onus on the absent lesbians of color by presenting the situation as an example of "self-inflicted invisibility" and an irresponsible disinterest on their part. By shifting responsibility onto lesbians of color, when she herself was not able to tap into her academic or political communities to contact any, she perpetuated the racism and homophobia that renders lesbians of color invisible. When a student suggested that the professor was partly responsible, she became defensive and said that, as a woman, she understood subordination and would never participate in it.

Academic segregation and selective responsibility reinforce each other when the responsibility for teaching certain substantive areas is restricted to people of color or white women while the rest of a department's faculty and curricula remain virtually unchanged. Academic ghettos of token people of color or white women and their scholarship may be created while the rest of the faculty is not required to expand its expertise. The underlying assumption is that people from dominant groups are not affected by sexism or racism and that these are problems only women and people of color need to confront. Thus, people may not recognize that they are affected by racism and sexism *and* are part of the problem. As a consequence, they may not see connections between their own social locations and their actions and words: whose work they support, who they encourage the department to promote, and so forth. They may say they are against sexism, racism, or classism but then act in ways that jeopardize the standing of those involved in race-, class-, and gender-conscious scholarship.

The Politics of Dismissal

Patterns of academic segregation and selective responsibility are furthered when faculty assume that scholarship about race, class, gender, or sexuality is "transparent" enough for anybody to teach, regardless of the person's personal and political preparation and ability or inclination to interrogate power inequalities. While this statement may appear to contradict our earlier formulations that only certain people are seen as having the privileged access to teach the material based on their social location, it is, in fact, merely the other side of the same coin. Ultimately, not considering scholarship about race, gender, or sexuality legitimate gives rise to the refusal to adopt it, in any meaningful way, within one's own scholarship — at the same time that it is considered "simple" enough to include when necessary regardless of the teacher's academic training or social location. This reductionist ideology allows male faculty and white faculty to include feminist scholarship and critical race scholarship in their own teaching without fully grappling with the implications for paradigm transformation or understanding the power relations inscribed in co-opting them. This continues to marginalize "outsider" scholarship at the same time that it does away with the need for "outsider" scholars. Clearly, if teaching feminist theory is so "transparent," then there is no need for a feminist scholar to teach it. This can effectively nullify recruitment and retention of a critical mass of feminist faculty.

One dangerous consequence of lack of expertise in "outsider" scholarship is that it leaves teachers unable to evaluate—and then promote—"outsider" scholars' work and contributions as they do each other's. Ignorance about a particular area of scholarship often leads to criticism that it reflects no recognizable theoretical tradition or fails to show substantial training in a discipline. Or, the faculty member may remain silent about the scholar's work (perhaps as a result of knowing that the scholarship is outside of his or her primary field of expertise). While silence may be more intellectually honest than rejection, the results are often the same, since intellectual growth, for "insider" and "outsider" alike, is dependent upon supportive critical engagement.

The significance of intellectual engagement with scholarship by people of color is underlined by legal scholar Mari Matsuda, who says that "citing outsider scholarship is a political act."[8] Inability to evaluate the scholarship of people of color ultimately undermines affirmative action, since intellectual support requires that white faculty take African-American, Latino, and Asian scholarship seriously enough to criticize and talk about it.

A teacher who disregards the scholarly work of people of color and white women may also be unwilling or unable to take seriously the work of students of color, lesbians and gay men, or women. For example, some white faculty do not have the same standards or expectations for students of color as they do for white students. When they are questioned about these dual standards, they explain that because the students of color have different experiences from their own, the white faculty cannot critique the students' work. In this way, the lack of lived experience (in relation to a particular identity) becomes a way to dismiss their own ignorance as well as their responsibility to teach *all* students effectively. This can have negative repercussions on teacher-student and student-student interaction. For example, a white teacher or a heterosexual teacher who fails to fully engage with students of color or gay students misses an opportunity to model positive across-race and across-sexuality behavior that the students can try to emulate. This leaves unchecked a common classroom dynamic in which white students marginalize students of color with the apparent assumption that, by virtue of their lived experiences, they must be either completely right or totally wrong; either way, there is no engagement of equals.[9] The few students of color in a class may be seen as representing or speaking for all people of color, and the onus of critically evaluating the work of students of color is placed solely on the backs of faculty of color.

When white faculty or male faculty argue that they cannot adequately evaluate or criticize the work of a student of color or a woman student, they fail to acknowledge the several other dimensions of the student's social status (such as class) that the faculty and students may have in common. As a consequence, the faculty of color and women faculty who do see students of color and women students as whole people — as people who may benefit from guidance and a critical engagement with their work — carry the burden of educating these students themselves.

The Politics of Inclusion

While we chronicle these examples to specify particular ways that inclusionary curricula and practices in higher education may be undermined, it would be unfortunate and ahistorical to interpret them as singular aberrations or simply reflections of individual limitations. In fact, forms of academic segregation, selective responsibility, and politics of dismissal are reinforced by converging structural conditions that weaken multicultural education. Many faculty came of age at a time when academic scholarship rarely included discussion about people of color, gay men and lesbians, or women, which means they now need to train themselves in this emerging scholarship. Elaborating on the effects of exclusionary scholarship, Elizabeth Higginbotham writes, "No one mentioned women of color when most contemporary college faculty pursued their degrees. . . . As the products of an educational experience which relegated people of color and women to the margins of our fields, faculty have to compensate for the institutionalized biases in the educational system."[10] Faculty who want to educate themselves in the work of African-American, Latin American, gay and lesbian, and women's studies scholars are then required to do a double shift in order to maintain existing disciplinary commitments while simultaneously expanding their scholarly boundaries.

Exclusionary practices in the curriculum are also reinforced by a sociopolitical climate in which the state continues to support discriminatory practices. For example, the denial of human rights to gay men and lesbians in the larger society reinforces their invisibility in the academy.

In addition, the academy supports the invisibility of subordinated groups when it fails to offer incentives for professors to examine and transform their own entrenched thinking and stereotypes.[11] This dynamic is further reinforced in environments where there is not a critical mass of teachers who are women, openly gay and lesbian, and people of color to correct distorted images of their communities. The professor who used the "empty lesbian-of-color chair" in teaching about sexuality merely reinforced this larger institutional process.

Curriculum transformation projects that have been initiated across the United States have provided some of the most significant institutionally sanctioned forums for initiating multicultural change. But many of the dynamics of exclusion continue to operate when curricular revision is seen as unrelated to and separate from attention to how social location shapes a traditional faculty member's relation to a new curriculum and new faculty. In addition to changing curricula and recruiting faculty of color, it is also crucial that people who historically have been represented in the academy reflect critically on their access to power and on their political and community commitments. This "theorization and politicization of experience," as Chandra Mohanty explains it, "is imperative if pedagogical practices are to focus on more than the mere management, systemization, and consumption of disciplinary knowledge" (see chapter 3).

We are suggesting that the long-term success of curriculum transformation and affirmative action hiring practices depends upon critical self-reflection about power and inequality. The problems resulting from the exclusionary practices we have discussed rest upon an inability or unwillingness to see connections between professed politics and academic commitments on the one hand and actual behaviors and practices on the other. Making such connections depends upon developing policies and training seminars that would enable faculty to critically assess their own lives, including their political involvements, friendships, and communities, and to develop a willingness to be changed. Our idea of "the politics of inclusion" assumes that a vital link between individual support of multicultural education and institutional implementation is a willingness to engage in reflection about one's own life and to accept accountability for one's own social and structural position and the unearned privileges that may accompany it. The politics of inclusion allows for the development of an "informed consciousness" that provides the impetus for long-term educational change.[12] A personally and institutionally supported politics of inclusion can undermine academic segregation, selective responsibility, the politics of dismissal, and other exclusionary practices.

Naming and Using Power

Adopting a politics of inclusion partly involves understanding one's own position in the social structure in order to use one's power to change it. Taking responsibility for teaching about race if the teacher is white, about gender if the teacher is male, or about heterosexism and homophobia if the teacher is heterosexual is one way to use power to help transform the curriculum. This involves reflecting on what teachers do and do not "choose" to teach and challenging personal and institutional barriers to curricular change. An example is the teacher of a gender course who recognized the need to include a section on physical and sexual abuse, given their prevalence across race and class.[13] She knew that by avoiding the topic of sexual abuse she would have little opportunity to highlight the strength, vision, and political organizing of many survivors, thus rendering invisible experiences that are common to at least one-third of girls and women in U.S. society. During the first two semesters she taught the course she hesitated to focus on sexual abuse because she had no personal experience of it, which she felt would have given her the authority and ability to talk about it. She did invite an expert on sexual abuse who was herself a survivor to do one lecture, but the teacher left the topic out of the rest of her course discussions, assignments, and lectures. Through exposure to and engagement with survivors, she began to analyze the implications of her decision and understood that she had avoided the steps she needed to take to teach effectively about sexual abuse. Instead she had relegated teaching about the subject only to those victimized by sexual abuse. For this teacher, recognizing her own vulnerability in teaching this subject was a crucial step in her understanding that not having experienced abuse should not stand in the way of teaching about it. Her "privilege" (of being spared sexual abuse), in fact, meant that she needed to learn about and teach the topic instead of leaving those who have been abused to do this work.

In this instance, the teacher's exposure to survivors enabled her to analyze her assumptions that those with experience are responsible for teaching (and are inevitably more qualified to teach) about what they have experienced. Critically examining what faculty teach can move us away from creating academic ghettos where faculty of color, women faculty, and gay and lesbian faculty are limited to particular subject matter and departments. Scrutinizing curriculum choices can reveal underlying essentialist logic. While a teacher's social location inevitably influences her or his perspective and approach, all faculty can take responsibility for teaching and learning about issues of race, class, gender, and sexuality. The task is to develop methods of articulating how social location shapes perspectives and outlooks. This process moves away from the continued consideration of "outsider" scholars and scholarship as somehow marginal to "real" scholars and scholarship and, in fact, contributes to the redefinition and broadening of what is considered mainstream.

Critical self-reflection allows people to use the power of "insider" status to make change within a collectivity since racism, sexism, and heterosexism are often most effectively undermined by those who have the most to gain from the maintenance of hierarchies. It can also spur new intellectual connections between faculty, opening up the range of people who consider the "outsiders' " work integral to progressive educational transformation.

Institutional implementation of individual engagement can include discussion about curriculum choices and pedagogical methods, but this requires breaking down the unwritten but powerful taboo against critically engaging with each other about what goes on in the classroom and with the course content. It is possible to maintain academic freedom and individual faculty autonomy while simultaneously engaging in dialogue about course content and process. But this dialogue requires the faculty's knowledge of, respect for, and engagement with scholarship about people of color, lesbians and gay men, and other groups along with a recognition of how power inequalities influence classroom dynamics. It also depends upon a critical mass of faculty of color, gay men and lesbians, and women "who could safely contest unfair and inadequate representations"[14] that inevitably occur as faculty who are white or male or both grapple with and learn about scholarship about and by people of color.

Such a commitment flies in the face of the positivist ideology that assumes that scholarship can and should be separated from faculty biases and perspectives — that there is such a thing as "objective" research that can be conducted regardless of one's social location and relation to the social structure. The politics of inclusion displaces false notions of objectivity by making explicit the influence of social location. It also contradicts the notion that the standpoints of, for example, people of color and white women are "biased" while those of white men are "objective" or "universal." Exposure to, involvement with, and commitment to "outsiders" enables people to understand their own standpoints and use their privileges to undermine exclusionary practices in the academy.

Expanding Community Ties
and Redrawing Political Commitments

Developing a politics of inclusion also involves exposing oneself to the ways in which oppression is experienced by the people who face it. Constant, long-term involvement with those who have ties to subordinated communities makes it possible for people to witness, firsthand, the effects of discrimination as well as the strength and vitality of communities struggling to change the conditions of their daily lives.

Involvement avoids the dangers of either distancing from or objectifying people, since it allows one to become invested in a community's issues and struggles. It also helps faculty to avoid the various ways in which the realities of people's lives are either made invisible or distorted in the classroom and removes the sole responsibility for teaching about race from faculty of color, ensuring that race issues are integrated throughout the curriculum and taught by all faculty. In the case of the professor who used the empty chair to symbolize the absent lesbian of color, for example, involvement in the culture and political struggles of gay men and lesbian women (both white and people of color) might have helped her understand the vicious ways in which heterosexism and racism function to keep many lesbians "closeted" and therefore invisible. Understanding the community's issues might also have created the required networks that would have helped her invite a lesbian of color to campus. Finally, the learning process would have given her the exposure, authority, and training to teach ethically and with integrity about gay and lesbian communities and the social construction of sexuality herself.

The formation of community ties with people who have traditionally been denied access to power in the academy allows faculty to examine and broaden their professional networks as well as redraw their political commitments. Clearly, it is difficult to envision how people can have effective and meaningful antiracist, antisexist, or antiheterosexist stances if their colleagues and professional networks continue to be all white, all male, or all heterosexual. If the people one associates with and ultimately relies on continue to be part of an exclusive, homogeneous group, then one's political commitment to "outsider" communities is token at best.

Maintaining peer relationships with people from diverse groups ultimately destroys one's stereotypes of these communities, and the relationships become the link that encourages people to make an "outsider's" struggles and priorities their own. Teachers' abilities to learn from colleagues can help them to identify ways in which they are making issues invisible. Developing a component in curriculum-change projects that would allow people to think through and evaluate to whom they hold themselves accountable could help draw connections between the personal and the political, showing that changing the intellectual content of courses depends upon rethinking our lives as well. This component could then serve as a model for classroom use. Finding ways for students to examine how their associations with others may relate to issues of power and inequality could encourage them to understand connections between their daily lives and the political, ethical, and intellectual decisions they make.

Nurturing peer relationships across race and class has especially important implications in the academy given the significance of colleague networks in spreading information about job openings and publishing opportunities. According to the level-playing-field ideology, this information is available to all interested people. In reality, the "qualifications" that are created to justify a particular hiring decision are often codes for whether someone will be a team player (i.e., be like "us"). Who is included in the "us" makes a huge difference in who may be invited in. Sustaining intellectual, social, and political relations with many people of different races, ethnic groups, classes, religions, and sexual preferences widens the definition of "us" while simultaneously helping people to see the subtle yet consistent ways "us" often effectively means an exclusive group. While it is illegal to ask about a job candidate's marital status, for example, it is not uncommon for it to become apparent during the hiring process. This information may be used (whether spoken or not) as part of the determination of whether the candidate might "fit in" among the faculty. While many gay and lesbian faculty have long known about this form of discrimination, it is through close working relationships with gay men and lesbians that heterosexual faculty also learn to recognize the parameters of exclusionary practices, and to intervene when heterosexist assumptions are made in evaluation and hiring decisions. We suspect that people of color and lesbians and gay men have long understood the politics of inclusion as a way to assess the extent to which someone who does not have the same experience as they have will "watch their backs" (stand in solidarity with them) when they are facing exclusion, silencing, or other forms of discrimination. This consciousness has often been used by "outsiders" as a strategy for survival in institutions where there are only a few women, people of color, and lesbians or gay men, since being in the minority demands that "outsiders" network with people who do not come from the same communities.

Developing community ties with people across race and sexuality can ultimately expand one's comfort zone and political expertise, creating new possibilities for building networks to undermine exclusionary policies and exclusionary scholarship. Developing new community ties, then, becomes a bridge between affirmative action and multicultural educational transformation. In fact, effective affirmative action depends upon expanding one's community ties. While we acknowledge the significance of colleague networks in the dissemination of knowledge, we do not want to imply that networking is without problems. Hiring through colleague networks can be reduced to whether people like each other and might feel comfortable working together rather than whether they respect each other's scholarship and teaching. In other words, while we recognize the centrality of colleague networks (and suggest that expanding these networks is vital for confronting exclusionary practices in the academy), political principles ultimately need to be placed before personalities. Developing respect for scholarship is far more important than simply feeling comfortable with people.

Nurturing peer relationships across race and class can also play a vital role in effective teaching. In their investigation of student responses to diversity at the University of California at Berkeley, the Diversity Project investigators found that students' most positive and influential cross-race experiences occurred when a teacher instructed the class to break up into small groups and work together on projects. This created a way for students to develop alliances with people of different races and ethnic groups without the interactions feeling forced or artificial.[15]

Exposure to people of different races and sexual identities is certainly not enough. The generations of white people who have maintained racist stereotypes and power although they were raised by black women is a powerful case in point.[16] Effective cross-race and cross-sexuality alliances depend upon both parties having equal access to power. In addition, effective long-term alliances require multiple connections through many individual relationships and extended involvement with a larger community so that individual friendships across race (or class or sexuality) do not drain and tokenize "outsiders." As Kate Rushin says in "The Bridge Poem":

> I'm sick of filling in your gaps
> Sick of being your insurance against
> The isolation of your self-imposed limitations
> Sick of being the crazy at your Holiday Dinners
> The odd one at your Sunday Brunches
> I am sick of being the sole Black friend to
> Thirty-four Individual White folks[17]

This truth again underlines why multicultural education starts with the empowerment of a critical mass of "outsiders" at all levels of authority.

Implementing a Politics of Inclusion

It is through the process of holding oneself accountable to diverse communities that one can deal ethically and responsibly with issues of diversity in the academy. A politics of inclusion enables people to analyze structural inequalities rigorously; although it recognizes that the perspectives of those who have experienced oppression is at the center of analysis, it neither tokenizes nor essentializes their voices. This stance recognizes the necessity of identity politics but also leaves room for people who do not have lived experience as "outsiders" and yet want to work with and teach "outsider" scholarship. Adopting a politics of inclusion offers a way to uphold identity politics without essentializing people's identities. As Russell Means writes, "When I use the term 'European,' I am not referring to a skin color or a particular genetic structure. What I am referring to is a mind set, a world view which is a product of the development of European culture. People are not genetically encoded to hold this outlook, they are *acculturated* to hold it. The same holds true for American Indians or the members of any other culture."[18] Institutional commitment to fostering the politics of inclusion is a way to move beyond the acculturation process that limits our abilities to speak and negotiate across differences. Multicultural education requires new skills. It opens a way for "outsiders" to avoid getting locked into certain disciplines or subfields and for "insiders" to engage with students and scholarship they might otherwise have dismissed (or were not trained to deal with). The politics of inclusion draws on the activist basis of gay and lesbian studies, black studies, and women's studies by encouraging institutional support for community- and activist-based scholarship. Institutional support for redrawing and maintaining political commitments would necessarily involve restructuring tenure requirements so that community activism would be considered a recognized and vital aspect of the production of knowledge; expanding the range of publications considered legitimate venues for scholarly achievement; and recognizing community service as a central aspect of one's educational contributions, not only rhetorically but in practice as well.

The politics of inclusion could also be incorporated into current curriculum transformation projects. In her pioneering work on race-, class-, and gender-conscious education, Elizabeth Higginbotham developed three steps for designing curriculum: gaining new information, reconceptualizing disciplinary boundaries and priorities, and designing pedagogical approaches that confront racism and other oppression in the classroom.[19] These steps could be complemented by attention to the personal and collective transformations that such work demands. Implementing the politics of inclusion institutionally could also supplement current strategies for increasing the numbers and power of men and women of color, white women, gay men and lesbians, and working-class people since the long-term success of maintaining a critical mass of these scholars requires reexamination of how they have been tokenized, ignored, and exploited. Such an examination depends upon concerted, long-term efforts supported by people traditionally in the academy to reevaluate their relation to scholarship, their communities and friendship networks, and their relation to power and privilege. This "politicization of experience" guards against co-optation of the knowledge and contributions of "outsiders" while setting in motion the possibility of transformative rather than reformist change.

As we continue to articulate the value and challenges of multicultural education, we are being asked to reflect upon the meaning of coalition politics for our daily lives. In "Coalition Politics: Turning the Century," Bernice Johnson Reagon explains that effective political strategy requires being careful to understand the historical differences between "home" and "coalition."[20] "Home" is where people have gone to feel comfortable, to be with people like themselves, to be rejuvenated, to see a reflection of themselves in those around them. History has shown that sustaining "home" has been essential for the political survival of groups who have experienced discrimination. It has also been the life source of identity politics. Nationalism, separatism, and "woman-only space" have all been political strategies used to create collective homes. But as we reach toward the twenty-first century, Reagon warns, we cannot afford to spend all our time in our homes, which means figuring out strategies for coalitions. Reagon explains that being "in coalition," unlike being "at home," is not comfortable, easy, or safe. In fact, it can be dangerous — but our political survival depends upon it.

Given that inclusionary practices rely upon nurturing supportive links between people from different "homes," it is time to rebuild the places we go to rejuvenate, recharge, and regenerate ourselves so that the meaning of "our" will be broader than it has been in the past. Home and coalition, then, are not inevitable opposites but rather interrelated strategies upon which multicultural education depends.

Notes

Thanks to Atreya Chakraborty, Cynthia Enloe, Mary Gilfus, Lisa Hall, Elizabeth Higginbotham, Charles Nero, and Kim Vaz for their critical analysis of and encouragement on this essay.

1. See chapter 3, "On Race and Voice: Challenges for Liberal Education in the 1990s."

98   Becky W. Thompson and Sangeeta Tyagi

2. Accounts of this movement include, for example, Margaret L. Andersen, "Women's Studies/Black Studies: Learning from Our Common Pasts, Forging a Common Future," in *Women's Place in the Academy*, ed. Marilyn R. Schuster and Susan R. Van Dyne (Totowa, N.J.: Rowman and Allanheld, 1985), 62-72; Troy Duster, *The Diversity Project* (Berkeley, Calif.: Institute for the Study of Social Change, 1991); Elizabeth Higginbotham, "Integrating All Women into the Curriculum," Research and Curriculum Integration Project (Center for Research on Women: Memphis State University, 1988).

3. The conservative backlash is evident in the writing of Allan Bloom, *The Closing of the American Mind* (New York: Simon and Schuster, 1987) and Dinesh D'Souza, *Illiberal Education: The Politics of Race and Sex on Campus* (New York: The Free Press, 1991); the political platform of the National Association of Scholars; and the funding priorities of the Madison Center and other right-wing think tanks.

4. Margaret L. Andersen and Patricia Hill Collins, eds., *An Inclusive Curriculum: Race, Class and Gender in the Sociology Curriculum* (American Sociological Association Teaching Resource Center, 1988); Maxine Baca Zinn, Lynn Weber Cannon, Elizabeth Higginbotham, and Bonnie Thornton Dill, "The Costs of Exclusionary Practices in Women's Studies," *Signs* 11 (1986): 290-303; Lynn Weber Cannon, "Fostering Positive Race, Class, and Gender Dynamics in the Classroom," *Women's Studies Quarterly* 1 & 2 (1990): 126-34; Laurie Crumpacker and Eleanor M. Vander Haegen, "Integrating the Curriculum: Teaching about Lesbians and Homophobia" (Wellesley College Center for Research on Women, Working Paper no. 138, 1984); Elizabeth Higginbotham, "Integrating All Women into the Curriculum," Research and Curriculum Integration Project (Memphis State University: Center for Research on Women, 1988); Barbara Omolade, "A Black Feminist Pedagogy," *Women's Studies Quarterly* 14 (1987): 32-39; Kathryn Ward, Christina Brinkley-Carter, Janet Morrison, and Karen Hampton, eds., *Faculty Curriculum Integration Workbook* (Southern Illinois University, 1991).

5. Members of the Combahee River Collective, a black feminist activist group, were pioneers in supporting identity politics; they assert that the most profound and potentially radical politics come directly out of our own identities as opposed to working to end oppression of others. See Combahee River Collective, "A Black Feminist Statement," in *All the Women Are White, All the Blacks Are Men, but Some of Us Are Brave: Black Women's Studies*, ed. Gloria T. Hull, Patricia Bell Scott, and Barbara Smith (Old Westbury, N.Y.: Feminist Press, 1982), 16. For further discussion of the historical roots and complexity of identity politics see Diana Fuss, *Essentially Speaking: Feminism, Nature and Difference* (New York: Routledge, 1989); Edward W. Said, "The Politics of Knowledge," in *Debating PC*, ed. Paul Berman (New York: Laurel, 1992), 172-89.

6. Johnnetta B. Cole, ed., *Anthropology for the Nineties: Introductory Readings* (New York: Free Press, 1988); Patricia Hill Collins, *Black Feminist Thought: Knowledge, Consciousness and the Politics of Empowerment* (Boston: Unwin Hyman, 1991); Cherríe Moraga and Gloria Anzaldúa, eds., *This Bridge Called My Back: Writings by Radical Women of Color* (New York: Kitchen Table, 1983); Dorothy E. Smith, "Women's Perspective Is a Radical Critique of Sociology," in *Feminism and Methodology*, ed. Sandra Harding (Bloomington: Indiana University Press, 1987), 84-96.

7. Patricia Hill Collins, "Learning from the Outsider Within: The Sociological Significance of Black Feminist Thought," *Social Problems* 33 (1986): 14-15.

8. Mari Matsuda, "Affirmative Action and Legal Knowledge: Planting Seeds in Plowed-Up Ground," *Harvard Women's Law Journal* 11 (Spring 1988): 5

9. Elizabeth Spelman, "Combating the Marginalization of Black Women in the Classroom," in *Gendered Subjects: The Dynamics of Feminist Teaching*, ed. Margo Culley and Catherine Portuges (Boston: Routledge and Kegan Paul, 1985), 242.

10. Higginbotham, "Integrating All Women into the Curriculum," 13.

11. For analysis of unearned privileges afforded to white people, see Peggy McIntosh, "White Privilege and Male Privilege: A Personal Account of Coming to See Correspondences through Work in Women's Studies," in *Race, Class, and Gender*, ed. Margaret L. Andersen and Patricia Hill Collins (Belmont, Calif.: Wadsworth, 1992), 70-81.

12. We thank Evelynn Hammonds for this term.

13. Diana Russell, *The Secret Trauma: Incest in the Lives of Girls and Women* (New York: Basic Books, 1986); Gail Wyatt, "The Sexual Abuse of Afro-American and White-American Women in Childhood," *Child Abuse and Neglect* 9 (1985): 507-19.

14. Ted Gordon and Wahneema Lubiano, "The Statement of the Black Faculty Caucus," in *Debating P.C.*, ed. Paul Berman, 252.

15. Duster, *Diversity Project*. See also Lynn Weber Cannon, "Fostering Positive Race, Class, and Gender Dynamics in the Classroom."

16. Legal theorist Patricia Williams writes about how white people in her neighborhood who had "seen me born and baked me cookies at Halloween and grown up with my mother" were the same people who fled the neighborhood when two or more black families moved in. Patricia J. Williams, "Defending the Gains," in *Beyond PC: Toward a Politics of Understanding*, ed. Patricia Aufderheide (St. Paul, Minn.: Graywolf, 1992), 193.

17. Kate Rushin, "The Bridge Poem," in *This Bridge Called My Back*, ed. Moraga and Anzaldúa, xxi-xxii.

18. Russell Means, "The Same Old Song," in *Marxism and Native Americans*, ed. Ward Churchill (Boston: South End, 1983), 28.

19. Higginbotham, "Integrating All Women into the Curriculum."

20. Bernice Johnson Reagon, "Coalition Politics: Turning the Century," in *Home Girls: A Black Feminist Anthology*, ed. Barbara Smith (New York: Kitchen Table, 1983), 356-69.

Chapter 6

Community Ties and Law School Faculty Hiring: The Case for Professors Who Don't Think White

Ian Haney López

The stultifying homogeneity of Harvard Law School's faculty directly and adversely affected my years as a student there. After three years of agitating for change, I wrote this essay to describe and explain the student diversity movement at Harvard Law School and to advance the core diversity arguments as they apply to minority hiring on law school faculties generally.

The Diversity Movement at Harvard Law School

Harvard Law School is being sued by its own students. On November 20, 1990, students calling themselves the Harvard Law School Coalition for Civil Rights filed suit in Massachusetts state court against the president and fellows of Harvard College, alleging discrimination on the basis of race, ethnicity, gender, sexual orientation, and physical disability in law school faculty hiring. The coalition's suit against Harvard Law School (HLS) provides a convenient starting point for a consideration of the diversity movement and its history.

The many groups that together make up the diversity movement at Harvard are listed on the roster of the coalition, including La Alianza, the Asian American Law Student Association, the Black Law Student Association, the Committee on Gay and Lesbian Legal Issues, the Disabled Student Association, the Native American Law Student Association, Students for Disability Rights, and the Women's Law Association. Each of these groups formed, in part, to push for the hiring of professors resembling their constituencies.

Students organized the Black Law Student Association (BLSA) in 1967. Reginald Gilliam, chair of the inaugural BLSA chapter, states flatly that "the issue of getting black professors on the faculty was what led to the organization of BLSA." Agitation by BLSA in conjunction with universitywide student protests, including an occupation of the university's administrative offices and a six-day student strike, impressed upon Harvard authorities the need to hire African-American faculty. In 1969, HLS hired Derrick Bell as its first Black professor and the college created the Afro-American Studies Program.

The few Mexican-American students at Harvard in 1970 founded the Chicano Law Student Association (ChLSA), La Alianza's predecessor. One of the first goals of ChLSA, besides increasing Latino admissions and financial aid, was organizing a seminar on Latino legal issues. Jaime Cervantes, who entered HLS in 1970, negotiated with the administration on behalf of ChLSA for three years before achieving a revealingly limited form of success. Harvard hired Mario Obledo as a teaching fellow, the lowest part-time teaching position, to lead an uncredited legal research and writing class. The position proved even more temporary than Harvard had intended. Within a few months, Obledo left to accept a post as California's secretary of health, education, and welfare. Obledo subsequently served as president of the League of United Latin American Citizens, then the Latino equivalent of the NAACP.

A decade later, student pressure and changing times had resulted in the appointment of a handful of White women and African-American men to full-time positions. Their small numbers ensured, however, that the issue of faculty hiring remained volatile. The departure in 1980 of Derrick Bell to become dean of the University of Oregon School of Law and the absence of anyone qualified to teach his course, "Constitutional Law and Minority Issues," emphasized the tenuous nature of the gains after a decade of struggle.

The 1982-83 academic year proved to be tumultuous. BLSA and other organizations created a Third World Coalition that boycotted a civil rights class taught by two visiting attorneys, one Black and one White, as a replacement for Bell's course. The boycotters protested Harvard's inadequate efforts to hire minorities and, more particularly, the hiring of a White lawyer to teach a subject about which scores of minority attorneys could undoubtedly have taught with distinction.

In a manner reminiscent of Jaime Cervantes and ChLSA a decade earlier, the Third World Coalition organized an alternative course in the spring of 1983. Entitled "Racism and American Law," the course featured a series of lectures delivered by visiting minority legal scholars and practitioners. The students intended not only to learn race law but also to showcase existing minority talent. As the spring came to a close, activism increased, culminating in a rally of six hundred students, two hundred of whom subsequently occupied the dean's office. Within the year, HLS extended offers to three Black scholars and, for the first time, to a Chicano, Gerald López. Harvard offered López only a temporary position, however, and after two years he left for a tenured post at Stanford Law School.

As the decade drew to a close, the number of tenured minority faculty remained small, and student disaffection rose again. In the spring of 1988 BLSA led an overnight sit-in at the dean's office. One year later, the Student Coalition for a Diverse Faculty, the predecessor of the coalition that is suing Harvard, formed to organize a study-in to support recruitment of women and minorities. On April 6, 1989, 125 students peacefully occupied Langdell Hall, the central building on the law school campus. La Alianza was particularly active in decrying the total absence of Latino faculty at HLS.

The agitation for representative faculty extended well beyond Harvard. The spring 1989 Harvard sit-in coincided with a nationwide law student strike organized by the Coalition for a Diversified Faculty at the University of California, Berkeley, Boalt Hall Law School. Students participated at thirty-five top law schools around the country, including Yale, Chicago, Michigan, Stanford, and the University of California at Los Angeles (UCLA). At Berkeley, police arrested forty-six students for occupying the dean's office, while hundreds of protesters cum punsters chanted "I see White men! U.C. Berkeley!"

Although the push for reforming hiring practices became national in scope, little of substance changed on law school faculties. At Harvard in 1990, for example, only five White women and three African-American men held tenured positions out of a total of sixty-two tenured faculty members. Nobody behind a Harvard podium was of another race, or openly gay or lesbian, or disabled. The students did not lose sight of these dismal numbers. That spring, students demonstrated, circulated petitions, and twice occupied the dean's office. However, the actions of Professor Derrick Bell, who by then had returned to Harvard, overshadowed all of these events. On April 24, 1990, in a rally to support the student diversity movement, Bell announced his intention to take an unpaid leave of absence until Harvard appointed a woman of color to a tenured or tenure-track position.

While Bell's announcement infused many with hope, it raised a storm of criticism among others. In one perhaps apocryphal exchange, Dean Robert Clark asked Bell whether he thought Harvard Law School was "a Southern lunch counter," and Bell responded that, yes, he did. Critics reserved the greatest ire, however, for a single comment Bell made during the rally. In calling for more minority faculty, Bell warned that "the ends of diversity are not served by persons who look black and think White."

Accusations of bigotry and intolerance erupted almost instantaneously. A letter to the editors of the law school's student newspaper, the *Harvard Law Record*, typifies the indignation of many who heard Bell speak: "Professor Bell's comment represents intolerance in its purest form. It establishes an orthodoxy of thought, and the African American must embrace it or be excommunicated for his 'white' views." Yet I understand Bell to be saying something different, albeit in stark terms: ways of thinking about the world may be highly correlated with community ties, and thus with race, and these must be considered in faculty hiring. I agree, for reasons illustrated throughout this essay.

Before turning to the concept of community ties, however, let me clarify and define certain terms. As the names of the Harvard and Berkeley student coalitions suggest, by about 1988 "the diversity movement" had become the nom de guerre and "diversity" the professed goal of those advocating increased faculty representation of traditionally excluded groups. The term "diversity" reflected an enlargement and evolution in the thinking of student reformers. Over the years, those clamoring for new hiring practices came to include Native Americans, Asian-Americans, women, openly gay and lesbian students, and the disabled, as well as African-Americans and Latinos. "Diversity" captured this breadth.

The inclusion of such disparate groups into a single movement facilitated an evolution in the students' conception of their own project, leading them to define more precisely the content of their demands. Genetic or physical variety seemed less important than the presence of professors with views shaped by their community affiliation and past experiences. The term "diversity" as used here reflects this understanding. By racial diversity I mean something more than the presence of persons with varied pigmentation. Rather, I mean the presence of people with significant and self-consciously held ties to the minority communities of their origins.

Community Ties

The concept of community ties can be illustrated by reference to *Sula*, a novel by Toni Morrison. In her novel, Morrison creates a place called the Bottom, a Black neighborhood in the hills above the fertile valley town of Medallion, Ohio, in the first decades of this century. The founding and naming of the Bottom resulted from a cruel joke played on a slave by a White from Medallion. The slave, promised rich bottomland and the freedom to farm it in exchange for particularly arduous labor he performed, was given only broken land in the high hills above the valley town. When the slave asked about the promised bottomland, the White farmer smiled and told him that when God looks down, the hills are the bottom of heaven.

The residents of the Bottom formed a community of friends and families who, over time, derived highly specific understandings of the world around them from the particularities of their daily lives. Growing up there, they knew almost by osmosis the intimate details of their community, such as the life history of Shadrack, who returned a crazy and broken man from the meaningless Great War in Europe. Every January third, people gathered to watch Shadrack celebrate his National Suicide Day by striding the length of the main road ringing a cow bell and swinging a hangman's rope. Every resident of the Bottom knew the literal fact of Shadrack's marches. More importantly, Shadrack's holiday became absorbed into the thoughts, language, and lives of those living in the Bottom. As Morrison explains, "easily, quietly, Suicide Day became a part of the fabric of life up in the Bottom of Medallion, Ohio." Those who lived their lives in the Bottom measured the world in a way no outsider could completely fathom or correctly interpret.

The Bottom constituted at the same time a subordinated community. The people of the Bottom looked down with a bird's-eye view upon Medallion, where most of them worked, but where they were nonetheless unwelcome upon penalty of violence. The etiquette of race hatred defined the parameters of their actions in Medallion, circumscribing their lives to terms acceptable to Whites. This White malevolence permeated the lives of all residents of the Bottom, whether they were immediate victims or not. Violence in the name of racial hierarchy foreclosed the possibility of Black residence in Medallion, or, stated more broadly, Black membership in the White valley community. The shared residence of the people of the Bottom bound them together, and so too did their shared forced exclusion from White Medallion.

At the same time, Whites from Medallion knew and understood little about the Bottom and its residents. Only a few Whites, trying to sell insurance or collect rent, ventured through the Bottom, and even then they saw the Bottom and its residents through eyes squinted against dust and poverty. The majority of Whites had no experience with the Bottom and imagined the community there, if they wondered about it at all, in the terms laid out by their myths of racial superiority.

The understanding possessed by residents of the Bottom of themselves and of Medallion, and the way Whites from Medallion saw the people of the Bottom, illustrate the broadest parameters of the community ties theory. Membership in a subordinated community greatly influences how one views both that community and the dominant group, while membership in the dominant group greatly skews how one views subordinated communities.

Both chance and choice play roles in the formation of community ties. Chance governs membership in a community in that individuals are born into racial communities and, depending on their physical characteristics, are treated as members of that community irrespective of their individual wishes. Membership requires choice insofar as individuals embrace, remake, or reject the cultural, moral, and aesthetic values of the community, either as a function of quotidian decisions or conscious reflection.

This densely packed description of community turns on notions of race and affiliation. Let me clarify the role of race and external pressures on the one hand and of affiliation and internal decisions on the other. Community ties implicate race in several indirect ways. First, the individual is almost always socialized into her community by parents and extended family, with whom she shares genetic traits. Generally, these superficial traits, including, for example, skin pigmentation and facial features, mark other members of the community as well. As a result, communities emerge as racially identifiable groups in that members of a community share certain readily recognizable physical attributes.

Second, physical attributes constitute a basis for racist treatment. Disparate treatment on the basis of physical appearance influences a community in complex and unexpected ways. Consider, for example, the de facto segregation of people into racially defined enclaves. On the one hand, such segregation destroys the fabric of established communities through the systematic geographical concentration of poverty and the denial of resources, such as schools and transportation. On the other hand, the act of segregation defines people who share certain features as a distinctive group, contributing to the formation of a community identity. Oppressed enclaves may create communities by enforcing physical proximity and providing a core of similar experiences—if only the experiences of fear, violence, exclusion, resistance, and struggle. As Black scholar Richard Ford has observed, the segregation of people on the basis of integument does not simply reflect preexisting communities or races. To a large degree, it creates them. Finally, race remains important in a third way. As I will argue later, racial identity serves as a useful proxy for community ties.

Thus, the discussion of communities requires the discussion of race. But, although I discuss "race" and refer to Blacks, Whites, Latinos, and Asians, I repudiate the idea of distinct biological groups marked by essential characteristics as a tragic and terrible absurdity. We do not exist as genetically separate races. Our common gene pool renders typological distinctions between individuals commonly considered Black, White, and so forth, biologically meaningless. Human beings fall across a tremendous spectrum of physical differences; we do not fall into the neat fictional categories commonly known as races. Obviously, these false biological races cannot be assigned essential characteristics except as a further and grievously harmful fiction. Indeed, the essentialist dualisms so central to racial mythology—black barbarity and white enlightenment, for example—starkly reveal the social and historical origins of the idea of race. In the words of Richard Ford, "Race is an ideological and not an ontological reality."

The term "race" in this essay refers alternately to the physical features commonly associated with different groups, or to these groups as they are socially defined. Similarly, "White" and "Black" refer to communities, defined through participation and experience. (I use a capital W to refer to Whites. This is done only rarely by others, as if in the United States there is no White community. However, the history of this country has witnessed the formation of a White culture distinct from the ethnic cultures of Europe.) White and black, light and dark, brown, olive, yellow, and red refer to skin pigmentation (and other physical characteristics). Uncapitalized, these terms refer to physical traits, but not to community. The color of one's skin does not determine community membership—not all browns are Latino, not all blacks are Black. Indeed, in the Latino community there are reds, whites, blacks, browns, and yellows.

Consider, in the context of Latino color and as a segue between race and affiliation, the way the social construction of race constitutes an aspect of people's chosen community identity. A recent survey of Latinos in California revealed that among first-generation residents, 25 percent describe themselves as "White" and 10 percent as "Indian." Among Latinos who are third-generation residents, a comparable 26 percent describe themselves as "White," but more than twice as many, 23 percent, describe themselves as "Indian." In biological terms, the Latinos who have been in the United States for three generations have no more, and probably fewer, "Indian" antecedents than those who are first generation here. The politics of community identity, not biology, explains the greater number of those who consider themselves racially Indian.

Several Latino scholars undertook the study I draw upon here in order to explore Latino social identity: "the part of an individual's self-concept that derives from his/her knowledge of various group memberships, together with the value and emotional significance attached to those memberships." The researchers relied upon interviews with more than 1,000 Latinos — defined as persons having at least two grandparents from Mexico, the Caribbean, or a Central or South American country. The results, published in 1992 under the title *Redefining California: Latino Social Engagement in a Multicultural Society*, document the importance of self-identification in the creation of communities.

The survey asked respondents to read through a deck of forty-nine cards with labels depicting ethnic, national origin, race, family, gender, religion, language, class, and political categories, and to retain the cards that in their opinion described themselves. More than eight out of ten respondents retained cards describing themselves, in descending order, in terms of family relationships, ethnicity or national origin, Catholicism, and the Spanish language. Only about half described themselves in racial terms. Communities do not rest upon the foundation of race. Instead, communities are built on shared values (the emphasis on family), shared culture (ethnicity and language), and shared beliefs (a common religion).

Community ties require choice broadly understood on at least two levels: the decision about which group relations most contribute to social identity, and the volition involved in maintaining those group relations. Thus, the emphasis on certain social relations and not others — for example, the maintenance of extended families — in part defines the Latino community. At the same time, the effort to maintain certain social relations also implicates volition. Thus, the celebration of ethnicity and the preservation of extended family relations depend on quotidian decisions, on the things people decide to do in their daily lives.

Choice reveals itself in community ties on a third level as well. As the ethnic militancy of the past several decades and even the rise of the diversity movement itself demonstrate, individuals often choose consciously and carefully to pursue and remake their own community identity as well as the community itself. The perennial debates on appropriate ethnic labels, such as Latino instead of Hispanic, reflect this conscious shaping of identity and community. Conversely, those who decide to leave the community of their birth also exercise conscious choice about community affiliation. Thus, James Weldon Johnson's ex-colored man chose to leave the Black community by passing as White to spare his children the pain of racial hierarchy.

I emphasize choice not to assert the preeminence of volition in the formation of communities, but to emphasize how human agency results in dynamic and fractured communities. Both popular and academic discourse commonly characterize communities, as they do races, as static, temporally transcendent, homogeneous, and monolithic. In this view, communities come preformed out of the dim past and recede unaltered and uniform into the future. To paraphrase Renato Rosaldo's telling critique in his book *Culture and Truth*, people award communities the objective status of systems: not unlike a grammar, a community stands on its own, independent of and uniform in application to the people who follow its rules. In this hierarchical view, a community arches over the individual, dictating her actions but immune to her decisions.

This view reduces communities from vibrant phenomena to rigid artifacts at the expense of the way people actually live. While communities mold people, people constantly reshape the community. Neither static nor temporally transcendent, communities change and evolve in relation to the lives of community members, upon whom the social, economic, and political forces of society operate. Similarly, the diverse lived experiences of community members insure heterogeneous, not homogeneous, communities. Comparing migrant Latino farm workers to their urban sisters and brothers, for example, reveals how geographic and class differences create a fractured mosaic within communities.

Finally, communities are not monolithic, either in the sense of being impermeable to outside influence or because people can be members of only one community. Instead, every community remains porous and closely linked to the society around it through the various extracommunity ties of its members. As protagonist Clemente Chacón explains in José Antonio Villarreal's book of the same name, "I am a Mexican and I am an American, and there is no reason in the world why I can't be both." Extending this sentiment, we can say that every American becomes to some extent a Mexican by virtue of Chacón's presence in this country, and there is no reason in the world why this too should not be so.

But how does the complex idea of community ties play out in the intellectual world of legal academia? While the rest of this essay addresses exactly that question, let me give a concrete example taken from the offices of the *Harvard Civil Rights-Civil Liberties Law Review*. The striking correlation between article topics, student editors, and authors in the Winter 1991 issue illuminates the value and limits of the community ties theory. One article, written by an African-American judge, concerned the legal status of Black freemen in antebellum Virginia. Two of the three student editors who worked on the piece are African-American. A second article reviewed the recently ratified Americans with Disabilities Act. The author and two of the three student editors who worked on that piece use wheelchairs. A third article explored feminism and the law. The author and two of five student editors are women. Finally, two of the three student writers of a piece examining a Massachusetts act prohibiting discrimination on the basis of sexual orientation are openly gay.

A theory of community ties does not tell us about those who are not Black, disabled, women, or openly gay who nonetheless worked on these articles. Nor does it explain the law review members associated with traditionally excluded groups who did not work on any of these articles. Nor can we always specify in community terms what precipitates an individual's decision to work on one thing as opposed to another. But a theory of community ties does explain, I believe, the strong correlation between affiliation with a particular subordinated community and the articles that the authors and editors chose to produce.

The Role Model Theory

Among the principal educational reasons for racial diversity, two arguments predominate. The first, the role model theory, anticipates that minority scholars benefit law schools by (1) symbolically challenging the stereotype of intellectual inferiority that burdens people of color; (2) serving as exemplars suitable for student emulation; and (3) acting as mentors to facilitate and aid the growth of students. While minority students benefit particularly, these advantages also accrue to nonminority students.

The challenge to racial stereotypes posed by minority professors lessens the inhibiting sense of inferiority and alienation often shouldered by students of color. Such disaffection commonly marks Harvard students. Nearly three hundred portraits and sculptures of prominent White, male lawyers and judges displayed throughout the school constantly remind HLS students of the historic absence of minorities and women at that institution and in the legal profession. In every hallway and in every classroom, the frigid gaze of these solemn White men coldly brushes over students and professors, causing many minorities and women to feel unwelcome and out of place. In 1988 the Women's Law Association pressured HLS to display portraits of successful women jurists. The school acceded by placing ten framed black-and-white photos of women in a single classroom, whereupon the association promptly hosted a party to celebrate the room's "liberation." In 1989, La Alianza members wore T-shirts bearing an empty portrait frame and the caption "Tenured Hispanic Faculty, Harvard Law School, 1817-1989." The back of the shirt posed this poignant question: "172 Years . . . A Harvard Tradition?" The somber message is that large groups of students suffer from a destructive sense of alienation from HLS.

Moreover, the overwhelmingly White composition of the faculty adds weight to negative stereotypes about the abilities of people of color. In an affidavit submitted in support of the coalition lawsuit, Margarita Prieto testified that "the lack of a diverse faculty is personally stigmatizing because it sends a false message to all students and to the entire law school community that . . . I could not teach at Harvard Law School simply because I am Latina." Similar comments have been made time and again by protesters willing to reveal publicly their private demoralization. Whether or not one agrees with the diversity movement's goals and tactics, this anguished testimony should convince everyone that the absence of minority faculty damages the self-esteem of many students.

The inclusion of scholars of color on faculties counteracts the sense of exclusion by conveying to minority students the affirmative message of belonging and instilling the belief that they can be similarly successful. All students, White and minority, benefit to the extent that the presence of minority faculty at the front of the classroom destroys derogatory racial stereotypes.

The role model theory also posits that professors of color benefit students as exemplars who inspire emulation. This expectation recognizes that professors implicitly legitimize certain types of professional conduct by their manner in class and in their relations with students. Susan Komisaruk, a member of the Committee on Gay and Lesbian Legal Issues, explains:

> I learn far more from my teachers than mere cases or rules. I absorb
> their methods of analysis, types of argument, and speaking styles, all of
> which will influence the way I conduct myself as an attorney. Yet
> techniques and mannerisms of heterosexual men can never altogether
> look right or sound right coming from me; nor will they ever altogether
> feel right, inside me. . . . I need professors who can teach me how to be
> successful as myself, not as a straight man.

The person behind the podium teaches not only law, but also how to act, analyze, and relate to others. Scholars of color show that one can be authentically Black, Latino, and so on—in touch with the hopes, struggles, and norms of one's own community—while also being a professional, whether as an academic or an attorney. Members of minority groups benefit from the validation of their own norms of conduct, and others gain from exposure to different norms.

The role of minority scholars as mentors for their students constitutes a third aspect of the role model theory. Scholars of color add to the mentoring capacity of law school faculties by their ability to relate to students from their own community on the basis of shared experience. In the Fall 1983 issue of its newsletter, *Raza Review*, La Alianza published a short article welcoming Gerald López, the first Latino professor to teach at HLS. The article noted with pride López's commitment to Latino culture, exclaiming enthusiastically that López "is to the fullest extent of the word—CHICANO." The article reserved its highest praise for the interest López took in the students, particularly students of color. Adding to the article's praise, an editor emphasized that "Prof. López's desire to help students at HLS was recently exemplified this semester when he conducted a rap session entitled 'Coping at HLS as a Third World [Student].' " The role model theory predicts exactly this sort of new and beneficial relationship between minority faculty and minority students.

The role model theory predicts as well that minority scholars transform mentoring for all faculty and students. Charles Lawrence, an African-American professor at Georgetown, describes the typical mentoring role at law schools as "passing the mantle of power from Father to Son." By this he means that mainstream scholars often consider their function as a mentor to be the molding of students in their own image. Lawrence suggests that professors of color, atypical themselves, realize that they need not force students into a procrustean bed. Evidence supporting Lawrence's contention can be gleaned from the observations of Derrick Bell. In *And We Are Not Saved: The Elusive Quest for Racial Justice*, Bell relates in semiautobiographical fiction what he often experienced in fact: "I had become the personal counselor and confidante of virtually all the black students and a goodly number of whites. The black students needed someone with whom to share their problems, and white students, finding a faculty member actually willing to take time with them, were not reluctant to keep my appointments book full." If Lawrence is right, it is not simply Bell's willingness to spend time with students that explains his popularity. It is Bell's willingness to facilitate students' personal growth, and this redounds to the benefit of minority and White students alike.

While for analytical reasons I distinguish between minority faculty as symbols, exemplars, and mentors, in practice these functions overlap and converge on a single point: the successful role model empowers students who might otherwise not believe in themselves or their capacity to succeed. Patricia Williams, a Black woman graduate of Harvard and a professor at Columbia Law School, explains simply that "diversity provides role models for students. I would not have been a law professor today had it not been for Derrick Bell." Yet a single role model cannot suffice for any community or individual. As Williams goes on to point out, "the expectation that Derrick Bell would represent all people . . . is a limited one, an unrealistic one." The complexity of minority communities requires not one but many representative role models.

Having outlined the role model theory, I want to be explicit about the importance of community affiliation to this argument. People often and mistakenly assert the role model theory without discussing community ties, as if the benefits accrue solely because a professor is brown or black. The role model theory is much richer than that. The impact of minority scholars as role models depends to a large degree on the extent to which they have retained ties to their community of origin. Consider the brown professor who stands behind the podium in gold-rimmed glasses and a navy three-piece pin-striped suit, eschewing any contact with the Latino community to which his family belongs. Imagine that he has adopted the personal philosophy that getting ahead means being White, and as a result not only attempts to act in a manner indistinguishable from his White colleagues but also tries to distance himself from his origins. He employs the Socratic method, carefully leading a doctrinal analysis of the case law, studiously ignoring the underlying facts or the implied social relations, calling on the students by their last names, Ms. So and Mr. Such. He anglicizes the pronunciation of his own name, and he disregards the particular historical circumstances that bind him in some way to other Latinos in the law school.

What does he symbolize? For some, merely by doing his job well he may symbolize the competence of minorities, a sort of Latino Colin Powell. To others, however, he may appear to be the exception that proves the rule of intellectual inferiority. Some students, not all of them White, will distinguish him from "other Latinos" and from this reason that the "others" remain incapable of teaching at Harvard Law School. Among students of color, some may be convinced that success requires conformity to traditional White norms, including patterns of dress, manners of speech, pedagogical style, and intellectual interests.

A scholar closely affiliated with her community of origin provides a very different role model from one who has shed community ties. If an ample number of minority scholars sat on a given faculty, the representation of individuals with varying and conflicting community ties would most benefit a school. But when, as now, we cannot expect that more than a very few scholars of color will be on any single faculty, it is imperative that they have strong community ties in order to provide the maximum range of difference. The role model theory thus supports Derrick Bell's assertion that hiring a professor who looks black but thinks White does not further diversity.

The Perspective Theory

The perspective theory provides the second educational argument for diversity. This theory, like the role model theory, draws heavily on the concept of community ties. It assumes that minorities often have distinct worldviews related to their close affiliation with traditionally subordinated communities and posits that law schools benefit when such views shape minority scholarship and pedagogy. The new insights associated with community ties generate: (1) distinctive methodologies; (2) the reconsideration of established legal debates; (3) the formulation of fresh legal controversies; and (4) the modification of pedagogical styles.

Until recently, legal scholarship reflected the stark homogeneity of law faculties. Legal academia viewed the sparse scholarship by people of color as marginal. The minority breakthrough in law schools, however, has affected legal scholarship out of proportion to the small number of new minority professors. More articles have been published by scholars of color in the Harvard, Yale, and Stanford law reviews since 1985 than in the preceding century. The strength of recent minority participation in legal debates required the recognition of a new school of legal thought that is known as critical race theory. The contours of this literature demonstrate the impact of minority professors on the methodology and substance of legal scholarship.

Derrick Bell paved the way for the sharp departures from conventional scholarship taken by many professors of color when, in 1985, he published his "Civil Rights Chronicles" in the *Harvard Law Review*. The "Chronicles" describe a series of allegorical fantasies in which Bell debates aspects of race relations with a fictional civil rights activist from the sixties who possesses startling visions. Bell continues to push for new methodologies and voices, saying in a 1989 interview that "the traditional way of doing legal scholarship doesn't do justice to our experience. We need new ways of addressing a situation many of us feel is abominable." A significant number of minority scholars have taken this call to heart.

Charles Lawrence begins his 1987 article "The Id, the Ego, and Equal Protection: Reckoning with Unconscious Racism" by describing his experiences as a child, and in watching his own daughter grow up:

It is 1948. I am sitting in a kindergarten classroom. . . .

> It is circle time in the five-year old group, and the teacher is reading us a book . . . *Little Black Sambo.* Looking back, I remember only one part of the story, one illustration: Little Black Sambo is running around the stack of pancakes with a tiger chasing him. . . . There is a knot in the pit of my stomach. I feel panic and shame . . . I am slowly realizing that as the only black child in the circle, I have some kinship with the tragic and ugly hero of this story—that my classmates are laughing at me as well as at him. . . .
>
> I am thirty-three. My daughter, Maia, is three. I greet a pink-faced, four year old boy on the steps of her nursery school. He proudly presents me with a book he has brought for his teacher to read to the class. "It's my favorite," he says. The book is a new edition of *Little Black Sambo.*

Two features of this passage characterize writings in the critical race genre and mark its departure from the conventions of traditional legal scholarship. First, Lawrence keenly feels his status as a minority, and second, he uses a story to convey ideas. The writings of critical race theorists often combine these two features.

Lawrence intertwines them in relating to the reader how he personally experienced the unconscious racism he discusses in his article. He makes no pretense of objectivity, but rather situates himself squarely within the discussed subject. He witnesses and participates. Lawrence's emphasis on identity and subjectivity finds echoes among other minority scholars. Patricia Williams describes her upbringing in "Alchemical Notes: Reconstructing Ideals from Deconstructed Rights": "I . . . was raised to be acutely conscious of the likelihood that, no matter what degree of professional or professor I became, people would greet and dismiss my black femaleness as unreliable, untrustworthy, hostile, angry, powerless, irrational and probably destitute. Futility and despair are very real parts of my response." Several articles by Williams draw not only on her life but also on the lives of her maternal ancestors, who were slaves in Tennessee. Many of the new methodological features of recent minority scholarship follow from the self-conscious reflection on history and society.

The emergence of narrative as a methodological innovation seems to be a product of this self-awareness. Critical race theorists maintain that consensus is unlikely, and the discovery of truth through reason impossible. The new style of legal discourse employed by many scholars of color eschews proof in favor of illustration. Offering evidence for the purpose of illustration acknowledges that individual and group identity inform beliefs and worldviews. Each reader must assign her own interpretive weight to the proffered evidence. Stories and personal experiences are not employed to prove assertions, only to make them clear. Minority scholars deploy subjective narration in academic discourse as much for political as for methodological reasons.

Armed with this new methodology, minority scholars jumped into the legal debates from which they were long excluded. This increased ferment particularly affects the area of jurisprudence, which encompasses the study of the nature of law, legal rights, and legal obligations. Scholars of color increasingly predominate in the jurisprudential debates known as critical legal studies (CLS). CLS radically critiques the inherent legitimacy of legal rules and rejects the definition of law as a coherent whole or a rational and predictable system for resolving disputes. Minority scholars have eagerly attempted to harness and mold the power of the change-oriented CLS critique. In one notable effort, law professor Mari Matsuda argued in "Looking to the Bottom: Critical Legal Studies and Reparations" that reference to the experiences of minorities would remedy many CLS weaknesses: "This article . . . suggests a new epistemological source for critical scholars: the actual experience, history, culture, and intellectual tradition of people of color in America. Looking to the bottom for ideas about law will tap a valuable source previously overlooked by legal philosophers." Others join Matsuda in her attempts to redefine CLS from a minority perspective. The titles of several other articles come to mind, including "Local Knowledge, Local Color: Critical Legal Studies and the Law of Race Relations" by Gerald Torres and "The Ethereal Scholar: Does Critical Legal Studies Have What Minorities Want?" by Richard Delgado, both Latino law professors. Persons of color talking as professors over lunch in faculty lounges, rather than serving in the silent role of waiter, transform legal discourse by injecting new insights into old debates.

The perspective theory also posits the creation of new areas of legal inquiry. The introduction into law school halls of debates long established in minority communities provides fresh grist for the academic mill. Important ideological battles, such as the integrationist-separationist debate raging in the Black community since before W. E. B. Du Bois and Booker T. Washington, divide many minority communities. These struggles offer alternative conceptions of how to order society, exactly the stuff most deserving of debate within the walls of legal academia.

In addition, minority professors create legal debates where none existed before. Richard Delgado fomented one such debate in a 1984 article entitled "The Imperial Scholar: Reflections on a Review of Civil Rights Literature" by calling into question the role of race in the sociology of legal knowledge. Delgado criticized "white scholars' systematic occupation of, and exclusion of minority scholars from, the central areas of civil rights scholarship," a process resulting in "an inner circle of about a dozen white, male writers who comment on, take polite issue with, extol, criticize, and expand on each other's ideas." Delgado's thesis has been supported and challenged by minority and nonminority scholars. But whatever side one takes, critical theory has, as one observer noted, "placed on scholarly agendas questions that have heretofore received little or no attention, questions that explore the nature and consequences of racial conflict within legal academia." This new debate cannot be understood without reference to the presence of minority scholars in the legal professoriat.

Racial diversity also leads to innovations in pedagogy. The relations between Professor Regina Austin, a Black woman and visiting professor at HLS during the 1989-90 academic year, and the students in her class exemplify this. In the fall of 1989, a White student announced at the close of class that Austin was discriminating against him by refusing to recognize his raised hand. These charges were repeated in a *New York Times* article entitled "Harvard Law School Torn by Race Issues." Several White male students complained that Austin favored minorities and women when calling on students to participate in class discussion.

Minority students are frequently ignored by White professors. In its brief against Harvard Law School, the coalition reported that "one professor went an entire semester without calling upon a single African American student. It was not until the last day of class, when an African American student interrupted the professor to state that he had waited all semester to present a case, that an African American student was finally recognized." In response to similar experiences, the Student Division of the Hispanic National Bar Association devoted half of its 1991 northeastern regional conference to a panel discussion of "silencing in the classroom." Several panelists reported that unless the case or issue being covered in class directly involved persons of color, their upraised hands seemed strangely invisible to the professor.

It seems likely that the students in Austin's class experienced not discrimination against Whites and men but rather an end to discrimination against minorities and women. As an article in the *National Law Journal* rightly observed: "The reality is that because subtle bias (against minorities and women) is the norm, it is equal treatment that may seem aberrant and objectionable." Austin, in giving more time to minorities and women, introduced a pedagogical innovation attributable, at least in part, to her status as a Black woman.

Kimberlé Crenshaw, another Black woman and a law professor at UCLA, provides an example of a minority scholar purposefully developing alternative pedagogical styles. In a recent article entitled "Toward a Race-Conscious Pedagogy in Legal Education," Crenshaw describes her efforts to "create an environment that presented an alternative to the traditional classroom experiences of minority students in majority-centered law schools." The perspective theory predicts, and experience shows, that minority scholars may practice a distinctive pedagogy, both unintentionally and by design.

Choosing Professors

Thus far, I have argued for explicitly seeking to hire minority scholars based on their minority status, citing benefits to students, to scholarship, and to pedagogy. These multiple benefits have been linked to the hiring of professors with close ties to minority communities rather than to the hiring of someone merely black or brown. But the question remains, how shall suitable professors of color be identified? Assessing their ties poses a number of difficult problems. To measure the "authenticity" of someone's membership in a community would require the articulation of a generally applicable standard. The delineation of evaluative standards by predominantly White institutions seems doomed to failure because of misunderstandings, distrust, and conflicts of interest between the institutions and the heretofore excluded communities. Moreover, ample cause exists to believe no standards could be set. Because the community groups and the variety of relations individuals maintain with their communities of origin are complicated, any standard would risk being so general as to lack force or so detailed as to be wrongly exclusionary. Finally, scrutinizing the authenticity of a candidate's place within a minority community would almost certainly entail an invasion of privacy and concomitantly cause resentment.

Rather than attempt to make institutional evaluations about the cultural identity of particular candidates, law schools should rely on some combination of race and self-identification as a proxy for community ties. While race does not determine community membership, there remains a strong correlation between the two. As Harvard Law School professor Christopher Edley, who is Black, argued in the *Washington Post*, "Race remains a useful proxy for a whole collection of experiences, aspirations and sensitivities." Edley explained that "it's not just a matter of having a particular slant on things; it's a question of what kind of glasses you've been wearing as the years roll by." Race should be used only because it approximates community ties, not because it determines any mind-set or establishes any claim of merit.

Self-identification by a candidate also constitutes a reasonable basis to infer community affiliation. Such identification can be either explicit or inferred from her public life. Inferences concerning community ties need to be made with care, however, lest they shade into the institutional judgments of legitimate minority status I criticized earlier. Relying on membership in certain organizations, publications, or employment as a proxy for community ties, if it was carried too far, would involve law school hiring committees in perilous evaluations of authenticity. Nevertheless, some cases of obvious public affiliation warrant an inference of community ties—for example, when a candidate has participated in a student organization like La Alianza or published an article exploring the concerns of her community or worked in a capacity that directly benefited her community (as an attorney with the Mexican American Legal Defense and Educational Fund, for instance). The use by law schools of race and self-identification in hiring decisions can greatly facilitate the achievement of racial diversity.

The Criticisms of Diversity

By asserting that community ties are important, that people of color may think and act differently from White people, and that race should be considered as a factor in faculty hiring, the diversity movement attracts a host of enemies. The most vociferous insinuate that the ideas propounded by the diversity movement are akin to those held by the Nazis. In a 1990 MacNeil/Lehrer broadcast, John Bunzell of Stanford's Hoover Institute and a member of the U.S. Commission on Civil Rights under President Ronald Reagan uttered this warning: "I think we have to be very careful incidentally about linking the whole concept of race to knowledge or race to scholarship or race to teaching. I'm old enough to remember over the last 50 years when we heard that kind of thing from the Nazis." I turn to less agitated criticisms of the diversity movement partly for purposes of refutation and partly to clarify still more the aspirations of the diversity movement.

Both proponents and detractors of diversity criticize the rhetoric of multiplicity and difference for disingenously masking a progressive ideological agenda. These critics commonly cast the diversity movement's response to the seating of Clarence Thomas on the Supreme Court as a litmus test of the true ideological colors of racial diversity's proponents. Paradoxically and—the critics contend—hypocritically, many who support increased racial diversity opposed the elevation of Thomas to the Court.

Examining the Thomas confirmation hearings deepens the paradox. Thomas embodies the paradigmatic diversity candidate. Thomas and others packaged and marketed him as a person profoundly influenced by his upbringing in Pin Point, Georgia: grandchild of slaves, witness to the humiliations of his family and neighbors at White hands, victim of segregation, recipient of the abiding faith that hard work and decency can triumph over even profound adversity. Again and again, Thomas tied his character and opinions back to his experiences in the small community of Pin Point, or the larger community of Black people. In his opening remarks, Thomas stated with obvious sincerity: "I have always carried in my heart the world, the life, the people, the values of my youth, the values of my grandparents and my neighbors, the values of people who believed so very deeply in this country in spite of all the contradictions." To this high note of community affiliation, Thomas added a very low one. Thomas decried the Senate's inquiry into Professor Anita Hill's credible allegations of sexual harassment as a "high-tech lynching" of himself as a Black man. Casting himself as a victim of White society, Thomas asserted that the Senate's behavior in giving a hearing to Hill could only be understood in terms of White and Black.

The importance of Thomas's "Blackness" to his candidacy cannot be overemphasized. The hollow protestations of President George Bush notwithstanding, Thomas's black skin explains his nomination. The Bush administration and private political groups did their best to craft Thomas's image as the "Black candidate." The private Citizen's Committee to Confirm Clarence Thomas, for example, flew some of the Black residents of Pin Point up to Washington to attend a Capitol Hill breakfast—and photo opportunity—with the nominee and key senators. The same campaign spent $300,000 airing national ads lauding Thomas, in language strikingly reminiscent of that used by the diversity movement, as "a role model we can all look to with pride."

At the same time, despite intense questioning, the intellectual grist of constitutional jurisprudence received little airing during the confirmation hearings. Thomas consistently refused to answer substantive questions— for example, on abortion. He declined to defend views he previously proclaimed in numerous public speeches, such as the primacy of natural law. And he was unable to name more than a couple of cases when he was challenged to cite significant Supreme Court decisions rendered in the last two decades. The hearings allotted even less time to a discussion of Thomas's skimpy qualifications, thin indeed in light of his ascension only one year earlier to the Court of Appeals and his poor showing at the hands of the American Bar Association, the worst of any Supreme Court nominee since 1955.

The only issue, it began to seem, was Thomas's community ties. The nomination process seemed an ironic satire, a caricature by conservatives of what a nomination staged by the diversity movement might look like: lots of heartrending testimonials on authentic ethnic experiences, an astounding paucity of intellectual substance, little evaluation of the candidate's qualifications, and a violent denunciation of racial bias in lieu of a considered response to legitimate and serious inquiry. During the confirmation process, Thomas and his supporters were "diverseniks" par excellence, in the fullest disparaging sense of that term.

Nevertheless, Thomas is an authentically Black candidate, and critics wrongly suppose that the diversity movement cannot identify him as such. Even as Thomas criticizes and castigates his community, he remains wholly within it. If all one were interested in was increased diversity, Thomas would be almost the ideal candidate. I say almost, because there remains a significant manner in which Thomas's appointment does not serve the ends of diversity. Thomas, as a critic of the mainstream of his own community, now occupies a position as the sole representative of that community. No other minority person will soon be seated on the Supreme Court. Thus, we are left with a justice whose views, while undoubtedly a product of his own lived experience as a member of the Black community, accord with those of only a small fraction of that community and, significantly, trace ideologically the views of the majority of the White justices already on the high court. The elevation of a Black critic of the Black community falls substantially short of the genuine increase in diversity many of us await. The fact that Thomas succeeds Thurgood Marshall, an ardent and abiding supporter of the Black community, makes the appointment of this Black critic doubly bitter.

Meanwhile, large segments of the Black community, including the NAACP and the National Bar Association, found themselves in the awkward position of opposing the "Black candidate." Awkward, that is, because a substantial synergy exists between the diversity movement and progressive politics. At root, similar ideals motivate both, including, for example, tolerance, political pluralism, concern for minority communities, and commitment to social justice. The Thomas candidacy pitted racial diversity against progressive politics. The case of Clarence Thomas illustrates the deep divergence that is possible between the ideal of diversity and the aspirations of left politics.

The greatest opposition to Thomas arose outside of the terms of the diversity debate. Most who opposed Thomas did so not because of his community ties, but because of his ideology, incompetence, and personal conduct. Thomas's conservative ideology, as evidenced, for example, in his actions at the helm of the Equal Employment Opportunity Commission under President Reagan, forced people to balance their desire for racial diversity against their progressive politics. Similarly, serious doubts surrounded Thomas's ability as a jurist, and his disingenuous and sometimes mean-spirited personal conduct offended many, not least those who support increased diversity.

The Pin Point paradox, in which supporters of diversity opposed an authentically Black candidate, is used as a basis for allegations of partisan affiliation and hypocrisy. But this paradox exists only if one assumes that the diversity movement espouses racial diversity as the sole criterion to be used in selecting a candidate. In fact, supporters of diversity also accept the importance of factors such as ideology, ability, and conduct. The diversity movement does not, and I do not, argue that community ties should be the decisive prerequisite in appointment decisions—only that community ties deserve a place in the perennial debates on faculty hiring.

A second criticism contends that the role model and perspective theories apply to just about every marginalized group, rendering them useless as a basis for faculty appointments. The advocates of diversity sometimes make this critique easy. One self-described proponent of diversity wrote to the *Harvard Law Record* that "three additional dimensions of diversity that cry out for inclusion are religious practice, military service, and legal experience." This critique is often lodged to disparage the various constituent groups of the diversity movement, or deployed as reductio ad absurdum.

The sympathetic commentator may yet ask, where will it all end? I respond, hopefully it won't. This critique nicely highlights the fact that many groups have been excluded from legal academia. To the extent that these different groups demand representation on the grounds posited by the role model and perspective theories, fair enough. That is not to say, however, that each group possess an identical claim to representation or that differentiating between competing claims is unfair or unjust. The terms of the role model and perspective theories suggest some relevant factors for consideration. Thus, it would be possible to distinguish among excluded groups by the extent to which they form a community, the manner in which shared characteristics shape group ties and worldview, and the nature of the community's historic exclusion from academia. No doubt the attempt to make such distinctions would result in fierce political battles. I prefer such pitched battles to the false tranquility of academic exclusion because they hold out the possibility of diversity and reveal the relationship between inclusion and power.

Allegations of cultural separatism and racism constitute a separate line of attack. The primitive version of the cultural separatism critique contends that the discussion of ethnic differences undermines the basically neutral ethnic character of American society. Most people seem to equate the transcendence of ethnic identity with progress and integration, and the explicit consideration of community identity with backsliding and racism. The sense that there is some antiseptic nonethnic character to which all citizens should aspire is often expressed to minorities in the statement "Why not say you're just plain American?"—instead of, for example, Asian-American or African-American. The term "American," however, like this society more generally, falls far short of ethnic neutrality. The term instead contains a presumption of Whiteness. Consider the introduction to "Diversity and Its Discontents," published in *Academe*:

> My name is Arturo Madrid. I am a citizen of the United States, as are my parents and as were my grandparents and my great-grandparents. My ancestors' presence in what is now the United States antedates Plymouth Rock, even without taking into account any American Indian heritage I might have.

> I do not, however, fit those mental sets that define America and Americans. My physical appearance, my speech patterns, my name, my profession (a professor of Spanish) create a text that confuses the reader. My normal experience is to be asked, "And where are *you* from?"

Depicting the ethnic character of American society as more or less neutral ignores the way that American institutions reflect dominant racial and ethnic characteristics. The predominant ethnic character of the United States is not neutral, it is White. At the same time, however, many non-White ethnic communities persist and even thrive within the borders of the United States. Some, like the Hispanic community of the Southwest to which Madrid belongs, have existed here since before the *Mayflower* arrived. This country, through a history of conquest, slavery, and economic opportunity, reigns as the most heterogeneous nation in the world. Eliminating the conscious recognition of community affiliation will not extinguish different communities in the United States, for these communities will persist whether they are consciously recognized or not.

A more sophisticated version of the cultural separatism critique accepts cultural heterogeneity in the United States but insists that the elimination of racism requires an attempt to achieve an ethnically neutral society of "Americans." There are two principal problems with this approach. First, those who espouse this argument very often do not intend the creation of an ethnically indistinct culture, but the vindication of White cultural norms. Proponents of "English only," for example, seek to create an integrated American society by banning the use of any language other than English. Second, and more troubling, the goal of a homogeneous culture implicitly rests upon a sociological belief in individuals as autonomous, undifferentiated units who are independent of others, and on a normative preference for sameness over difference.

Those who propound a homogeneous country suggest a whitewashed world of equal, undifferentiated monads.

The diversity movement repudiates the idea that individuals exist without community ties, as well as the preference for conformity. The role model and perspective theories rely on the empirical fact that community ties shape how and what each of us thinks. The assertion that people resemble ciphers bereft of cultural identity seems more a product of philosophical speculation than self-conscious observation. Student activists also reject the view that uniformity is the norm, and is good. Indeed, the word *diversity* itself reveals the deep commitment its proponents have toward multiplicity and difference. A pejorative view of difference and divergence seems entirely misplaced in our tremendously variegated world. The diversity movement focuses on minority communities to legitimate and celebrate the variation that exists between cultures, not to create it.

Charges of racism often follow allegations of cultural separatism. One version of this accusation maintains that the call for diversity demeans minorities. In *Newsweek*, Harvard Law School student Brian Timmons criticized the assumption that if an institution hires "members of disadvantaged groups, diverse ideas will follow": "This assumption," he charged, "is both prejudiced and implausible. That black people think differently from white people is a racist premise."

Timmons's charge warrants a brief dissection of the nature of racism. As an attitude, "racism" derives from a belief in the superiority of one race over another. In much of the world, as in the United States, notions of white supremacy over nonwhite peoples drive racism. Racism detracts from an individual's humanity by ascribing to her degenerate traits and withholding human characteristics, such as the ability to reason and to exercise moral choice. Myriad conscious and subconscious motivations for racism overlap. They include fear, socialization (often erroneously referred to as "ignorance"), the generation and maintenance of wealth, the accumulation or preservation of political power, and the rationalization of privilege. Racism manifests itself between groups and individuals in multiple forms including (either separately or together) violence, subjugation, segregation, and disempowerment.

Recently and unfortunately, however, many equate racism with differential treatment on the basis of race. In the legal field, this abstraction underlies an equal protection jurisprudence in which every action taken in cognizance of race is presumed constitutionally infirm, irrespective of context or motivation. Under this view, the harm of racism lies in the violation of meritocratic norms. That is, the evil of racism lurks in the willingness of some to base actions or beliefs on skin color, since skin color is arbitrary and unrelated to individual worth. This abstraction fails entirely to capture two key elements of racism: the nature of racial hierarchy and its cruel and dehumanizing force.

To see the difference between race consciousness and racism, consider a hypothetical campaign commercial pitched to Latino voters in Southern California. The producer of the ad will almost certainly take note of race in choosing between actors, in this case by employing a Latino. If the producer then hires an all-white technical staff in the belief that Latinos can act but cannot film, direct, or edit, she again decides on the basis of race. Both decisions offend meritocracy equally because of the equal arbitrariness of white and brown skin. Yet, an all-important difference exists.

In choosing a Latino actor, the producer is not racist; in hiring an all-White technical staff, she is. The producer throws no derogatory aspersions on the capabilities of whites by casting someone with brown skin to whom the intended Latino audience can relate. By contrast, the producer's decision to hire only white technical workers brands all people of color inferior. The producer has organized her world in accord with a formal structure of racial exclusion and domination predicated on the superiority of whites and the inferiority of people of color. Skin color is not arbitrarily unrelated to worth—it defines worth. Racism malevolently strips people of their humanity and serves as a rationalization for barbarism in the interests of hierarchy.

Keeping this discussion in mind, let us examine once again the role model and perspective theories. Both call for professors with ties to minority communities. But neither theory justifies its position on the supposed superiority or inferiority of racial groups. The worst that can be said about these theories is that they violate certain debatable norms customarily relied upon in faculty hiring. No tenable basis exists for comparing those who push for diversity to the zealots of race hierarchy.

A less crude version of the racism critique charges that by employing generalizations about minority groups, proponents of diversity derogate from the individuality of group members. These generalizations, often erroneously referred to as stereotypes, allegedly constitute racism because they ascribe characteristics to individuals based on their perceived affiliation with a certain group. But generalizations based on group affiliation engender no injustice. To suggest that, typically, Asians eat rice while Latinos eat tortillas is not racist; as a generalization, it is true. A generalization abstracts on the basis of large numbers, with no pretense of specificity, while stereotypes ascribe unvarying characteristics to every individual within a group. Unlike those who engage in stereotyping, those who generalize remain acutely aware of the partial nature of their statements. For example, in discussing Black and White perspectives, Professor Kimberlé Crenshaw tells her readers explicitly: "I rely on no empirical data to support [my] generalizations. I realize that any conclusions drawn from such generalizations are tentative at best and are compelling only to the extent that the underlying generalizations seem plausible." The diversity movement's use of generalizations and the student reformers' care in emphasizing the partiality and incompleteness of their observations distances the movement from those who disparage people of color through mechanical stereotyping.

Another version of the racism critique asserts that the diversity movement racially demeans Whites by implying not only that people of color have special insight but also that Whites lack such insight. Unfortunately, some sectors of the diversity movement on occasion have been motivated more by the color of a person's skin than by the person's knowledge. The 1983 course boycott led by the Third World Coalition at Harvard provides one such case. The White visiting instructor, Jack Greenberg, possessed nearly impeccable credentials as a civil rights activist. Greenberg litigated *Brown v. Board of Education* on behalf of the NAACP Legal Defense and Educational Fund, succeeded Thurgood Marshall as head of the organization in 1961, and held that position at the time of the boycott. The Third World Coalition organized the boycott for two reasons: to protest Harvard's inadequate efforts to achieve diversity and to protest the hiring of a White attorney to teach a civil rights class. The second rationale reflected the belief that in an area where many minority practitioners and professors held significant sway, the hiring of a White person was unacceptable, but it also reflected an animus toward Greenberg because he was white. There are some White people who have tremendous insight into what it means to belong to a racial minority in the United States and some people of color who have almost no conception of racial identity. Greenberg has that insight, so it is unfortunate that in protesting Harvard's stultifying homogeneity students also criticized Greenberg's race. To uncritically give or deny legitimacy to scholars or scholarship on the basis of race per se seems to me to be inconsistent with the cultural pluralist underpinnings of the diversity movement.

Nevertheless, generalizations about Whites resemble the many generalizations made about minorities. These generalizations reflect the existence of racially identifiable communities—among them, the White community—in the United States. Moreover, the assertion that being White generally skews how one views subordinate communities is a valid and integral part of the community ties idea.

I use the word *skews* on purpose. Minorities and Whites are not equal but separate groups viewing each other across a simple divide. Instead, the divide polarizes light asymmetrically across two different planes. First, like the Whites from Medallion, Whites in contemporary America often understand minority communities in terms dictated by White myths of racial superiority. Second, racism in the United States creates and perpetuates material differences between the races. These differences further distort White views regarding subordinate communities by seeming to confirm nonwhite indolence and incompetence. While minorities are tragically not free of these warped views, people of color challenge far more persistently the slanders of racial hierarchy. The inability of most Whites to break out of the closed circle of their racist perceptions, vistas of minority poverty, and back again to racist views shows how being White skews understanding of minority communities.

The Problems of Diversity

While the demands of the racial diversity movement are not hypocritical, ridiculous, separatist, or racist, as some would paint them, they *do* raise vexing problems. Most prominently, the role model and perspective theories threaten to exhaust scholars of color by fastening on them all the expectations enumerated in this essay. Native American professor Rennard Strickland makes this point in his article "Scholarship in the Academic Circus, or the Balancing Act at the Minority Side Show." In an effort to advise new scholars of color on how to balance the demands placed on them, Strickland writes: "It is time some of us stood up and said, 'Sorry, I don't do windows.' I cannot be a model teacher, an effective, dynamic minority counselor, an understanding community-relations director, a respected role model, and a Pulitzer Prize-winning scholar all at the same time." By stressing the distinctive and multifarious functions that professors of color can fulfill, the diversity movement increases the danger that individuals will be expected to fulfill every function.

The role model and perspective theories also create a specter of segregated hiring standards in which hiring committees expect more of minority candidates than of White applicants. The stress placed by the arguments for diversity on the importance of minorities as role models and teachers makes this peril particularly pronounced with respect to teaching. When coupled with potential suspicions concerning intellectual prowess, the result may be fatal to a minority professor's candidacy. A White professor of mediocre pedagogical ability may benefit from a favorable presumption of scholastic promise while a minority professor equally lackluster at teaching may labor under the presumption of little scholarly talent. In this way, the minority professor who is a bland teacher may soon find herself with two strikes against her candidacy. Appointment committees *should* consider teaching ability in faculty hiring, but not only in the case of minority scholars.

Another source of potential difficulty comes from the perspective theory's emphasis on the existence of a distinct minority voice. By insisting that some minorities possess special insights largely unavailable to White scholars, the diversity movement may unwittingly support a system of segregated scholarship in legal academia. A presumption that scholars of color are narrowly focused or lacking in intellectual depth already exists. Expressing frustration at the tenacious hold of this presumption, Professor Arturo Madrid notes that "whatever our history, whatever our record, whatever our validations, whatever our accomplishments, by and large we are perceived uni-dimensionally and treated accordingly." The diversity movement's insistence that some minorities speak with unique voices may serve to confirm the suspicion that minorities are one-dimensional intellectuals, fit for addressing the marginal subject of race, but not subjects at the core of the curriculum.

In addition to lending unintended support to segregated scholarship, the diversity movement's arguments may provide a basis for further stigmatizing people of color. As Anita Allen, a Black professor of law at Georgetown, warns, arguments that attempt to give a separate rationale for taking race into account in the hiring of people of color affirm our worth while whispering our inferiority. Similarly, Stephen Carter, a Black law professor at Yale, writes that "racial preferences—adding points for skin color—often carry an implicit denigration of the abilities of scholars of color, the unspoken suggestion that we cannot really compete." In articulating a rationale for hiring minorities, the efforts of the diversity movement will be seen by some as confirmation that people of color need help because they are intellectually inferior to Whites.

The negative repercussions of the diversity movement's arguments are not limited to misinterpretation by the unsympathetic. The heightened emphasis on community ties exposes minority scholars to the hazards of uncritical reliance on perspectives influenced by experience and group affiliation. Ignoring the role subordination plays in shaping experiences creates the possibility that minority scholars will unintentionally support the system of domination under which their communities labor.

In the related context of gender relations, Frances Olsen notes in "The Sex of Law" that some feminists accept without challenge the conventional distinctions between men and women—that men are rational and women emotional, for example—while seeking to reverse the accepted hierarchy, for instance, by arguing that emotion trumps reason. Alison M. Jaggar's "Love and Knowledge: Emotion in Feminist Epistemology" fits this pattern. Jaggar correctly argues that "emotion may be helpful and even necessary rather than inimical to the construction of knowledge," but then asserts that women's superior receptivity to emotions gives them an "epistemic advantage" over men. Olsen chastises this approach for uncritically accepting conventional gender stereotypes and warns that "to reverse or invert the hierarchy between rational and irrational, active and passive, and so forth, could simply reinforce the dualisms and ultimately maintain dominant values." To avoid this possibility, people of color must examine their voices by asking unabashedly: What are the origins of my voice? Which forces helped shape the voice I have? Whose interests does my voice serve? Only by asking such political questions can minority scholars avoid internalizing oppressive norms even while they are rebelling against subordination.

The discursive modes of critical race theory give rise to a final trap for minority scholars. The reliance on narrative that draws upon experience and fantasy threatens the ability of scholars of color to hold a dialogue with individuals from other communities. In a talk given at Harvard Law School, professor Gerald Torres cautioned that storytelling can be an essentially authoritarian methodology if heavy reliance on personal experience insulates the speaker from intellectual challenge and cross-examination. Experience must be generalized and interpretative acts made clear before a narrative format that relies on insights acquired through community ties can adequately serve as a methodological tool. Scholars of color should foster forums for intercultural communication through careful explication of their community-based perspectives.

Conclusion

By way of conclusion, I wish to make a few remarks about the way Harvard Law School authorities react to the call for faculty diversity, and about the happenings since the 1990-91 academic year. The law school administration repeatedly alleges that diversity requires a trade-off of "excellence." Responding to Derrick Bell's push for a woman of color, Dean Robert Clark remarked: "We do have high standards, and we aren't going to compromise them." Some members of the faculty echo this sentiment. Also responding to Bell, Professor Emeritus Clark Byse flatly concluded, "To me, it's more important to maintain Harvard's standards of excellence than to improve the diversity of the faculty."

I object to the use of the word *excellence* for two reasons. First, as deployed in this context, "excellence" seems to disparage the intellectual ability of minority scholars. While in every faculty hiring decision there are some trade-offs, the statement that a loss of "excellence" will be the cost of considering race in faculty hiring is derogatory. Second, by relying so heavily on "excellence" but declining to give the term substantive content, the administration impedes debate about the implications of considering community ties in hiring decisions. The student activists have often been accused of using the term "diversity" as a slogan. Yet proponents of diversity have explicitly articulated their goals and explained the key words that constitute the rhetoric of their movement. University authorities should abandon the bloody shirt of excellence and join in open dialogue with the student insurgents about diversity in the halls of academe.

Unfortunately, recent events suggest Harvard's continued intransigence and unwillingness to diversify. In the academic year after the first version of this article was published, Harvard appointed no minority scholars to tenured, tenure-track, or visiting positions. The 1992-93 academic year repeated the same distressing pattern: among the six new faculty members, two were women and all were White. The tenuring of Black professor David Wilkins, an exceptional teacher, mentor, and scholar, constitutes the only positive turn of these two years.

After a quarter century of student agitation for increased diversity and despite Derrick Bell's act of conscience, which in 1992 cost him his tenured position at the law school, there remain on the tenured Harvard faculty only three African-American men and five White women. No woman of color yet stands behind a podium at Harvard Law School. The ideals of the diversity movement demand otherwise.

References

Ansley, Frances L., "Stirring the Ashes: Race, Class and the Future of Civil Rights Scholarship," 14 *Cornell Law Review* 993 (1989).

Austin, Regina, "Sapphire Bound!" 1989 *Wisconsin Law Review* 539 (1989).

Ball, Milner S., "The Legal Academy and Minority Scholars," 103 *Harvard Law Review* 1855 (1990).

Bell, Derrick, *And We Are Not Saved: The Elusive Quest for Racial Justice* (New York: Basic Books, 1987).

Carter, Stephen L., "The Best Black, and Other Tales," *Reconstruction*, no. 1 (1990): 6; "Academic Tenure and 'White Male' Standards: Some Lessons from Patent Law," 100 *Yale Law Journal* 2065 (1991).

Chused, Richard H., "The Hiring and Retention of Minorities and Women on American Law School Faculties," 137 *University of Pennsylvania Law Review* 537 (1987).

Crenshaw, Kimberlé W., "Foreword: Toward a Race-Conscious Pedagogy in Legal Education," 11 *National Black Law Journal* 1 (1989); "Race, Reform and Retrenchment: Transformation and Legitimation in Antidiscrimination Law," 101 *Harvard Law Review* 1331 (1988).

Culp, Jerome, "Autobiography and Legal Scholarship and Teaching: Finding the Me in the Legal Academy," 77 *Virginia Law Review* 539 (1991).

Delgado, Richard, "Mindset and Metaphor," 103 *Harvard Law Review* 1872 (1990); "When a Story Is Just a Story: Does Voice Really Matter?" 76 *Virginia Law Review* 95 (1990); "The Imperial Scholar: Reflections on a Review of Civil Rights Literature," 132 *University of Pennsylvania Law Review* 561 (1984); "The Ethereal Scholar: Does Critical Legal Studies Have What Minorities Want?" 22 *Harvard Civil Rights-Civil Liberties Law Review* 301 (1987).

Espinoza, Leslie, "Masks and Other Disguises: Exposing Legal Academia," 103 *Harvard Law Review* 1878 (1990).

Freeman, Alan, "Racism, Rights and the Quest for Equality of Opportunity: A Critical Legal Essay," 23 *Harvard Civil Rights-Civil Liberties Law Review* 295 (1988).

Hurtado, Aída, David Hayes-Bautista, R. Burciaga Valdez, and Anthony Hernández, *Redefining California: Latino Social Engagement in a Multicultural Society* (Los Angeles: UCLA Chicano Studies Research Center Publications, 1992).

Johnson, Alex M., "The New Voices of Color," 100 *Yale Law Journal* 2007 (1991).

Kennedy, Duncan, "Legal Education as Training for Hierarchy," in *The Politics of Law: A Progressive Critique*, 2nd ed., ed. David Kairys (New York: Pantheon, 1990); "A Cultural Pluralist Case for Affirmative Action in Legal Academia," 1990 *Duke Law Journal* 705 (1990).

Kennedy, Randall, "Racial Critiques of Legal Academia," 102 *Harvard Law Review* 1745 (1989).

Lawrence, Charles, III, "Minority Hiring in AALS Law Schools: The Need for Voluntary Quotas," 20 *University of San Francisco Law Review* 429 (1986); "The Id, the Ego, and Equal Protection: Reckoning with Unconscious Racism," 39 *Stanford Law Review* 317 (1987).

López, Gerald, "Training Future Lawyers to Work with the Politically and Socially Subordinated: Anti-Generic Legal Education," 92 *West Virginia Law Review* 305 (1990).

Matsuda, Mari, "Affirmative Action and Legal Knowledge: Planting Seeds in Plowed-Up Ground," 11 *Harvard Women's Law Journal* 1 (1988); "Looking to the Bottom: Critical Legal Studies and Reparations," 22 *Harvard Civil Rights-Civil Liberties Law Review* 323 (1987).

Olsen, Frances, "The Sex of Law," in *The Politics of Law*, ed. David Kairys.

Peller, Gary, "Race Consciousness," 1990 *Duke Law Journal* 758 (1990).

Rosaldo, Renato, *Culture and Truth: The Remaking of Social Analysis* (Boston: Beacon, 1989).

Strickland, Rennard, "Scholarship in the Academic Circus, or the Balancing Act at the Minority Side Show," 20 *University of San Francisco Law Review* 491 (1986).

Torres, Gerald, "Local Knowledge, Local Color: Critical Legal Studies and the Law of Race Relations," 25 *San Diego Law Review* 1043 (1988).

Williams, Patricia, *The Alchemy of Race and Rights* (Cambridge, Mass.: Harvard University Press, 1991).

Mil gracias are due Rey Rodríguez, Dana Shelley, Juan Zúñiga, Gerald Torres, and, especially, Randall Kennedy and David Wilkins. *Reconstruction* magazine published an earlier version of this article under the title "Community Ties, Race, and Faculty Hiring: The Case for Professors Who Don't Think White," and has generously allowed it to be republished here.

Chapter 7

The Responsibility of and to Differences: Theorizing Race and Ethnicity in Lesbian and Gay Studies

Earl Jackson, Jr.

In the process of teaching, writing, and thinking "queer theory," I have come to the conclusion that if lesbian and gay studies is to achieve its full radical potential and intellectual integrity, those of us involved in this process need to pay long-term and committed attention to "Third World" feminisms and the critical and cultural practices of black gay men.[1] This is neither an expression of white guilt nor a goodwill gesture, but an empirically developed observation motivated by practical necessity and self-interest. The writings of feminists of color represent one of the longest and most richly varied critical traditions for conceptualizing differences inclusively and dynamically, providing places for gay male cultural and political activism that are *not necessarily* either intrusive or imperialistic. More than any other cross section of gay communities, black gay male critics, writers, and artists have consistently reflected in their work the politics of Third World feminisms, and have creatively engaged with both Third World and "hegemonic" feminist theory.[2]

In this light, I would like to sketch ways in which gay male studies within a multicultural lesbian/gay studies program can specifically contribute to and benefit from—in Cornel West's term—the cultural politics of difference.[3] To do this, I write against the general assumption that men (especially white men) formulate theories and women and people of color (and especially women of color) have experiences. After offering experiential inroads into my topic, in responsive reading of theoretical texts of lesbians of color, I will propose a redefinition of sexual difference that allows for specifying sexually marginalized subject positions outside of (hetero)sexist paradigms. Envisioning the lesbian/gay "subject" as an unstable constellation of localized, particular, and codependent differences leads to a consideration of the other variables constituting the subject: race, class, and ethnicity, as well as their mutual overdeterminations. I will formalize these observations in a four-term model of identity construction that will provide a means of analyzing the discursive processes that configure social identities. I will also use this model to sketch an ethics of dialoguing across differences and between marginal and nonmarginal subjects.

Learning/Teaching from Experience

As a white gay man from a lower working class family, teaching Japanese literature and lesbian and gay studies in a state university, I constantly find myself within networks of dazzling and often exhilarating contradictions. These contradictions stimulate and inform much of my current work, which both shapes and evolves within my classes. To illustrate some of the questions we face in these fields, I offer two anecdotes and some educated guesses at the negotiations of identities that were going on both explicitly and implicitly.

The Incidents

1. In 1991, I participated in a University of California "think tank" symposium on Japan and otherness. Approximately half of the highly regarded specialists in cultural criticism who took part were people of color, but to the best of my knowledge I was the only "queer." When I ventured the (admittedly polemic) opinion that a heterosexual male could not have written Michel Foucault's *History of Sexuality*, the room erupted. I was roundly accused of being "essentialist" and "exclusionary," and my premise was declared "simplistic" and "reductionist." The male participants were more immediately and visibly outraged than the women, and among the men, the white men more than the men of color.

2. A black lesbian graduate student visiting my comparative lesbian and gay literature class asked why I was ignoring lesbians and gay men of color. She did not have a syllabus, so I outlined it for her, indicating that over half the texts were by lesbians and gay men of color, and that in fact we were entering a week-long discussion of Latin American lesbian writ-

ing, at which point a white gay male student in the class asked me where I got the authority to teach such texts and why he should listen to a white man's interpretation of them. I agreed with him that such questions have to be continually asked, but said that the logic of his objection could actually be used to justify the exclusion of such texts from courses under the guise of "liberal discretion." The student's intervention angered a Chicana lesbian in the class, who told him that as a white man, he had no experience of racial oppression from which to launch his argument. This in turn angered him, because, as a Jewish man, he felt he indeed had had just such experience. Later I found out many of the heterosexuals in the class felt entirely silenced by this interchange, but the differences in the qualities and scope of this feeling were divided along gender lines.

The Readings

1. The first incident, at the symposium, is a good illustration of how little explanatory value "homophobia" has. Regardless of the degree to which the initial reactions of the participants might be attributed to "homophobia" (not very much, in fact), simply labeling their reactions "homophobic" closes analysis and discussion rather than opening them up. First of all, the attribution of any minority status at all to Foucault — not only a white male, but part of the French academic elite — may have been insulting to those whose attainment of institutional validation was the hard-won result of social and political struggles against racist and sexist ideologies, beyond the considerable effort required to establish intellectual credentials. Secondly, the composition of the group and the nature of the symposium implied that by convening we had all agreed, at least generally, on what are the significant aspects of an individual's social identity and focus of oppression: race, ethnicity, national identity, and gender. By raising the issue of sexual orientation, I introduced a "difference" that had not been part of the implicit consensus — and not merely as a significant, but as an *enabling* difference. The force of the reaction could have been partially resistance to the unanticipated change in paradigm my suggestion implied.

I also have some educated guesses regarding the sexual and racial divisions in the intensity of responses to my intervention: the women were the least involved perhaps because their own experiences of gender oppression (not merely in terms of sexuality) may have made them more readily empathetic. The non-U.S. men of color may have felt outside this debate, or simply not threatened by it. I have had other experiences in which heterosexual U.S. men of color have regarded white gay male discussions of "gay rights" with suspicion, as a way of displacing racial injustice with white interests. The white heterosexual male reaction I find the most interesting. In academic situations such as this one, white male scholars tend to feel uneasy regarding their own relations to marginality and hegemony, and even slightly envious of those whose visible differences seem to exonerate them from the need to justify their authority (I speak for myself here as well). In claiming an enabling difference for same-sex orientation, I was "pulling rank" on the other white men. Beyond this, my assertion contained a subtextual assertion that at a certain level in my identity politics I ultimately refused identification with them.

My statement, however, was not innocent. In emphasizing Foucault's sexuality, I did not address the elision of race, class, and gender in his analyses of sexuality and power, something I never fail to do in a lesbian/gay-focused class or conference.[4] What I found most amazing in this exchange, however, was that, in their adamant refusal to accept Foucault's sexuality as an enabling difference in his work, none of the participants mentioned his inattention to race and gender. To put this most bluntly, *the immediate defense of the operative but nonexplicit identity politics against one "difference" was carried out at the expense of the differences already recognized.* This valuable lesson will be one of the guiding theses of the present essay.

2. In my lesbian/gay courses, my "difference" as a gay man is virtually neutralized by the centralization of my marginality and the gendered politics of traditional pedagogical structures, which means that as a white man, I am more susceptible to the unease regarding my right to teach other "differences" in this setting than I was in the heterosexual cultural studies symposium. I think the speed with which the black lesbian graduate student challenged my syllabus was partially a result of the ways in which the history of academic indifference to race/gender/sexuality places her in the role of social conscience (it would be her job to ask where the women were in an Afro-American literature class, and where the lesbians were in a black women writers class, too). Because the context (which I had established myself) had reduced me to a "white male," my reaction to the graduate student's intervention was one of expedience instead of engagement. After all, a black lesbian has hit the jackpot of difference. My recitation of authors' names was a response in deference to her differences—which amounts to defensive dismissal of those differences, and is ultimately not very respectful of the complexities of all those differences in shifting alignments and conflicts within the classroom and the larger communities we were discussing.

My tone in listing those authors may have prompted the gay man to challenge my right to teach them. He did this within an implicit identification we shared as gay men, and even the pointed nature of the question served to confirm that identification rather than threaten it. The Chicana lesbian student, however, read the gay student's inquiry as a white man's attempt to remove the works she wanted to read, "for her own good." Her response to him shifted both the premises of discursive intervention and the identifications in play: her argument assumed the experience of racial oppression as a necessary condition for interrogating the grounds by which white males could teach texts by people of color. (She was not questioning *my right to teach them*, but *his right to question* my right.) Here again, sexual orientation becomes a nonenabling difference—in that his experience of oppression as a *gay* man did not justify his objection. This required him to effectively "pull rank" on me with his "hidden difference" as a Jewish man, triggering the debate about the status of Jewish identity as a racial identity and the torturous calculus some engage in to weigh the contemporary comfort of some Jewish communities in the United States and the luxury of whiteness for many Jews against the history of the Holocaust to produce credentials of oppression.

The student's need to assert Jewish identity as a focus of marginalization would be at least doubly painful, since it was one of his two invisible and diasporic differences, both of which, revealed in the wrong contexts, could immediately disqualify him from the privileges of or membership in the group to which he had belonged (as a Jew in an anti-Semitic group—either straight or gay—or as a gay man in a homophobic group—gentile or Jewish—including his own family of origin) and even place him in very real physical danger. Some of the white heterosexual women told me that these exchanges made them painfully aware that their personal histories of oppression as women were not guarantees of unproblematic identifications; the white heterosexual males were rather therapeutically traumatized, forced to confront a social context in which their perspectives had to be localized and their subject positions made relative to others. These incidents were not an interruption in learning but central to it, and actually attest to the students' active participation in their education.

Gay Men, Gay Male Studies, and "Difference"

How do we begin to account for differences in ways that do not end in competition for civil rights, in-different harmonies, or ranked marginalizations? How do we envision empathetic exchange and political alliances without reductive formulas or appeals to the tranquilizing (and by no means benign) effects of "tolerance"? How do we learn that many contradictions are most empowering and enriching when they are not resolved but lived?[5] Our responsibilities as lesbian and gay scholars to such questions and conflicts gain in clarity and urgency as lesbian and gay studies continues to attain various degrees of recognition in the academy, and as universities become increasingly alienated from the stultifying homogeneity of national "family values" and the vehement reduction of "American" identity to its lowest (and most exclusionary and illusory) common denominator. White gay male writers, artists, and academics have specific responsibilities here.

Gay men's historical and contemporary positions relative to male privilege and traditional masculinities (varying in different ethnic and racial communities)[6] condition their various modes of self-understanding and complicate the ways in which gay men situate themselves in terms of other political struggles. White gay men have had a purchase on power and privilege unique to otherwise disenfranchised individuals. These power relations are central to the historical configurations of white gay male identities and their modes of articulation, which cannot be assumed to be applicable to gay men of color or other marginalized groups. Any consideration of gay male studies as a critical endeavor, and of the homosexual/gay male cultural practices that form some of its objects, entails confronting the ways in which both are inscribed in dominant traditions, reflecting the paradoxical relations between male homosexuality and racist, classist, and sexist hegemonies.

In its foundational assertion of its own intellectual validity and social importance, the critical study of gay male literature is as much a countercultural practice as the texts that are its object of investigation. While the continuity of cultural resistance between texts and interpretation is something gay studies shares with feminist and "minority" critical theories, this comparison requires qualification.[7] As a discipline, gay studies differs fundamentally from women's studies and "minority discourse" in terms of the divergences in their respective histories of exclusion. Central to feminist and "minority" literary studies are archival projects crucial to "the recovery and mediation of cultural practices which have been and continue to be subjected to institutional forgetting."[8] Such "recoveries" in gay male studies would be redundant, as many of the texts and writers we would wish to "recover" are already in the canon. The canon re-formations in feminist/minority discourse projects are not merely alternative literary inventories, but also strategies consonant with the overall theoretical goals of these discourses and their reconceptualizations of "literature," "history," and sociopolitical categories of identity and criteria of legitimacy.[9]

This would not be true of similiar maneuvers in gay literature. I appreciate the heuristic force of Eve Kosofsky Sedgwick's hyperbolic (and largely hypothetical) declaration that "not only have there been a gay

Socrates, Shakespeare, and Proust, but . . . their names are Socrates, Shakespeare, and Proust; and, beyond this . . . hundreds of the most centrally canonic figures in what the monoculturalists are pleased to consider 'our' culture";[10] to subscribe to these identifications unqualifiedly, or to incorporate literal vindications of such suppositions into an agenda for gay literary studies, however, would be to foreclose the radical potential of the discipline itself. Uncritically claiming "gay forefathers" from Euro-American traditions would reify sexual identities that gay studies should complicate, and would continue to foster the conception of male homosexuality as a noncontestatory variation of phallocentric patriarchy. To characterize Plato's *Symposium* as a tribute to gay love is to identify gay sexuality with the misogyny and imperialism of male citizens in classical Athens. On the other hand, an examination of the *Symposium* from a more self-consciously gay perspective may have precisely the opposite effect.[11] An initially nonidentificatory insistence on the literal sexuality of such male–male bonds can in fact demythologize masculinity, thus providing a means to specify the historical and cultural variations in the manifestations and social meanings of homoeroticism and to distinguish contemporary gay male sexuality conceptually and politically from the "male supremacism" of the canon and its guardians.

Studying the writings and films of lesbians and gay men of color should not be done as a corrective appendix to the canon, but as a challenge to the processes of valorization and exclusion that produced *the* canon or the unexamined need for *a* canon in the first place. Furthermore, these texts are uniquely helpful in foregrounding the negotiations of identity constantly under way not only in the lives of the writers who chronicle them, but also in the classroom itself, as my second anecdote illustrates.[12] Michelle Cliff, a light-skinned black Jamaican writer who can easily pass as white, offers very rich examples in her work. Writing of her college days in London, before she came out as a lesbian, Cliff describes one evening with a straight, darker skinned male cousin, in which her identity in relation to him and her surroundings is reconfigured at least three times.

They began their evening waiting in vain in a hotel bar until a light-skinned Jamaican professor informed them that people of color were not served there. At first her cousin refused to believe it and made excuses for the waitress. Cliff writes: " 'No, man, the girl is just busy.' (The girl is a fifty-year-old white woman, who may just be following orders. But I do not mention this. I have chosen sides.) All I can manage to say is, 'Jesus Christ, I hate the fucking English.' "[13] Cliff then took her cousin to a restaurant owned by gay Italians she knew. There her cousin joined white male fellow patrons (some of his co-workers among them) in mocking the "faggot" waiters. On the way home, Cliff's cousin tried to persuade her to sleep with him, which she refused without telling him that she was a lesbian. "I pretend I am back home and start patois to show him somehow I'm not afraid, not English, not white."[14] In the bar Cliff suppressed her possible identification with the waitress as a woman to identify instead with her cousin as black because of the racism of the incident—even though the difference they shared was visible in his case, and invisible in hers. In the restaurant her cousin identified with the white men as a heterosexual man (two hegemonic identities—sexuality and gender), which suppressed his identification as black and realigned Cliff's identification with the waiters as "queer," yet again her shared difference was invisible. In the final confrontation with her cousin, despite Cliff's experience of the division imposed upon them by the dominant sex/gender system, she refused his advances in a way that preserved—and even asserted—her identification with him in racial and national terms.

Differences and Feminisms

The complexity and volatility of the differences described by Cliff cannot be fully accommodated by analyses based either on a gay politics giving priority to a hetero/homo opposition or on a feminist politics giving priority to a male/female division. Of course, we cannot afford to ignore the organic relations between the patriarchal sex/gender system and homophobia. We must also remember that "sexual difference" provides the deep structure for all other hierarchically divided binarisms central to Euro-American epistemologies; the reified and mutually exclusive divisions of "Self" and "Other," of unmarked universal subject and particular, material-bound object, are based on a "masculine-feminine" paradigm.[15] These gendered polarities are easily projected onto imperialist versions of the world: colonizer-colonist; anthropologist-native; the "West"-the "East"; and so forth.[16]

Although many feminist writers have attacked the sexism inherent within these divisions, white feminists have not traditionally challenged the presumptions regarding the primacy of sexual difference that grounds this dichotomous worldview. The earliest and most sustained critique of the mythically totalizing force of sexual difference has been from feminists of color. Chela Sandoval points out that Francis Beal was among the first to criticize the centrality of male-female binary oppositions as a dangerous oversimplification in the analysis of the oppression of women and their political response.[17] The Combahee River Collective is one group among many women of color who have addressed the implicit racism and indifference to class in some of the theories and practices of radical feminists and lesbian separatists:

> Although we are feminists and lesbians, we feel solidarity with progressive Black men and do not advocate the fractionalization that white women who are separatists demand. We have a . . . loathing for what men have been socialized to be in this society. . . . But we do not . . . [believe] that it is their . . . biological maleness that makes them what they are. As Black women we find any type of biological determinism a particularly dangerous and reactionary way to build a politic. We must also question whether lesbian separatism is an adequate and progressive political analysis and strategy . . . since it so completely denies any but the sexual sources of women's oppression, negating the facts of class and race.[18]

Cherríe Moraga's autobiographical essays draw intricate connections between the flattening out of sexuality and the indifference to race and culture in radical feminist sexual politics. Moraga found that the contradictions within her own acculturated sexuality, deeply implicated in the mythopoetics of female sexuality within Mexican traditions, often exceeded the boundaries of "politically correct" lesbianism. Like countless Mexican women and Chicanas, Moraga had to articulate her sexuality against the figure of Malintzin (or La Malinche), an Aztec noblewoman who was presented to Cortés upon his arrival in 1519. Having served as his interpreter, adviser, and mistress, she is traditionally seen as the archetypal traitor of the Aztecs in the Spanish Conquest, and the mother of the mestiza race. Her betrayal is focused in her sexuality, particularly apparent in her other appellation, La Chingada, "the fucked one."[19] Octavio Paz has added to the contemporary burden of these sexualized divisions with his gloss on the verb *chingar*: "Chingar . . . is to do violence to another. . . . The verb is masculine, active, cruel: it . . . wounds, gashes, stains. . . . The person who suffers this action is passive, inert, and open, in contrast to the active, aggressive, and closed person who inflicts it. The chingón is the macho, the male; he rips open the chingada, the female, who is pure passivity, defenseless against the exterior world."[20]

As Moraga grew more aware of her own sexuality, her experimentation reflected her rebellions against and internal contradictions regarding her gendered and sexual identities and their relation to her culture. In these struggles to demystify her sexuality, her sexual practices and the forms her desires took put her in conflict with the pastoralizing sexual orthodoxy of the cultural feminists.[21] She felt cast out by the unnuanced assertions of white radical feminists that "lesbian sexuality was naturally different from heterosexual sexuality. That the desire to penetrate and be penetrated . . . would vanish. That retaining such desires was 'reaction-ary,' . . . 'male-identified.' "[22]

It is at this nexus that the unexpected common interests emerge between lesbians of color and gay men. The centrality of the binary opposition of male and female in white feminist analyses of gender oppression and the decontextualized prescriptive semantics of sexual practices in radical feminism both erase sexual orientation as a significant difference or variable just as they do race, class, and ethnicity. Marilyn Frye discerns in gay male demands for sexual rights an identification with the "male supremacist" heterosexual male's "cosmic male arrogance" manifested as "the almost universal right to fuck—to assert his individual male dominance over all that is not himself by using it for his phallic gratification or self-assertion at either a physical or a symbolic level."[23] This is the same indifferent essentializing of sexual practices that invalidated Moraga's emergent sexuality. Frye's comparison of male supremacism and gay male sexuality hinges upon a definition of fucking as a self-evident exercise of phallic dominance on a victim. "When a man who considers himself firmly heterosexual fucks a boy or another man, generally he considers the other to be a woman or to be made a woman by this act."[24]

While I concur with Frye's description of male heterosexuality and the degradation of the person who is "fucked" being associated with becoming a "woman," I question the easy parallel between heterosexual intercourse and gay male intercourse, the emotional and political equivalence in terms of the presumed nonreversibility of the positions, and the superior status attributed to the penetrator. Frye denies that the biological sex of the "passive" partner will affect the social identity of the "active." While this is exceptionally the case in special homosocial male environments such as prison, Euro-American homophobia among men is still more pervasive a controlling principle than that. In several Latin American countries, and in certain Latino and Chicano communities in the United States, however, there is little or no social stigma attached to men exclusively "active" with men and women.[25] In northern Mexico, for example, sexual classification divides men into macho, or chingón—who penetrate either women exclusively or women and "homosexual" men—and chingada—women and jotos, the men who voluntarily allow sexual penetration.[26] By describing a politics of penetrative sex indifferent to the sex of the recipient partner, Frye is in effect ascribing to the sociosexual system that oppresses Mexican, Latina, and Chicana women and that makes sexism and homophobia mutually determining social psychologies.

One of the trickier aspects of Frye's essay is that in many respects she is right: her depiction of the sexual ideology of dominant heterosexual males is accurate, but she universalizes it; her arguments against the gay rights movement of the late 1970s are well founded, but she dehistoricizes them. White gay movements then were undeniably sexist, and the way gay activists conceived their politics certainly derived from a white male sense of entitlement. Just as gay male politics had not benefited from feminism, the feminist politics espoused by Frye here, and by the radical lesbian feminists confronting Moraga, had not benefited from the more complex and inclusive accounting of differences in the theorizing of feminists of color.

Certain forms of black nationalism place black gay men in double binds similar to those in which (white) lesbian "nationalism" places lesbians of color. Francis Cress Welsing is a black child psychologist famous for her analyses of "white supremacy" as a repressed sense of inferiority and a defensive response necessary to protect the recessive albinism that produces "whiteness." Because the "phenotypic condition" of "whiteness" could be "annihilated" by reproducing with people of color, "white survival" depends upon bringing "all 'non-white' men . . . into cooperative submission."[27] Welsing concludes that black male homosexuality is a capitulation to white supremacy, a complicity in the self-extermination of the race. Welsing writes within a tradition of reviling the black male homosexual as traitor to both race and sex, exemplified by Eldridge Cleaver's brutalization of James Baldwin.[28] Essex Hemphill discerns the danger in Welsing's unsophisticated account of sexuality in her ability to ground

> her homophobia and heterosexism . . . in an acute understanding of African-American history and an analysis of the psychological effects of centuries of racist oppression and violence. . . . Welsing's seductive fusion of her own ideology with widely held Black nationalist concepts only shows how potentially misdirected the effort to counterattack racism can be, even for those intelligent enough to see the connections between racism, homophobia, heterosexism, classism, and all other oppressions spawned by patriarchal and white-supremacist domination.[29]

Welsing's connections between sexuality and race obviate any coherent analyses of their relations, because she makes those connections within a sexist and heterosexist ideology, just as Frye's text cannot admit differential dynamics between sexuality and gender because her indictments of gay male politics are also contained within a heterosexually based sex/gender system.

Radical feminist analyses of cultural representations of sexuality often suffer from a confluence of underdeveloped conceptions of sexual difference and inattention to racial imbalances. When antipornography feminists see the same eroticization of power and exploitation in gay and heterosexual male pornography, they willfully ignore the differences in cultural contexts in which the two forms circulate (including safer-sex education) and fail to address the histories of oppression specific to compulsory heterosexuality and the "biologically authorized" rhetoric of unilateral penetration that inform and condition heterosexual pornography, and thus essentialize a "feminine" position as inherently and transcendentally passive and the victim of desire.[30] Imposing a heterosexually defined gender disequilibrium onto gay porn also detracts attention from a problem actually inherent in it: the racism of white gay culture and the meanings of objectification, fragmentation, and sexual roles in pornographic images of men of color.[31]

These problems also extend to radical feminist readings of "nonpornographic" cultural production. Andrea Dworkin's critique of James Baldwin's fiction is a case in point. While there is some basis to Dworkin's claims that sexuality for Baldwin is a form of "revenge," her illustrations and priorities in her reading of *Another Country* need some further examination.[32] Two of the main characters, Rufus, a suicidal black musician, and Eric, a white actor, have had an affair before the story commences. The novel opens in the last days of Rufus's life and tells in flashbacks of his destructive relationship with Leona, a white woman whom he beat and abused until she lost her mind. Eric is not introduced until nearly halfway through the novel. He is in Paris, having dinner with his lover, Yves, on the night before Eric returns to America to appear in a Broadway play. Although Yves will join Eric later, the last dinner provides a scene of remembered intimacy and reflection on the refuge each found in the other.

Dworkin alludes to Rufus's story first, but she extracts her first example of "fucking" as hatred from the interior monologue in Eric's mind at this dinner with his lover. There is not only no sex in this scene, there is no action, and the two men are fairly harmonious. Nevertheless, Dworkin quotes part of the indirect discourse meditation here as an insight into Eric's mind and the inherent violence and hostility of male sexuality. Her statement dovetails into a peculiar form of quotation: "For Eric, fucking is 'a confession. One lies about the body but the body does not lie about itself; it cannot lie about the force which drives it. And Eric had discovered, inevitably, the truth about many men, who then wished to drive Eric and the truth together out of the world.' "[33] I quoted Dworkin's quote, to contrast her version of the first sentence with that of the original: "For the act of love is a confession."[34] Even assuming that Dworkin's Anglo-Saxon paraphrase is a more accurate picture of the practice than Baldwin's "euphemism," the passage itself is far more ambivalent than Dworkin's interpretation allows. If "fucking is a confession" it is a confession for *both parties*—not just the "penetrator." Furthermore, her assumption that Baldwin reveals Eric's subjectivity from the "penetrator" perspective is not only textually unsubstantiated but also heterosexist in assuming "the act of love" is necessarily intercourse; sexist in automatically identifying the subject of discourse with the penetrator; and racist in assuming that the white Eric was the "active" partner in his relations with his black ex-lover Rufus. The equation of heterosexual and homosexual penetration also obscures the much more explicitly sexualized hatred across race and gender and its expressions in the heterosexual relations in the novel—particularly the horrific scene of Rufus and Leona's first sexual encounter.[35]

Frye's equation of heterosexual and homosexual "fucking" and the cultural feminists' emphasis on the "feminine" position in sexual encounters are both derived from heterosexual paradigms that are contested politically but whose epistemological pertinence is never questioned. The connatural fusion of male homosexuality and patriarchal self-aggrandizement (and gay sexuality and phallic violence) found in both the dominant political imaginary and in some feminist analyses of male hegemony can only be rigorously deconstructed by demonstrating that such identifications are only "inevitable" within the discursive frameworks of heterosexual normativity. I am not suggesting that there are not many gay men who have enjoyed, continue to enjoy, and even actively participate in this collusion between homosexuality and patriarchal values. What I do contest is the belief that such connections are structurally innate, inevitable, or "natural"; such a belief can only support sexist and heterosexist norms. It is obvious that definitions of gender, sexual practices, and sexual difference derived from heterosexual traditions are conceptually inadequate for deviant critical interventions in sexual politics.

Sexual Difference and Discursive Formations

Central to the definition of "sexual difference" I will develop here are three terms that are often conflated, or whose relations are otherwise mystified: sex, gender, and sexuality. By "sex" I simply mean the biological division of male and female; by "gender" I mean the representations of one's sex. These representations include appearance and behavior, but also status, privileges, and restrictions differentially imposed on the sexes. One's gendered visibility is further inflected by the relative adherence to or transgressions from the representational norms enjoined by the social order. "Sexuality" includes acts, fantasies, object choice, and orientation. "Object choice" denotes the sex of the person desired and reflects both contingent and variable choices as well as fully defined sexual orientations. I distinguish between "object choice" and "orientation" because "object choice" does not always imply an "orientation" and because either a variable or a consistent "object choice" has a different impact on an individual's gender identity according to the system. As I have noted, in some cultural constructions of male sexuality, the sex of his partner does not affect the gender status or "sexual orientation" of the exclusively penetrative male. The receptive partner, however, is either "feminized" or otherwise rendered a "noncitizen" in the phallocracy, a "non-person."[36] In the dominant system of sexual regulation in the United States, however, any admission—or suspicion—of desire between men is often feared as something that will disqualify those individuals for full social recognition as "men" (the military makes this quite literal).

The relations among these elements contribute to the discrete signifying totalities that I call discursive formations, partially derived from Foucault, but closer to the definition of "discourse" developed by Ernesto Laclau and Chantal Mouffe:

> If I kick a spherical object in the street or if I kick a ball in a football match, the *physical* fact is the same, but *its meaning* is different. The object is a football only to the extent that it establishes a system of relations with other objects, and these relations are not given by the mere referential materiality of the objects, but are, rather, socially constructed. This systematic set of relations is what we call discourse. . . . It is the discourse which constitutes the subject position of the social agent . . . the same system of rules that makes that spherical object into a football, makes me a player.[37]

Accepting this definition and removing sexuality from the dominant sex/gender polarities, we perceive that the meanings of any sexual act depend upon the sex, gender, status, race, and so forth of all the parties involved, this fluid totality constituting a discursive formation. Studying sexual expression through discursive formations yields a far more rigorous critical basis for a coherent and supple sexual politics. For example, take the sexual act of deliberately revealing one's penis to another's view. Now place it in the following discursive formations: (1) a flasher in a park at night, exposing himself at random to lone women; (2) a man posing for a *Playgirl* centerfold; (3) two gay men cruising each other at the baths, removing their towels. The first is obviously an act of sexual violence. The second is more ambivalent: ostensibly it is a gesture toward "sexual equality" for middle-class white heterosexual women, based on an unexamined equation between male and female arousal or pleasure in looking. It also questions the "masculinity" of the model, since submission to a desiring gaze is marked "feminine."[38] In the third, both men are equally subject and object, at once asserting masculine privilege and contraverting its conditions.

If we return to gay male sexuality in terms of alliances with other sexually oppressed persons, our interpretations of each case may be more complexly empowering than any one of them in isolation. Take, for example, the sexism faced by Chicana lesbians and the mythopolitics of penetration in their cultural heritage. The sexuality of Chicana women is regarded with suspicion, as the women are envisioned as descendants of La Malinche, La Chingada, "the fucked one," a native Mexican woman who is paradoxically considered a traitor to Mexico and the mother of the new "Mexican race" through her sexuality.[39] Chicana women are therefore marked as traitorous through an act of sexual submission to a man, which is the same act (in marriage) that confirms a Chicana's loyalty to her family and community; indeed, the refusal of that act (through lesbianism) would prove a cataclysmic betrayal.[40] In fact, Mexican and Chicana women who rebel against gender and sexual norms are referred to as *malinchistas*.[41] Gay men, on the other hand, by actively allowing the "male body" to be penetrated, betray the phallic order that places the Chicana in this sociosexual stalemate.

Community-specific sexual and gender-based oppressions also entail painful double binds for the lesbian and gay members of those communities and often lead to cross-cultural strategies with various consequences, as Moraga's personal history illustrates:

> What looks like betrayal of women on the basis of race originates . . . in sexism/heterosexism. Chicanas begin to turn our backs on each other to gain male approval or to avoid being sexually stigmatized by them as puta vendida jota. . . . I gradually became anglicized because . . . [it seemed] the only option available to me toward gaining autonomy as a person without being sexually stigmatized. . . . This . . . meant resisting sex roles . . . [which was] . . . easier to do in an anglo context than in a Chicano one. That is not to say that anglo culture does not stigmatize its women for "gender transgressions"—only that its stigmatizing did not hold the personal power over me that Chicano culture did.[42]

This leads to other double binds: "Chicanas are denied one another's fidelity. If women betray one another through heterosexism, then lesbianism is a kind of visible statement of our faithfulness to one another. But if lesbianism is white, then the women I am faithful to can never be my own."[43]

Proliferating Differences

At this point, we have a critical apparatus through which we can appreciate and even intensify the proliferation of differences to which our discursive positionings afford a conceptual space. With this, however, come harder questions as well. Our redefinition of sexual difference allows us to specify a "gay male subject" distinct from the heterosexual male, but what else is missing? What about race, ethnicity, class, nationality, age? Just as a sexually unmarked subject under patriarchy is always male, a racially unmarked subject under racism will be white. How many elements are sufficient for a minimal description? At what point does the number of components exceed the viability of the model? I, of course, do not have the answer. I do, however, believe that this step allows us to ask these questions from less stratified assumptions, and to begin decentered and unforeclosed explorations of them.

To expand our discursive formations to include racial, ethnic, and class considerations in the intrapsychic and social productions of subject positions, I want to introduce some new distinctions and formalize distinctions I have made in passing. In these discursive formations, the elements that make up one's phenomenal and social identities can be divided into "aspects" and "differences" that can be qualified as "significant," "privileged," and "enabling." By "phenomenal identity" I mean the collocation of visible and tangible elements by which one is recognized as an individual. Some of these "aspects" are more significant than others in terms of social identity: hair color and white skin are both aspects of one's "phenomenal identity" but only the latter (in contemporary U.S. culture) is a significant (and privileged) aspect of social identity. I define aspects as elements that either are unmarked or are consonant with features important to a standard social identity (either the hegemonic standard or a subcultural one); "differences" are elements that deviate from the standards.

Which elements are aspects and which are differences, and whether they are significant, enabling, neither, or negations of those categories depends on the totality of the discursive formation. For example, the whiteness of a white male's skin is not a difference but a significant and privileged aspect. The whiteness of Cherríe Moraga's skin is enabling in comparison to the skin colors of the Mexican people and Chicanos with whom she identifies—"enabling" in terms of access to educational and professional advancement in "mainstream" white society—but a disenabling difference within Chicano communities who do not recognize her as "one of us" or regard her with suspicion because of her ability to pass and the values she may have acquired because of her use of this difference. This is also a problem for Michelle Cliff in Jamaica. In the part of Frye's argument I addressed earlier, gay men, on account of their maleness, cannot become allies to other oppressed groups: their sexuality is a nonsignifying, nonenabling difference.[44] In Welsing's view, black gay men are traitors to their race: their sexuality is a negatively signifying, disenabling difference.[45]

Who determines the significant differences in the multiply marginalized subject? Where do liberal politics fail? Samuel R. Delany provides intriguing answers (and questions) in his autobiography, *The Motion of Light on Water*. In his adolescence he kept a notebook of masturbation fantasies, which included dramatic scripts featuring hostile encounters between black and Jewish kings that become sexual. The internal antagonism between desire and narrative chronicled in the notebooks gave way to a greater antagonism between Delany's lived experience and the institutionally imposed interpretation of that experience, when his mother discovered his notebooks and secretly handed them over to his psychiatrist. The psychiatrist discussed them with Delany, "though not with much comprehension on his part . . . of their erotic function," a lack of comprehension shared by the psychiatrist's supervisor, Kenneth Clarke, who "excerpted them . . . in an article on 'Prejudice and Your Child' for *Harper's Magazine* and later in a book of the same title."[46]

This incident is refracted through reified racial definitions, misdiagnosis, and the utter refusal to recognize homosexuality. Clarke categorizes the incident as "an extreme example of the effects of the confusion of racial problems in the total pattern of development of personality difficulties of an intelligent Negro boy of twelve":

> One of a few Negroes in a school for exceptional children, he was referred to a child-guidance center because he was unable to concentrate on his school work. . . . He was assigned to a white psychiatrist, who was soon able to win the boy's respect . . . [and] the child began to express directly and indirectly many feelings and frustrations about race and his racial identity. His preoccupation with racial stereotypes and frustrations was indicated in a fantastic play he wrote . . . called "Morlow, King of Blacks, of the NiggIlses," and its characters are divided into "Niggers," "Kikes" and "whites."[47]

After quoting short excerpts featuring angry racial exchanges between the black man and the Jewish leader, Clarke concludes: "For this boy, symbols of racial and religious inferiority, conflict, and ambivalence have been deeply imbedded in his feelings."[48]

There are several major omissions and inaccuracies here. Delany had initially been sent to counseling because his teachers were at a loss to explain why a student who was remarkably gifted and articulate in class would hand in papers so outrageously misspelled that they were often indecipherable. Because dyslexia was not a widely recognized condition at this time, Delany's difficulty was assumed to be an attention-getting maladjustment. Furthermore, Clarke never met Delany; had they met, Clarke might have realized that Delany was so light-skinned that he could pass for white. Besides this, the school Delany was attending was Dalton—the progressive school for gifted children that was parodied in *Auntie Mame*—which made racial issues less a daily reality for him than for most black schoolchildren. The "white psychiatrist" was a Cuban man who, in his first session with Delany, expressed his astonishment that Delany considered himself "Negro," given his light complexion and that of his mother. The psychiatrist in fact told Delany that he himself probably had "just as much Negro blood" as Delany, but because "things are much more mixed up down in Cuba," that he was "white."[49] This was the only discussion of race that Delany recalls. Delany also felt inhibited from discussing sex with this man, and never did so.

Clarke's version of the circumstances surrounding the play suggests that this was a text the child had deliberately displayed, neglecting to detail the invasions of privacy involved in the play's coming to Clarke's attention. He also omits any mention of the sexual content, to Delany the most pervasive part of these texts, which were an attempt, in his words, "to integrate my sexuality into the rest of my world as best a twelve-year-old could in 1954 and 1955."[50] Delany took the name Morlow, from Marlowe, intrigued that he had written a homosexual play, *Edward II*, in which someone was killed with a hot poker up the anus. Secondly, the obscenities he heard outside of home took on a great sexually arousing charge because of their forbidden nature.[51] The racist hatred depicted in the play provided a context in which such obscenities could be used. Clarke never mentions that the exchanges between the black man and the Jewish man proceed from spitting at each other to French kissing to anal intercourse. Nor did Clarke suspect that these elements were not merely "unresolved conflicts" surrounding "racial stereotypes" but "gratifying sexual fantasies that regularly—two or three times a day—brought me to orgasm."[52]

In Clarke's text, race is the totally signifying difference, even though it was not experienced as such by Delany at the time. The insistence on race as a self-evident pole in a black-white binarism required Clarke to impose "blackness" on a child he had not seen (and for whom at the time it was often not part of his phenomenal identity), and to suppress "blackness" as any factor in the psychiatrist's social identity. The psychiatrist's "whiteness" also illustrates that racial identity itself is a discursively dependent phenomenon. Delany's "real" disenabling difference, and the actual cause of his having been referred to therapy—dyslexia—does not figure here because of the diagnostic limits and political agendas of the discursive practice determining this version of Delany's childhood history. And Delany's sexuality is neither a difference nor even an aspect.

The concrete demonstration of discursive construction of identities may help close the theory and activism divide.[53] While my gay male student may be "white" in my classroom, he is "colored" according to the Australian Immigration Code. Dr. Clarke's "twelve-year-old black boy" would have been "white" if the history had been written by Clarke's Cuban colleague.[54] In fifth-century Athens, neither a citizen's intercourse with his wife nor with his male slave was an expression of a sexual identity, but rather an enactment of his political entitlements.[55] A man who cheats on his wife or girlfriend by fucking other men would be a *chingón* in Mexico, a *bugaron* in Cuba, an *activo* in Brazil, a *machista* in Nicaragua, but a "homosexual" in none of these countries. The "mainstream U.S." would consider the same man as queer as his partner, but in San Francisco he might be granted the trendy and woefully undertheorized epithet "bisexual." In phallocentrically restricted discourses, lesbians become "asexual," "frigid," or simply noncategories.[56]

The focus on discursivity can also illuminate the political relevance of "literary studies" and the often life-saving potential of language itself. Three years after Moraga had graduated from a private college, one of her friends made an observation that proved revelatory: " 'Cherríe, no wonder you felt like such a nut in school. Most of the people there were white and rich.' It was true. All along I had felt the difference, but not until I had put the words 'class' and 'race' to the experience, did my feelings make any sense."[57] Language also plays a major role in Samuel R. Delany's recovery from his nervous breakdown (a decade later), in his retrospective making coherent early experiences of sexuality and racial identifications, using contemporary conceptual tools to make sense of a past that could not have provided them: "at that time, the words 'black' and 'gay'—for openers—didn't exist with their current meanings, usage, history . . . . There were only Negroes and homosexuals, both of whom—along with artists—were hugely devalued in the social hierarchy."[58] Rydra Wong, the protagonist of Delany's science fiction novel *Babel-17*, observes that "until something is named, it doesn't exist."[59] She makes this observation while attempting to teach the meanings and uses of "I" and "you" to someone whose native language apparently did not contain them. Wong's lesson is more than lexical supplementation, since "I" and "you" are not merely words but also concepts and positionings that articulate intersubjective possibilities, which is also true of Delany's resignifications of "gay" and "black," particularly in the section of his autobiography focusing on recoveries of identity through "memory not history" — counterhegemonic reflective reevaluations of his differences.

Responsibilities to Differences: Classroom Politics/ Identity Politics

The model for identity negotiations developed here can also serve to map the ethical dimensions of cross-cultural dialogue, which includes the specification of oppressions and formation of alliances. Here I would like to suggest some axioms that I use as rules of thumb to assess the implicit politics of particular interactions that focus on social identities, and as ground rules for responsible positioning within, across, and between communities:

1. One cannot claim oppression based on a privileged "aspect."
2. To claim pride in one's differences neither parallels nor justifies claiming pride in one's privileged "aspects."
3. It is rational and socially productive to identify with others based on shared differences.
4. It is irrational and socially oppressive to identify with others based on shared privileged aspects.
5. Empathizing with others based on unshared differences is rational, and can lead to creative alliances.
6. Identifying with others based on unshared differences is irrational, and can be obfuscatory and alienating.

Oppression (1): Marilyn Frye writes that men cannot be "oppressed" and that claims by men to the contrary threaten to rob "oppression" of all meaning.[60] She points out that women "are oppressed *as* women," and racial and class "minorities" of both sexes "are oppressed *as* members of those races and/or classes. But men are not oppressed *as men*."[61] I am not oppressed as a man, or as a white man, but I am as a gay man. Marilyn Frye is oppressed as a woman and as a lesbian, but not as a white woman. Audre Lorde was oppressed as a black person, as a woman, and as a lesbian.

Pride (2): Pride in being black and pride in being white are two very different social phenomena: the former reflects cultural struggle and san-

ity under seige; the latter is a sociopathology conducive to criminal behavior. Declaring English the "official language" of the United States
makes a national policy out of pride in ignorance. Because it is usually
imbedded in the faith of the universality and transparency of white ways
of being and white culture, "white pride" is paradoxically pride in having
no characteristics whatsoever.

Identifications (3 and 4): There is an enormous difference between identifications based on differences and identifications based on privileged aspects. This distinction grounds one of the differences between black feminists and white radical feminists: "Our situation as Black people
necessitates that we have solidarity around the fact of race, which white
women of course do not need to have with white men, unless it is their
negative solidarity as racial oppressors."[62] When Michelle Cliff's cousin
joined the white men in homophobic slurs, he identified with them based
on heterosexuality (a privileged aspect), with the same kind of men
(white, bigoted) who had refused him service earlier in the evening. This
is another example of a defense against a nonaccepted difference at the
expense of the accepted ones. Contrarily, in my conversation with the
gay male student in my second anecdote, we identified as *gay* men, but
not as *white* men, and not as *men.*[63] One of the reasons I find men's
groups like Robert Bly's theoretically incoherent, politically retrograde,
and ethically reprehensible is that their members identify solely *as men.*
Why should we want to "return to the fathers"?—where does the word
patriarchy come from, anyway?

Empathy/identification across differences (5 and 6): The histories of lesbian
and gay politics and the early associations of "gay studies" with women's
studies encouraged gay men to identify with lesbians and women in general in unreflective ways that often led to greater divisions and alienation.
When "gay" liberation covered both lesbians and gay men, the differences between the two groups were erased in favor of male visibility and
interests and at the expense of women's oppressions and political goals,
essentially repeating the gender injustices of heterosexual patriarchy.[64]

A marginal sexual identity does not warrant reductive identifications
across other differences. Although Audre Lorde observed that "lesbians
were probably the only Black and white women in New York City in the
fifties who were making any real attempt to communicate with each
other," she hated hearing her white lover, Muriel, say, "We're all nig-
gers." Apparently believing that all lesbians were "outsiders and all equal
in our outsiderhood," Muriel made such statements out of "wishful
thinking based on little fact; the ways in which it was true languished in
the shadow of those many ways in which it would always be false."

Blackness was something Lorde discussed only with her black lesbian friend Felicia.[65]

Accepting a lesbian or gay identity, however, often becomes a conduit for a reaffirmation of a racial or ethnic identity in new terms. Marlon Riggs's film *Tongues Untied* (1990) treats gay sexuality as a new basis for black male solidarity, as do Joseph Beam's "Brother to Brother: Words from the Heart" and many of the narratives of the performance group Pomo Afro Homos.[66] Ana Castillo observes that many Anglo-assimilated Chicanas and Latinas reclaim a Spanish language "heritage" and ethnic identity after "the affirmation of their sexual identity."[67] Both Cherríe Moraga and Gloria Anzaldúa draw explicit connections between the two affirmations. This is very different from white gay men claiming spiritual affinity with either extant or extinct Native American peoples because of variously documented and contextualized accounts of gender-transgressive or same-sex eros accepted within those cultures. Neither "queer nationalism" nor restitution of alternative sexualities "hidden from history" can justify imperialist appropriations of Native American practices for a white gay mythography or the pederastic rituals of Micronesian peoples as strategies of legitimation for white gay men.[68]

By the same token, the question of the heterosexual in lesbian and gay studies needs to be examined. In establishing our disciplines as legitimate areas of research, we certainly cannot claim their exclusive relevance to "our people" or stipulate a specific sexual orientation as a necessary condition for the ability to contribute to the field.[69] The queasiness and suspicion invoked by the image of a heterosexual teaching or writing on these topics needs to be addressed, but we must also acknowledge that such discomfort has just cause with the same seriousness granted the uncertainties surrounding male academic involvement in feminism or white academic involvement in African-American studies. There are differences that make this particularly difficult. First of all, men teaching in women's studies and white people teaching in "ethnic" studies positions impinge upon affirmative action hiring practices in ways that heterosexuals in queer studies would not.[70] Secondly, the history of "gay male studies" is marked by profound and sustained involvement of heterosexual women.

The roles heterosexual women have played in the development of gay male studies illustrate both the shifting quality of aspects and differences and the problems surrounding the means by which the nonmarginalized observer situates himself or herself. Eve K. Sedgwick published her book *Between Men* during more oppressive days, when the likely professional approbation more generally prevented men from writing on gay topics. Sedgwick's privileged aspects—as a white upper-class heterosexual married woman—allowed her to write what many regard as seminal works in the field of gay male studies, effectively protecting her from the suspicions and the dire consequences of being a gay man. It was also important that it was *gay men* she studied, and not lesbians, since this not only further assured her freedom from suspicion of belonging to a sexually anomalous group, but also allowed her to stay primarily within the traditional white English/American canon. Furthermore, a research commitment to male homosexuality both coincides with the hegemonic engendering of women that ascribes to them a devotion to men and male culture and resonates with the masculinist order's exclusive interest in itself. Given the contradictions in patriarchal systems, however, it is conceivable that seriously subversive work could be accomplished within this seeming adherence to gender norms and reliance on white heterosexual privilege.

There is a fascinating shift in Sedgwick's work from the materialist analyses of male-gendered power through a critique of homophobia in *Between Men*, to a performative critical fantasmatic exemplified in her two-person impersonation of and meditation on Divine (with Michael Moon), which seems to be a further elaboration of her extraordinary declaration that she identifies as a gay man, primarily because of her proclivity for anal erotism: "Among the many ways I do identify as a woman, the identification as a gay person is a firmly male one, identification 'as' a gay man."[71]

It would be interesting to explore in class how Sedgwick's statement differs from a white man declaring himself "Chicano" in spirit because of his love of jalapeños or a heterosexual male's claim to a "lesbian" identity based on his exclusive sexual desire for women and his obsession with lesbian pornographic films. Sedgwick's identification is a good test case for introducing the four-term grid for cross-cultural dialogue developed here. Under the present heteropatriarchal regime, desire for penetration is a significant difference only for a man; for a woman, desire for penetration is an aspect—not a difference. A woman's desire for *anal* penetration is a nonsignifying difference[72] (except technically in some never-enforced or -remembered statutes in certain localities, or in some religious communities). Therefore Sedgwick's identification as a gay man is an attempt to identify with a difference based on a "privileged" aspect (female desire for penetration)[73] insufficiently qualified by a nonsignifying difference (female anality). Of course, empathetic alliances based on gender oppression as a woman or hate crimes as a Jewish person would be perfectly understandable.

I write this not as an attack on Professor Sedgwick, but as an illustrative example to implement the aspect/difference grid as a guideline for cross-difference dialogue and analysis and as a structuring contract in multiculturally conscious lesbian and gay studies classes. Nor am I suggesting that Sedgwick's identity politics are morally remiss because they fall outside the premises of my system—we have far too many real enemies to nominate more. I merely wish to use her formulation as a contemporary and well-known instance of political identifications, to demonstrate the complexities of identities and contradictions that occur even outside of direct antagonisms. This will be particularly important in the preliminary stages of a lesbian/gay studies class, to make it clear to the white lesbian and gay students why their "differences" do not give them authority to speak for "Difference" itself, particularly at the expense of the students of color of whatever orientation. It should also provide ways to dialogue nondestructively with and about "political lesbians," "academic lesbians," and students who identify as "bisexual." When a heterosexual student voices the opinion that "we're basically all bisexual," assuming it will break the ice and establish trust, reliance on the identity-negotiation grid aids in explaining why it does not and in rechanneling angry responses into an exercise in identity negotiation.

Attention must be paid to how heterosexual students relate to the subject, the other students, and the classroom dynamics. But it is also important to pay attention to how these students are received. They cannot be permitted the position of thrill-seeking tourist, enlightened bridge builder, or objective anthropologist. Nor can the lesbian and gay students or the classroom ethos be allowed to silence them, to preempt or demonize them for their privileged aspect that becomes a disenabling difference in the lesbian/gay class.

To return to my intervention in the "think tank," my real point in saying that a heterosexual male could not have written Foucault's *History of Sexuality* was to draw certain parallels among dominant groups in terms of their privilege to disregard their own contingencies. For a heterosexual male, "sexuality" has no "history"—or at least there would be no reason for its historicity to occur to him, just as for white people race has no history (in fact, "whiteness" as a race has no ontology). By the same token, the ability of radical feminists to discard their own cultures for the sake of a feminine essentialism and separatist utopia is actually derived from the belief in the transparency of a white, middle-class subject position—in other words, the same assumption of unmarked "universality" that benefits straight white men. The willingness and capacity to shed one's culture is in fact a specific aspect of the contemporary constructions of white as a race and the middle class as a class (and "male" as a gender). Reemphasizing the specificities of the first two of these elements opens the possibility of more responsibly positioned dialogues between white women and women whose cultures are more intimately woven into their individual identities, communal identifications, and strategies of cultural, political, and literal survival. Reinstating the historical contingencies of white, middle class, male, and heterosexual opens up the dialogue even further, and provides a way for white heterosexual men to interact in lesbian/gay and other difference-centered classes without serving merely as the iconic lightning rod for the resentment of the "Others"—but this also obligates them to take responsibility for their positive participation, and not to turn their history of privilege into an *advantageous* disenabling difference within the class, which would make their needs the center of attention, thus reproducing through inversionary logic their status in the society at large.

A final classroom anecdote. I recently taught a required introductory course for all literature majors that also fulfills writing and distribution requirements for several other majors. I chose to focus on texts by lesbians of color, with some gay male works. The initial resentment from the eighty-some students was only intensified in the second week of class, when I ended the lecture by reading Monique Wittig's description of the intensity of passion one feels when meeting the object of desire in the confines of a homophobic social order. I prefaced this passage by stating that "the lesbians and gay students in the class will understand this text perfectly, and the heterosexuals will not." The hostility was tangible. At the beginning of the next class I asked the heterosexual students how they felt about my pronouncement. After fielding several expressions of their anger and frustration, I asked them how they had wanted to respond to me. Many of them said they wanted to write their own experiences down to prove me wrong. I replied, "Now you have a concrete inkling of what the stakes are in writing for people whose perspectives have been systematically ignored or delegitimated." A collective light bulb went on over the students' heads, and the class went much more smoothly after that. Exercises such as this allow the straight white students to *empathize with* but not to occupy the marginal subject positions under discussion. It also demonstrates that "understanding" is not guaranteed, granted, or to be taken for granted but is something that is earned, contingent, intersubjective, often contradictory, traumatic, and as transformative as it is susceptible to transformation.

Notes

My focus and critical direction benefited tremendously from Becky Thompson's conversational imagination and generous critical attention. I would also like to express my deep appreciation to the following people, who made this essay possible: Gloria Anzaldúa, Trinidad Castro, Samuel R. Delany, Lourdes Martínez Echazabal, David Jansen-Mendoza, Nora Muntañola Thornburg, Ekua Omosupe, Chela Sandoval, Benjamin G. White, and Magdalena Zschokke, and a special thank you to Gilberto Martínez, for making everything more than possible.

1. One of the most important essays to date on Third World feminism and its history and strategies is Chela Sandoval, "U.S. Third World Feminism: The Theory and Method of Oppositional Consciousness in the Postmodern World," *Genders* 10 (Spring 1991): 1-24. Sandoval's own theory of "differential consciousness" is compelling and suggestive, and deserves more examination than space allows here.

2. See Joseph Beam's introduction to *In the Life: A Gay Black Anthology*, ed. Joseph Beam (Boston: Alyson, 1986); Melvin Dixon, *Ride Out of the Wilderness: Geography and Identity in Afro-American Literature* (Urbana: University of Illinois Press, 1987); and the work of Samuel R. Delany, Essex Hemphill, Kobena Mercer, and Isaac Julien. I do not mean to ignore the work of gay men of other races, but only to reflect on the breadth of black gay male achievements. In terms of fascinating and subtle syntheses of gay identity politics, feminism, postcolonial theory, and cultural critique, the work of Canadian-Trinidadian Chinese videomaker Richard Fung should be mentioned here, particularly his magnificent video "My Mother's Place" (1990).

3. See chapter 2.

4. On race, see Emma Perez, "The Discourse of Sexuality: Notes from a Chicana Survivor," in *Chicana Lesbians*, ed. Carla Trujillo (Berkeley: Third Woman, 1991), 165-66. On gender, see Biddy Martin, "Feminism, Criticism, and Foucault," *New German Critique*, no. 27 (Fall 1982): 3-30; Teresa de Lauretis, *Technologies of Gender* (Bloomington: Indiana Universitiy Press, 1987).

5. For some of the best examples of this see Gloria Anzaldúa, *Borderlands/La Frontera: The New Mestiza* (San Francisco: Spinsters/Aunt Lute, 1987), 79-80 and passim.

6. R. J. DiClemente, C. B. Boyer, and E. S. Morales, "Minorities and AIDS: Knowledge, Attitudes, and Misconceptions among Black and Latino Adolescents," *American Journal of Public Health*, no. 78 (1988): 55-57; Maxine Baca-Zinn, "Chicano Men and Masculinity," *Journal of Ethnic Studies* 10, no. 2 (1982): 29-44; Joseph M. Carrier, "Cultural Factors Affecting Mexican Urban Male Homosexual Behavior," *Archives of Sexual Behavior* 5, no. 2 (1976): 103-24; Richard Rodriguez, "Masculinity, Femininity and Homosexuality: On the Anthropological Interpretation of Sexual Meanings in Brazil," in *The Many Faces of Homosexuality*, ed. Evelyn Blackwood (New York: Harrington Park, 1989), 155-64; Robert Staples, *Black Masculinity* (New York: Black Scholar, 1982); Kobena Mercer, "Racism and the Politics of Masculinity," in *Male Order: Unwrapping Masculinity*, ed. Rowena Chapman and Jonathan Rutherford (London: Lawrence & Wishart, 1988), 110-25.

7. In using "gay studies" I do not mean to collapse "lesbian" and "gay" into the old undifferentiated category, nor do I mean to ignore lesbians or lesbian studies. I use "gay" only here because many of my observations will not apply to lesbian studies. In short, my use of "gay studies" is in order to preserve—not erase—the differences. I address these differences in "Explicit Instruction: Teaching Gay Male Sexuality in a Literature Class," in *Professions of Desire: Lesbian and Gay Studies in Literature*, ed. George Haggerty and Bonnie Zimmerman (New York: Modern Language Association, 1993).

8. Abdul JanMohammed and David Lloyd, "Introduction: Toward a Theory of Minority Discourse" in *The Nature and Context of Minority Discourse*, ed. Abdul JanMohammed and David Lloyd, *Cultural Critique* 6 (Spring 1987): 8.

9. Afro-American literary histories are part of a radical intervention in cultural epistemologies, which also includes alternative histories and new topographies of histories

(Houston A. Baker, Jr., *Blues, Ideology, and Afro-American Literature: A Vernacular Theory* [Chicago: University of Chicago Press, 1984]). The same is true in different venues for black women's literary interventions (Barbara Smith, "Toward a Black Feminist Criticism," *conditions: two* [1977]: 25–44; Valerie Smith, "Gender and Afro-Americanist Literary Theory and Criticism," in *Speaking of Gender*, ed. Elaine Showalter [London: Routledge, 1989], 56–70) as well as Latina literary studies (Eliana Ortega and Nancy Saporta Sternbach, "At the Threshold of the Unnamed: Latina Literary Discourse in the Eighties," in *Breaking Boundaries: Latina Writings and Critical Readings*, eds. Asuncion Horno-Delgado et al. [Amherst: University of Massachusetts Press, 1989], 3–23). Some radical disciplines redefine others—as feminist theory is clearly doing in a rewriting of Latin American literary history (Sara Castro-Klarén, "La crítica literaria feminista y la escritora en América latina," in *La sartén por el mango*, ed. Patricia Elena González and Eliana Ortega [Río Piedras, P.R.: Huracán, 1985], 27–46) and black lesbian critical theory is doing for black women's literary studies (Barbara Smith, "The Truth That Never Hurts: Black Lesbians in Fiction in the 1980s," in *Third World Women and the Politics of Feminism*, ed. Chandra Talpade Mohanty, Ann Russo, and Lourdes Torres [Bloomington: Indiana University Press, 1991], 101–28).

10. Eve Kosofsky Sedgwick, "Pedagogy in the Context of an Antihomophobic Project," *South Atlantic Quarterly* 89, no. 1 (Winter 1990): 143.

11. An excellent example of this is David M. Halperin's brilliant "Why Is Diotima a Woman?" (in his *One Hundred Years of Homosexuality* [New York and London: Routledge, 1990]) and Teresa de Lauretis's use of that essay in "Sexual Indifference and Lesbian Representation," *Theatre Journal* 40, no 2 (1988): 155–77.

12. These in-class exchanges would seem much more an "interruption" in a class whose "gay" syllabus centered on Plato, Shakespeare's sonnets, Forster, and Whitman, for example.

13. Michelle Cliff, *The Land of Look Behind* (Ithaca, N.Y.: Firebrand, 1985), 68.

14. Ibid., 69.

15. Simone de Beauvoir, *The Second Sex*, trans. H. M. Parshley (New York: Knopf, 1953); Evelyn Fox Keller, *Reflections on Gender and Science* (New Haven and London: Yale University Press, 1985); Carolyn Merchant, *The Death of Nature: Women, Ecology, and the Scientific Revolution* (San Francisco: Harper & Row, 1980).

16. Homi K. Bhabha argues convincingly that the colonized subject serves the same fetishistically consoling purposes for the colonizer, which can be seen in the ambivalent fascination with Otherness in the stereotype. Homi K. Bhabha, "The Other Question," *Screen* 24, no. 6 (1983): 18–36. I have argued elsewhere that the deepening castration anxieties of Western culture brought on by widespread emergence of other subjectivities is at times alleviated by a fetishization of Japan and identification with a samurai ideal, most clearly illustrated (including its sexual ambiguities) in the Western canonization of the homosexual novelist Yukio Mishima. "Phallic Imperialism: Sexual Politics in and around Mishima Yukio," *Critical Japan* 2, forthcoming winter 1994.

17. Sandoval, "U.S. Third World Feminism," 4. Francis Beal, "Double Jeopardy: To Be Black and Female," in *Sisterhood Is Powerful*, ed. Robin Morgan (New York: Random House, 1970).

18. "A Black Feminist Statement," in *This Bridge Called My Back: Writings by Radical Women of Color*, ed. Cherríe Moraga and Gloria Anzaldúa, 2nd ed. (New York: Kitchen Table, 1983), 213–14. See also Audre Lorde, "An Open Letter to Mary Daly," *Sister/Outsider: Essays and Speeches* (Freedom, Calif.: Crossing, 1984), 66–71 and Cherríe Moraga, *Loving in the War Years* (Boston: South End, 1983), 128–30.

19. See Moraga, *Loving*, 99–101; Anzaldúa, *Borderlands*, 20–23.

20. Paz, *The Labyrinth of Silence*, quoted in Moraga, *Loving*, 118–19.

21. Moraga, *Loving*, 124–25. For her working out the *chingón/chingada* paradigm, see her *Teatro, Giving Up the Ghost* and Yvonne Yarbro-Bejarano, "The Female Subject in Chicano Theatre: Sexuality, 'Race,' and Class," in *Performing Feminisms*, ed. Sue-Ellen Case (Baltimore: Johns Hopkins University Press, 1989), 145–47.

22. Moraga, *Loving*, 125–26. See also Amber Hollinbough and Cherríe Moraga, "What We're Rolling Around in Bed With: Sexual Silences in Feminism," in *Powers of Desire: The Politics of Sexuality*, ed. Ann Snitow, Christine Stansell, and Sharon Thompson (New York: Monthly Review Press, 1983), 394–405.

23. Marilyn Frye, "Lesbian Feminism and the Gay Male Rights Movement: Another View of Male Supremacy, Another Separatism," in *The Politics of Reality: Essays in Feminist Theory* (Trumansburg, N.Y.: Crossing, 1983), 133. Frye's essay stems from and is addressed to a specfic moment in gay and lesbian political situations in the late 1970s in the United States. Since she wrote the essay, the politics and the configurations of alliances between lesbian and gay men have also changed dramatically, partially as a result of internal divisions in feminist communities over sexuality and heterosexism, and partially as a result of the new coalitions among lesbian and gay men in response to the AIDS crisis. See Gayle Rubin, "Thinking Sex: Notes for a Radical Theory of Sexuality," in *Pleasure and Danger: Exploring Female Sexuality*, ed. Carole S. Vance (Boston: Routledge, 1984), 267–319; Pat Califia, "Gay Men, Lesbians, and Sex: Doing It Together," *Advocate* 7 (July 1983): 24–26; B. Ruby Rich, "Feminism and Sexuality in the 1980's," *Feminist Studies* 12 (1986): 525–61; Julia Creet, "Daughter of the Movement: The Psychodynamics of Lesbian S/M," *differences* 3, no. 2 (Summer 1991); Cindy Patton, *Sex and Germs: The Politics of AIDS* (Boston: South End, 1985).

24. Frye, "Lesbian Feminism," 134.

25. See Roger N. Lancaster, "Subject Honor and Object Shame: The Construction of Male Homosexuality and Stigma in Nicaragua," *Ethnology* 27, no. 2 (1987): 111–14; Tomás Almaguer, "Chicano Men: A Cartography of Homosexual Identity and Behavior," *differences* 3, no. 2 (Summer 1991): 77–79.

26. Ana Maria Alonso and Maria Teresa Koreck, "Silences: 'Hispanics,' AIDS, and Sexual Practices," *differences* 1, no. 1 (Winter 1988): 110–11.

27. Francis Cress Welsing, "Black Male Passivity," quoted in Essex Hemphill, *Ceremonies* (New York: Plume, 1992), 55–56. Understanding black gay men's situations in the face of this tradition and the racism of white gay communities aids a fuller appreciation of the urgency of the ongoing self-creation through creating a black gay culture that Daniel Garrett writes of in "Creating Ourselves: An Open Letter," in *In the Life*, 93–103.

28. *Soul on Ice* (New York: McGraw-Hill, 1968), 97–109.

29. Hemphill, *Ceremonies*, 54–55.

30. Kathleen Barry, *Female Sexual Slavery* (Englewood Cliffs, N.J.: Prentice-Hall, 1979), 206; Gloria Steinem, *Outrageous Acts and Everyday Rebellions* (New York: Holt, Rinehart & Winston, 1983), 250. See also Moraga's critique of the emphasis on antiporn political action in radical feminism, *Loving*, 128–29.

31. Kobena Mercer, "Imaging the Black Man's Sex," in *Photography/Politics: Two*, ed. Pat Holland, Jo Spence, and Simon Watney (London: Methuen, 1987), 61–69. Richard Fung, "Looking for My Penis: The Eroticized Asian in Gay Video Porn," in *How Do I Look?* ed. Bad Object Choices (Seattle: Bay Press, 1991), 145–60.

32. Andrea Dworkin, *Intercourse* (New York: Free Press, 1987), 53.

33. Ibid., 52.

34. Baldwin, *Another Country* (New York: Dell, 1971), 180.

35. Ibid., 23-25.

36. For another variation on this in one perspective of Chicano culture, see Salas's novel, which depicts as the outcome of male rape the necessary self-expulsion from the Chicano community. See Floyd Salas, *Tattoo the Wicked Cross* (New York: Grove, 1967), 37-39, and the discussion of this scene in Juan Bruce-Novoa, "Homosexuality and the Chicano Novel," *Confluencias* 2, no. 1 (1986): 72-73.

37. Ernesto Laclau and Chantal Mouffe, "Post-Marxism without Apologies," *New Left Review* 166 (November-December 1987): 80-81.

38. On the inability of the male to "bear the burden of objectification," see Laura Mulvey, "Visual Pleasure and Narrative Cinema," *Screen* 16, no. 3 (Autumn 1975): 6-18. On the ambivalence of heterosexual male objectification, see Richard Dyer, "Don't Look Now: The Male Pin-Up," *Screen* 23, nos. 3 and 4 (September-October 1982): 61-73.

39. The parallels to Eve are striking, but on the differences see Norma Alarcón, "Chicana's Feminist Literature: A Revision through Malintzin: Putting Flesh Back on the Object," in Moraga and Anzaldúa, *This Bridge*, 183-84.

40. Heterosexual Mexican women are placed in the double bind of being required to cheerfully submit to the sexual needs of their husbands and to be susceptible to suspicion and even contempt if they manifest signs of enjoying sex themselves. Ana Castillo, "La Macha: Toward a Beautiful Whole Self," in Trujillo, *Chicana Lesbians*, 28-29.

41. Yarbro-Bejarano, "The Female Subject," in Case, *Performing Feminisms*, 135.

42. Moraga, *Loving*, 98-99.

43. Ibid., 116. See Essex Hemphill on betrayal and loyalty in racial and sexual contexts, particularly "Does Your Mama Know About Me?" and "Loyalty," in *Ceremonies*, 37-42, 63-64.

44. Later in the essay Frye does suggest this possibility (147-48), which is rather confusing since none of her critical formulations would account for it.

45. I distinguish "nonenabling" and "disenabling" here: "nonenabling" because the difference as gay does not "enable" the men to transcend the moral state of the male dominant heterosexual men; "disenabling" because for Welsing, the black man's gay desire negates the moral superiority over whites that would have been integrally his in his black identity. The first does not give them access, the second takes it away.

46. Samuel R. Delany, *The Motion of Light on Water* (New York: New American Library, 1988).

47. Kenneth B. Clarke, *Prejudice and Your Child* (Boston: Beacon, 1963; reprint, Middletown, Conn.: Wesleyan University Press, 1988), 98.

48. Ibid., 98-99.

49. Personal communication in a letter Samuel R. Delany wrote to me concerning this incident.

50. Ibid.

51. Samuel R. Delany, "From Erik, Gwen, and D. H. Lawrence's Esthetic of Unrectified Feelings," *Callaloo* 14, no. 2 (1991): 505-23. In this autobiographical fragment, Delany discusses the sexual charge he found in forbidden language as a child. The section of the fragment that illustrates this, however, is excised from its published version. I am grateful to Professor Delany for providing me with copies of both versions.

52. From Delany's letter to me.

53. See chapter 8.

54. Stuart Hall was "colored" in Jamaica, and first became "black" in Britain—and the social valences of these terms changed radically across cultures and in contemporary political history. Stuart Hall, "Signification, Representation, Ideology: Althusser and the Post-Structuralist Debates," *Critical Studies in Mass Communication* 2, no. 2 (June 1985): 109-11.

55. David M. Halperin, *One Hundred Years of Homosexuality, and Other Essays on Greek Love* (New York and London: Routledge, 1989).

56. For example, in David Ruben's *Everything You Always Wanted to Know about Sex but Were Afraid to Ask*; the exemption of women from the sodomy law in England; and the sex/orientation line on the Centers for Disease Control statistical information form given to people seeking HIV testing, which gives the following options: heterosexual male, bisexual male, homosexual male; woman.

57. Moraga, *Loving*, 54–55.

58. Samuel Delany, *Motion*, 242. See also Anzaldúa, *Borderlands/La Frontera*, 55–64.

59. Samuel R. Delany, *Babel-17* (New York: Ace, 1966), 152.

60. Frye's reasons for objecting to men identifying themselves as victims of "oppression" support my arguments for the importance of sexual difference ("Oppression," *Politics*, 1–16). The differences in the political, social, and cultural histories of men and women that make it senseless for men to claim to be "oppressed" also render suspect interpretations of gay male sexuality based on male heterosexual history.

61. Frye, "Oppression," 16.

62. Combahee River Collective, "Statement," in Moraga and Anzaldúa, eds., *This Bridge*, 213.

63. He later limited his identification with me through his assertion of his Jewish identity, but for me to limit my identification with him through my gentile upbringing would be unconscionable.

64. Adrienne Rich, "Compulsory Heterosexuality and Lesbian Existence," in Snitow et al., eds., *Powers of Desire*, 177–205. Before "lesbian/gay studies" was clearly envisioned as an academic possibility, many gay men took women's studies courses, which provided the only political and social analyses of gender and sexuality generally available. Early "gay culture" courses were taught under a women's studies rubric.

65. Audre Lorde, *Zami: A New Spelling of My Name* (Freedom, Calif.: Crossing, 1982), 179, 203. In a related vein, see also Olivia Espín, "Issues of Identity in the Psychology of Latina Lesbians," in *Lesbian Psychologies: Explorations and Challenges*, ed. Boston Lesbian Psychologies Collective (Urbana: University of Illinois Press, 1987), 35–55.

66. Beam, *In the Life*, 230–42. Beam's text is featured in Riggs's film. See also Ron Simmons, "Other Notions: Interview with Marlon Riggs," *Black Film Review* 5, no. 3 (Summer 1989): 22–23.

67. "La Macha," in Trujillo, *Chicana Lesbians*, 40.

68. Ramón A. Gutiérrez, "Must We Deracinate Indians to Find Gay Roots?" *Out/Look* 1, no. 4 (1989): 61–67. On the Micronesian strategy, see the paper given by Walter L. Williams at the Harvard University Lesbian and Gay Studies Conference, October 1991.

69. Two of the most gifted, insightful, and serious students I have ever worked with in gay male courses were heterosexual men, and I would support their continued professional pursuit of lesbian/gay studies and look forward to their contributions. Henry Louis Gates once wrote forty-nine letters of recommendation for a "talented white job candidate in African literature," all of which were "unsuccessful." This indicates the resistance to hiring white scholars for such positions, but also attests to Gates's acceptance of qualified white scholars in the field. "Tell Me Sir . . . What Is 'Black' Literature?" *PMLA* 105, no. 1 (January 1990): 12.

70. This also obscures the other racist or sexist assumptions within traditional patterns of affirmative action: simply reserving the African-American position for a black professor does not address the issues of hiring that professor for the Shakespeare position, or the Chinese linguistics position, etc. There is also an assumption that African-American

studies—or any "ethnic studies" discipline—requires few formal qualifications apart from belonging to that racial or ethnic category. See chapter 5.

71. Eve K. Sedgwick, "A Poem Is Being Written," *Representations*, no. 17 (Winter 1987): 129-30, 133.

72. Sedgwick states this herself: "There has been no important and sustained Western discourse in which women's anal eroticism means. Means anything." "Poem," 129.

73. I put scare quotes around *privileged* in this case, since this aspect's "privilege" is the entry into the heterosexual sex/gender system, which for women seems anything but.

Chapter 8

Compromising Positions

Lisa Kahaleole Chang Hall

Warning: This is not a universal essay. I am writing from a very specific location—as a feminist lesbian of color academic, activist, and nonacademic writer with ties in a multitude of communities—to a very specific audience: academics involved with feminist and multicultural theory who are committed to social change. This is the "we" that informs this essay.[1]

Our Situation: 1992

What's politics got to do with it? The last several years have seen increasingly virulent attacks on progressive ideology and academics in the university system. By "progressive," I mean scholars and scholarship that assume that the academy is profoundly interconnected with the world beyond the university; that the interplay of race, class, and gender permeates our scholarly life as theorists and teachers as well as the larger world; and that we are at some level trying to rectify inequalities. In contrast to more traditionally situated scholars, academics in women's studies and ethnic studies cannot deny the political origins of our work because these departments and fields of study were created as a direct result of political action and protest; we are the legacy of students and communities who literally took to the streets. The student strikes for ethnic studies at San Francisco State and the University of California at Berkeley in the 1960s were the hammer that forced the universities to take seriously the power of these communities, if not the validity of their demands.[2] Women's studies programs were implemented through a similar coalition of academic and nonacademic feminists. The original push focused on the inclusion and recognition of the specific issues of those who had been excluded from traditional scholarship. As academics involved in feminist and ethnic studies, we first had to struggle to prove that we existed as artists, as thinkers, and as historical subjects and agents. Then came the project of articulating theoretically how our exclusions have been institutionalized, dismantling notions of "objectivity" and "universality" that somehow always covered the objective universal experience of straight white Western men. The political implications of the construction of what counts as knowledge and who counts as scholars became an arena for argument.

The contemporary liberal movement toward a "multiculturally" expanded curriculum throughout the university has caught up with the first part of this struggle—a project that has been characterized as "just add women (other races, cultures, etc.) and stir." "Multiculturalism" is an ideology; the many wildly various cultures of this country produced through and around class, race, ethnicity, sexuality, geographic location, and ideology are lived realities with lengthy histories only now beginning to be widely acknowledged and explored. "Multicultural education" at its most limited is the liberal ideal of "cultural pluralism," the idea that we just provide a space for all kinds of people, all kinds of ideas on an equal basis, a "level playing field." There is nothing wrong with this per se, but it does beg several questions. First, who is doing the conceptualizing; who gets to choose which ideas get represented? Too often a common agenda is presupposed rather than analyzed and thought through. This leads to situations like the struggle for women's reproductive rights being conceptualized as the universal right for individual women to have abortions, ignoring the class stratification of the current availability of abortion and the importance of the sterilization abuses perpetuated on black, Latina, Native American, and poor white women. There is no possibility of meaningful representation if only bodies are represented in someone else's agenda and not their histories, issues, and affiliations.

In academia, the question of who decides what issues count is even more problematic given a situation in which work by and about marginalized groups has not been read or understood by the dominant majority, and is made worse by the lack of female and colored players on the "level playing field." We do not all come to the "dialogue" from positions of equality—the dynamics of gender, race, and class skew how others perceive the validity of speakers and ideas. In institutional settings where tenure and real administrative power are overwhelmingly concentrated in the hands of white men, who will educate the educators?

When the political implications of *all* knowledge construction are not acknowledged, the drive to implement "multicultural" courses becomes just another form of academic ghettoization in which particular departments and scholars are to be the different "other" while the rest of the university carries on with the real, "universal" scholarship. Consequently, the only people perceived to experience the dynamics of race, class, gender, and sexuality are those who are *marginalized* by those dynamics because the theoretical scholarship on the institutionalized privileges of men, white people, and heterosexuals has, with rare exception, not been written.[3] The theorizing of "difference" has all too often been read as though difference is only a synonym for marginalization, leaving the center to the dominant once again. This is what enables cultural conservatives to stigmatize liberal and progressive scholarship as being uniquely political. Traditional academics claim to inhabit politically neutral territory, taking refuge in the conceptual split between "knowledge" and "politics" that is precisely what we have been deconstructing.

There was a moment, long past, when the democratization of higher education seemed imminently possible, and when the line between "community" and academia was blurred and merged in places like the Open Admissions Program of New York's City College, at San Francisco State, and at other urban institutions. This was the historical moment about which artist/activist/teachers such as Adrienne Rich, Audre Lorde, and Toni Cade Bambara have written, a moment in which all things seemed possible.[4] Our contemporary historical moment is different. A deteriorating economy and conservative political and cultural retrenchment have created a situation in which access to education is increasingly curtailed by devastating budget cuts at public institutions and the demolition of student loan and work-study programs. In the early 1980s political debate about public education used the real inadequacies of the educational system to argue that innovative programs and methods designed to empower students as thinkers rather than passive receivers of knowledge were the cause of the deficits of the traditional education system. The solution to this, of course, was to be authoritarian discipline, a common (traditional Western) curriculum, and increased reliance on standardized tests to evaluate learning. As money for any kind of education dried up, the need to justify experimental course content and methods intensified.

For those of us ensconced in disciplines with explicit political commitments, such as women's studies and ethnic studies, the dissonance between political and professional commitments is often profound as the institution becomes more conservative. The "professionalization" of these fields has meant that some have begun to downplay the original political commitments in search of an intellectual validation that is permeated with conservative concepts of "objectivity" and "scholarly worth" that are assumed to be apolitical. This is obviously a losing game; the status quo is always seen as apolitical while critiques of the status quo are seen as uniquely political. The problems we face are not the result of our overpoliticization but of our ineffectiveness at dealing with our contemporary political situations.

Between a Rock and a Hard Place

In contemplating the relationship between academia and political activism, I have ricocheted between the faith of the true believer and paralyzing despair. That dynamic has everything to do with the dilemmas that progressive academics face every day. The standard response by academic feminists to criticisms from nonacademic activists about the political usefulness of academic work has been that the university is not an ivory tower removed from a "real world," that constructing theory is a form of activism, and that critical debates and canon formation and revision are all legitimate and valuable forms of political activity. This is all very true and at the same time not enough. I say this recognizing only too well how huge our tasks are. As critics of dominant ideologies, we do the intellectual "second shift": we are constantly forced to defend our basic assumptions as well as to do the theoretical work we are led to because of them. What invokes the most despair is that we are also then led by our intellectual commitments to a third shift—breaking down the constrictions of race, class, gender, and sexuality, the dichotomy between public and private, personal and political upon which the university is in fact founded. We bite the hand that feeds us and we are not well fed. To be a truly radical academic is to be unemployed, unless you are lucky enough to have become a star in a cross-over nonacademic forum or find a place in a unique and marginalized institution.[5] (Sometimes there is more pedagogical and course content flexibility in community and city colleges, where teachers then become crazed from the inhuman work requirements of systems under siege.)

Those who have taken seriously even those community commitments supposedly valued in the tenure process have often been dismissed as "nonscholarly" or the deadly "biased." Active community commitments are not even given neutral weight in academic evaluation, but are viewed as illegitmate uses of time better spent in trying to appear in prestigious publications. These struggles are rooted in the university system's pervasive assumption that scholarship can be value-neutral and thus objective and that scholarship requires disinterested, value-free scholarly individuals. Because membership in dominant communities means the freedom to conceive of oneself as an individual voluntarily participating in the university community, investment in other communities and group identities of race, gender, or sexuality is either inexplicable or a betrayal of the community of individuals and "objective," "disinterested" scholarship.

The Theory of Practice

The desire for systemic global change is the root of our work, and the magnitude of the project easily becomes overwhelming. The disjuncture between theory and practice stems both from the conservative pull of the institution toward disembodied universal theory and from the draining realities of trying to implement concrete, material changes. In women's studies and ethnic studies departments, it is also the legacy of the purging, attrition, and exhaustion of activist-academics throughout the late 1970s and the 1980s. The institutional gains of these departments in terms of number and prestige did not come without a price. In many places part of that price was the deliberate removal of founding faculty and staff who retained serious commitments to extra-academic communities.

I have no unified field theory that will save us: I believe the desire for one is a manifestation of the kind of all-or-nothing dichotomy that keeps us from making the small changes and gains that will never seem like enough. Radical change is the ultimate goal, but if the available options are reformist acts or political paralysis the choice seems clear. Incremental change should be valued as the means to a goal; the global begins in our backyards but obviously does not end there. With this in mind, I have some modest proposals about the possibilities of progressive political action within and through the university system. I take seriously the assertion that the university is a site for political struggle; what this encompasses is the real issue.

Why the University?

The short answer is because we are here, but the long answer is quite complicated. What most of us share, I think, is a history in which, at some point, books and teachers literally saved our lives and sanities by giving us both a critical framework to envision our lives and the knowledge that there were communities for us we had never before conceptualized or experienced. The shift from passive receiver of knowledge to critically engaged thinker is profound. My undergraduate mentor described it as "never being bored again. You're either enraged, excited, or arguing." Once we begin to question authority, life is never the same. That critical engagement is the foundation of our investment in analyzing how traditional academic discourses construct, erase, or distort the existences and meanings of our communities of origin and affiliation. The urgency of that investment is a product of the very real concrete effects of "discourse" on our existence as women, postcolonials, queers, and people of color. What has been theorized about us — the pathology of homosexuality, the inherent savagery of native peoples, the compliant acceptance of slavery by African-Americans, the hysteria of women who claim to have been sexually abused, and so forth — has been and continues to be used as the basis for public policies and "private" actions that radically affect our lives. "Representation" in all of its meanings has been a consuming problem for us; the dissonant pressures of representing selves, communities, and ideologies have been a painful and intellectually fruitful spur to our scholarship.

What's Politics Got to Do with It?

The contemporary claiming of the university as a political site has primarily focused on curriculum revision and development, faculty hiring and firing, and, to a much lesser extent, pedagogy and classroom relations. These first responsibilities fall well within traditional areas of concern for faculty; they are hotly contested, yet can be assimilated within a preexisting university structure. Departments may shift and reform, but while critical studies, ethnic studies, cultural studies, American studies, and feminist studies become interdisciplinary, potentially multicultural, potentially radical havens, other departments are free to carry on their monodisciplinary, monocultural business-as-usual agendas. Traditional departments can solve their internal dilemmas by adding Maxine Hong Kingston and Toni Morrison to the English Great Books syllabi, say, or by picking up a "race and gender" theorist for the sociology department. It is academic consumer capitalism in which we just buy one and add him or her to our collection.

The energy we must expend on these traditional battles draws us away from addressing a much larger and more challenging set of political issues within the university. Like the classmates I encountered at the University of California at Santa Cruz who were willing to travel to Nicaragua on coffee brigades but were woefully ignorant of and uninterested in the Mexican farm worker strikes of neighboring Watsonville, progressive academics have often missed the trees while theorizing the forest. Why, for example, have departments with explicit commitments to theoretically dismantling racial, gender, and class inequalities not been in the forefront of staff unionization battles on campus? Or of restructuring a system in which senior tenured faculty have almost no accountability as teachers while the heaviest burden of teaching falls on the least well paid, least secure echelon of expendable lecturers?

The class stratification among those teaching in universities has long been accepted as an apprenticeship program where we work our way up from the least-paid, most-burdened ranks of graduate student teaching assistants along a preordained path to the power and privileges of tenure, and maybe an endowed chair. This might have been true in a past when the university teaching pool was more homogeneous, prestratified against a diversity of race, gender, and class, but it certainly is not now. We are not all going to become "old boys" reaping later benefits from current exploitation. The continuing erosion of public education has made job security even more uncertain for those who have chosen or been forced into the circuit of state schools, city colleges, and community colleges. The fate of nomadic scholars teaching at several local institutions simultaneously for little money, no benefits, and no job security has only recently received any public attention. The struggle of graduate students to unionize as teaching assistants and research assistants at Berkeley, Michigan, Yale, and elsewhere reveals the extent to which the education of undergraduates at large research universities is dependent on the use of underpaid graduates who the universities then claim are not "really" employees. Similarly, yearlong "minority" postdoctoral awards at elite universities have become the latest dog and pony show demonstrating the university's commitment to "diversity" in a conveniently disposable format.

Power, Power, Who's Got the Power?

Power is a particularly complicated issue for those of us working from the margins. The depth and complexity of the issues we face are exacerbated as the climate surrounding us becomes increasingly reactionary — including upsurges in racial, sexual, and anti-Semitic hate crimes; the economic devastation of a decade of accelerating transferral of wealth from the bottom to the top; and the renewal of struggles for legal abortion, civil rights, and access to public education that we had hoped were partially resolved. It is easy to feel powerless against the vastness of the problems. Feeling powerless and being powerless, however, are two different things.

One reason for our ineffectiveness at examining and using what power we have is the simplistic dichotomization of good/bad, oppressor/oppressed. If we take seriously our theoretical vision of multiple overlapping identities formed around race, gender, sexuality, class, nationality, and so forth, it is clear that each of us exists within, and acts from, a multitude of roles and locations whose privileges and power are often both contextual and provisional. For us, the failure to recognize this is grounded in essentialized concepts of identity that revolve around the inherent "innocence" of our particular oppressions. To build effective coalitions in the service of the liberation of all requires addressing our shared complicity in the oppression of others, without implying that "shared" means "identical" in terms of power and consequences. To recognize that none of us is innocent is not to say that we are equally guilty.

One thing that prevents many of us from taking action is the equation of power itself, rather than the abuse of power, with evil. Powerlessness and victimization are equated with innocence, and this holds ugly implications for communication and organizing. If the only possibilities are good/bad or all-powerful/powerless, everyone is frozen on one or the other side of the dichotomy. This is what leads people to brandish any badge of oppression they can claim, in order to trump themselves into a position of nonresponsibility for anything. Everyone becomes the done-unto, never the doer. It is dangerous to rely on an identity founded on being innocent because the truth of the matter is that none of us is ever completely innocent. The African-American gospel group Sweet Honey in the Rock sings a song about the journey of a polyester and cotton shirt through several countries and groups of exploited women workers before its arrival at J. C. Penney to be sold to working-class women in the United States. The last line of the song asks, "Are my hands clean?" We all need to remember that though our hands are not equally dirty, neither are they clean.

Seeing innocence as the necessary condition for action means that not a lot gets done. Trying to be the most powerless and innocent is a morality play useful only for personal redemption. It is an activity that prevents making connections with others—first, because it involves having to hide the often messy facts of our lives, and second, because it usually involves making others feel guilty. Seeing power as inherently bad means having to deny and thus waste any power we have. This longing for radical purity is what prompts some to ask why we are in the university at all since we assume its structures are so deeply oppressive. Yet the reality of the situation is that we have not been able to effectively organize with the institutional resources available to us. What is the likelihood that we would be more successful outside existing structures? This is the kind of thinking that got us Ronald Reagan as president, as liberals and progressives were unable to mobilize around Walter Mondale in 1984. Clearly, electing Mondale would in no way have altered the fundamental political problems of the United States or the Democratic party, but I hope those on the left who saw no substantive difference between the two enjoyed the twelve Republican years.

Another factor that works against the effective use of power is the tendency to look upward in hierarchies in order to gauge the extent of our power. Because we are all marginalized to greater or lesser degrees within the dominant institution, there is always someone else to point to who "really" has the power. Students see the teachers, graduate students see the departmental faculty, the untenured see the tenured, the tenured see the department chair, the department chair sees the larger university, and so on, like the farmer in the dell. A more useful way of considering what kinds of power we have access to is to look down the hierarchy, examining the situations of those we perceive as having less power than we do.

Another way to identify power within the university is to examine its relationship to groups outside the university system. One example is the relationship between academic feminists and nonacademic feminist activists. On the whole, activist feminists have access to far fewer resources than academic feminists, from as basic a level as photocopiers, money for long-distance phone calls, and free or discounted books to the more obvious advantages of adequate salaries and an institutionalized network of communication through university-funded conferences, journals, and so forth. Nevertheless, there are at least two areas in which grass-roots cultural and political activists have created unique and invaluable institutions—health care and the production and distribution of feminist writing.

A Modest Proposal

In the 1992 education edition of *The Women's Review of Books*, Nancy Bereano, publisher of Firebrand Books, highlighted the financial stability and increased visibility of feminist presses that would result if the more than three thousand women's studies courses and six hundred women's studies departments in the United States had at least one of their titles on required reading lists.[6] As a worker at a small multicultural feminist press, I am admittedly partisan, but I believe that feminist presses are invaluable precisely because they are motivated by politics rather than profit.

Still, developing and publishing a wide range of underrepresented voices and keeping them in print requires an institutional and financial stability that would be easily acquired if university feminists as a whole supported feminist presses. This is not charity work, because the developing literature has a cutting-edge impact far beyond sales figures. One small example: Aunt Lute Books published Gloria Anzaldúa's groundbreaking *Borderlands/La Frontera* in 1986. It took four years for the book to reach its audience and become economically self-sustaining. It then came into use as a textbook in scores of college classrooms across disciplines and is repeatedly cited as a major influence in a new wave of theoretical writing. Even if (and that is a big if) the book had been published by a mainstream press, it would have died, out of print years before its audience grew into it. Cleis Press's *Sex Work: Writings by Women in the Sex Industry*, Kitchen Table's *Home Girls: A Black Feminist Anthology* and bringing back into print of *This Bridge Called My Back: Writings by Radical Women of Color*, Seal Press's Women in Translation series, Spinsters' *Look Me in the Eye: Old Women and Aging*, and Third Woman's *Chicana Lesbians: The Girls Our Mothers Warned Us About*, are just a few examples of invaluable and irreplaceable work that would not exist without the commitment of feminist presses.[7]

Thinking Globally/Acting Locally

One of the many ironies currently facing us is that the right wing has effectively learned lessons about grass-roots organizing that were previously the strong suit of the left. The 1992 campaigns against gay civil rights in Oregon and Colorado and antiabortion assaults on clinics and health care providers are founded on a coalition of national right-wing institutions and local organizers. As progressives, we need to redevelop the combination of coalition institution building that propelled the civil rights movements of the 1960s and the feminist movements of the 1970s. We have been talking about the necessity of coalitions for a long time, but conceptualizing how to do this *and* prioritizing that need have not been high enough on our collective agenda.

Unfortunately, there is no way to tell what would happen if we took coalition building seriously. In an address at the 1990 conference on "Women and the Law" at Stanford, Mari Matsuda offered an analytical strategy gained from her students that she called "ask the other question." She described her experience organizing after the murder of Vincent Chin, a young Chinese man who was bludgeoned to death by a white father and son who thought he was Japanese and saw him as responsible for the loss of their auto-worker jobs. Clearly, racism was the most obvious element in the murder. But the point of "ask the other question" is to take seriously what we have been claiming for some time—that oppressions such as racism, sexism, homophobia, and so on are interlocking, inseparable, and not able to be hierarchized. Matsuda asked herself and her predominantly Asian-American audiences, "Where is the sexism in this story?" She went on to underline the culture of masculinity that glorifies violence as a solution to frustration, and then the homophobia that underlies the sexism: to object to this system of masculinity is to be a faggot. Classism turns the rage of disenfranchised working-class people onto demonized "others" rather than the economic system that exploits and the economic elite that perpetuates this system. Matsuda concludes that to ask where the racism exists in a homophobic incident, the sexism in a racist incident, and so forth is to begin to truly understand the interlocking nature of oppression and is thus a way to avoid single-issue politics.

It is not the diversity and multiplicity of our issues that keep us from coming together; it is the failure to create a framework large enough to encompass our specificities while seeing their interrelationships. If our questions are too narrow, how can activists and academics expect our alliances to be any bigger? When our questions are as big as they can be, we are thinking globally. When we address those questions strategically with the shifting resources available to us, we are acting locally. It's not just a bumper sticker; it's an agenda.

Notes

1. Grateful thanks to the "we" that literally informed this paper: Becky Thompson, Sangeeta Tyagi, and, most especially, Rudiger Busto, *mi compadre.*

2. See Mike Murase, "Ethnic Studies and Higher Education for Asian Americans," in *Counterpoint: Perspectives on Asian America* (Los Angeles: UCLA Asian American Research Center, 1976), 205-33. Also see *Amerasia Journal* 15, no. 1 (1989).

3. Elizabeth Spelman's *Inessential Woman* (Boston: Beacon, 1988) is a notable exception. See also Minnie Bruce Pratt's essay "Skin, Blood, Heart," in *Yours in Struggle*, Elly Bulkin, Minnie Bruce Pratt, and Barbara Smith (Brooklyn, N.Y.: Long Haul Press, 1984).

4. See, for example, "An Interview: Audre Lorde and Adrienne Rich," in *Sister Outsider* (Ithaca, N.Y.: Firebrand, 1984).

5. For example, Gloria Anzaldúa, June Jordan, Audre Lorde, and Trinh T. Minh-ha are some of the most brilliant and influential cultural theorists currently writing. Yet within the academy, their status as theorists is consistently undermined by their primary status as "artists."

6. Advertisement in *Women's Review of Books* 9, no. 5 (February 1992): A7.

7. Frédérique Delacoste and Priscilla Alexander, eds., *Sex Work: Writings by Women in the Sex Industry* (Pittsburgh: Cleis, 1987); Barbara MacDonald, *Look Me in the Eye: Old Women and Aging* (San Francisco: Spinsters, 1992); Cherríe Moraga and Gloria Anzaldúa, eds., *This*

Bridge Called My Back: Writings by Radical Women of Color (Ithaca, N.Y.: Kitchen Table, 1983); Barbara Smith, ed., *Home Girls: A Black Feminist Anthology* (Ithaca, N.Y.: Kitchen Table, 1983); Carla Trujillo, ed., *Chicana Lesbians: The Girls Our Mothers Warned Us About* (Berkeley, Calif.: Third Woman, 1991).

PART III

New Directions for Critical Engagement

Chapter 9

Education for a Change: The MOST Program

Carole C. Marks and Margaret L. Andersen

As a black person in a society dominated by Whites, I was always an outsider. . . . What was actively communicated to me was that Black people and other people of color are on the periphery of the society. . . . At the same time, I also learned that the information I accumulated about Black people—and, later, other people of color—was nice to know, but basically irrelevant for understanding society. . . . I did not begin by discovering that women were missing from the curriculum—instead I have always perceived schools as foreign institutions.

—Elizabeth Higginbotham, sociologist

Despite the operating myth of the day, school did not erase my otherness. It did try to deny it, and in doing so only accentuated it. To this day, schooling is more socialization than education, but when I was in elementary school . . . socialization was everything. . . . There was a pervasive and systematic denial by the society that surrounded us that we were Americans. . . . Our absence from the larger cultural, economic, political and social spaces . . . reminded us constantly that we were the other. And school was where we felt it most acutely.

—Arturo Madrid, Chicano literary critic and policy analyst

I hope I will never relinquish values that are dear to me just to fit into the mainstream.
—Gina Masequesmay, Vietnamese-American MOST student

Throughout the educational process, people of color remain invisible. When they appear, they are distorted through the eyes of dominant groups and are rarely studied on their own terms or seen as active agents in history, society, and culture. How, in the face of invisibility and oppression, can education be developed to educate, support, and empower people of color? Exclusion from the curriculum reinforces a sense of disconnectedness. It robs students and faculty of the ability to think in ways that are centered in multiple experiences and the interrelatedness of all groups. Whites come to see people of color as other. All students learn to think in segregated ways, as if studying society, history, and culture is about white society, with black, Latino, Asian-American, and Native American experience being only specialized topics or separate concerns. Instead, students need to learn about the connections between the experiences of different groups and to learn that the study of society is the study of black experience, white experience, Latino, Asian, and Native American experience—not just the study of separate groups. As Alice Walker writes, "Black and white writers seem to me to be writing one immense story—the same story, for the most part—with different parts of this immense story coming from a multitude of different perspectives" (1983: 5).

Calls for the transformation of the curriculum have by now become common, yet faculty often find themselves alone in classrooms where trying to be inclusive contradicts everything else that students learn. And building an inclusive community requires more than individual effort: it requires the construction of new communities where participants are committed to the development of education that will support and enable all students, especially those who have been defined as other.

Sy Kahn, a Southern community organizer, has developed principles for building effective race relations within community organizations and other groups that we found instructive:

1. An institutional commitment to racial equity which is clearly and forcefully stated.
2. Leaders, both people of color and whites, who are personally committed to racial equity.
3. A political will, shared by all participants, to enforce the structures and rules relating to equity, even under enormous pressure.
4. Safe spaces within which these processes can be worked through. . . .
5. Social occasions as well as public events in which personal as well as political relations can develop. (Kahn 1991: 36)

Although implementing these principles is often difficult, they represent a necessary beginning for the institutional change we envision. The Minority Opportunity Summer Training (MOST) Program is a project of the American Sociological Association. It is designed to identify promising minority students who have an interest in sociology and to encourage them to pursue doctoral degrees in the field.[1] In this essay we discuss our experience as codirectors of the MOST Program at the University of Delaware in 1990 and 1991. As a disciplinary-based project, the MOST Program provides a model for developing multicultural education; at the same time, it informs us about the possibilities for and obstacles to creating more inclusive educational programs.

Developing new educational communities is not merely altruistic. America at the turn of the century will be a "nation in which one of every three of us will be non-white" (Epps 1989: 26). The impact on higher education will be dramatic. An April 1992 article warned that "by the year 2000, American colleges and universities will be lean and mean, service-oriented and science-minded, multicultural and increasingly diverse—if they intend to survive their fiscal agony" (Elson 1992). Yet, while diversity is a priority for survival, it remains elusive. As Edgar Epps, professor of urban education at the University of Chicago, explains, "When we ask colleges and universities to

Table 1. ASA minority fellowship program Ph.D. completion rates by cohort

Year	Fellowships Awarded	Dropped	M.A. only	Number	Percent
1974–75	21	5	0	11	52
1975–76	29	4	3	19	66
1976–77	42	8	4	23	54
1977–78	34	8	1	18	53
1978–79	18	2	1	11	61
1979–80	14	0	0	11	79
1980–81	10	0	1	5	50
1981–82	11	1	0	7	64
1982–83	11	0	1	9	82
1983–84	17	1	0	0	58
1984–85	12	1	0	6	50
1985–86	5	0	0	3	60
1986–87	12	0	0	5	42
1987–88	13	1	0	2	15
1988–89	15	1	2	3	20
1989–90	9	0	0	1	11
1990–91	19	0	0	0	0
1991–92	14	0	0	0	0
Total	306	32	13	134	
		(10.5%)	(4.3%)	(43.8%)	

expand opportunities for low-status groups and persons, we pose a serious threat to the claim of exclusivity upon which their hallowed status rests" (1989: 23). This crisis was a starting point for the development of the MOST Program — a program intended to support students of color in completing Ph.D.'s in sociology.

The Development of the MOST Program

The MOST Program selects students early in their junior year and recruits them to an intensive summer research institute held on two university campuses each summer. The program evolved from a successful, long-standing minority graduate student fellowship program within the American Sociological Association (ASA) — the Minority Fellowship Program. Established in 1973 with funding from federal and private sources, the fellowship program has supported more than 144 minority Ph.D.'s (table 1).[2] By the mid-1980s, funding for the program had declined significantly. Reagan administration budget cuts had eroded support from the federal government, and the ASA was worried about the program's future. Thus, in 1987, the Council of the American Sociological Association appointed a task force of senior sociologists to identify new sources of funding for the Minority Fellowship Program.[3]

Members of the task force quickly learned that foundations and federal agencies had little interest in further funding for minority graduate fellowship programs. But, as a result of these discussions, several sociologists from the task force formed a subcommittee that began to imagine a bigger project—one that would develop a "feeder" program for the graduate fellowships by identifying potential minority sociologists earlier in their educational careers. This group, informally calling itself the "longitudinal committee," began to work on an expanded program.[4] From this collaborative work, the MOST Program was created.

MOST was developed by an interracial group of sociologists, all of whom have strong commitments to minority scholarship and professional development. The group, which became the MOST advisory board, consisted of people with a vision for a more inclusive and racially just discipline and unique and diverse talents in fund-raising, program and curriculum development, minority recruitment and retention, and scholarship on race.

Over a three-year period, this group developed the MOST Program from a theoretical foundation informed by sociological research, which shows that students need information, financial support, and mentoring to succeed in higher education. These elements of support are especially crucial for minority students, who often do not have social networks in the academic community and whose experiences in schools and graduate departments lead them to perceive education as alien and unsupportive.

James Blackwell, a member of the original task force and a black sociologist known for his work on mentoring, argues that it is the quality of social supports—mentors, role models, and sponsorship—that most strongly influences students' ability to complete educational programs (1987). Creating a community of students and mentors was the keystone of the new MOST Program, which, like the Minority Fellowship Program, is designed to increase the number of minority students who ultimately will become faculty mentors for other students. As Blackwell shows, there is a tendency for students to select mentors who are like them in terms of race, gender, social class, and religion. Given the underrepresentation of people of color in sociology and the shortage of them in college and university teaching positions, more underrepresented minorities must be recruited and supported in order to expand and facilitate a broader universe of mentors. The idea is that this will encourage other minority students to pursue professional careers in sociology and will make the content of sociology more reflective of diverse racial-ethnic experiences.

According to Blackwell, mentors are those who have a manifest commitment to the total development of the protégé, whether the individual is an undergraduate student, graduate student, or junior colleague. Mentors assist protégés in attaining career goals and in scholarly endeavors. True mentoring is not merely a matter of supporting specific tasks; rather, it is a deliberate, conscious, and sometimes subtle effort to promote the overall success of the person under the tutelage of the mentor. While facilitating the development of important coping strategies, the mentor, often by example, fosters socialization into the profession. Furthermore, the mentor offers encouragement and is sufficiently involved in the protégé's life to understand when it is important to listen, to criticize constructively, or to reward. If the mentoring relationship is fully successful, students are incorporated into a network of professionals whose common goals and ideals result in a sense of group identity and solidarity (Blackwell 1987). As one MOST student wrote to us after her experience in the summer program: "It's really kind of funny when I see something you've written in the library or on one of my professors' bookshelves. I always say, 'Yea, I know her . . . in fact we practically lived together this summer . . . yea, we're basically like mother and daughter!' "

The MOST Program was designed to provide extensive mentoring while also giving the information and financial support necessary for students to consider graduate school in sociology. The program was conceived as a community of scholars—minority and majority—in which undergraduate students would develop close working relationships with senior scholars and with peers. The summer institute would provide advanced training in the logic of social inquiry, but would also introduce students to minority sociologists so they could learn how the life experiences of minority sociologists shaped their research interests and careers.

The MOST Summer Institutes

The plan created by the MOST advisory board was to gather some of the most talented students from across the country, give them advanced research skills and strong mentoring systems through the summer, and help them find faculty mentors at their home institutions. After the summer program, students return home to work with these sponsors in their senior year, completing research projects, finishing graduation requirements, taking graduate school entrance exams, and applying to graduate schools.

Each summer institute is open to fifteen students at each of two campus sites. The small size is important because it allows for the development of meaningful primary group relationships and encourages close mentoring. Selection for the program is competitive and is based on a national recruiting effort. Students selected for the program receive stipends of $1,000, plus travel and book expenses. The length and format of each summer institute varies, but is typically six to eight weeks.

The MOST Program is funded through a major grant from the Ford Foundation, with additional support from the Maurice Falk Medical Foundation and the American Sociological Foundation. Host universities also contribute a substantial amount of funding. The nature of university contributions varies, but may include support for faculty salaries, remission of tuition or room and board or both, graduate assistant summer salaries, administrative support, and honoraria for visiting lecturers.

Site Selection

MOST programs are held on two campuses each year. The University of Delaware and the University of Wisconsin at Madison hosted the first MOST programs in the summers of 1990 and 1991. The 1992 and 1993 programs were at the University of Michigan, Ann Arbor, and the University of California, Berkeley. This pattern—two years on each of two campuses, then moving to two new locations—will be repeated in the future.

The rotation of sites is intended to encourage departments to think of innovative ways to attract minority students, thus developing effective minority recruitment and retention programs while competing for selection as a MOST site. It also brings the program to different regions of the country, attracting regionally concentrated minority populations. The MOST advisory board selects sites from proposals submitted by interested departments of sociology.[5] There is no single model for the MOST Program; participating institutions are encouraged to call on their particular strengths in designing a curriculum for the students.

The board looks for innovative proposals designed to enhance the success of minority students. Departments are expected to propose a curriculum that emphasizes development of research skills. Preference is given to sites with (1) a significant presence of tenured minority faculty; (2) a Ph.D. program; (3) a location favorable for recruiting minority students; (4) a record of producing successful minority students; (5) strong institutional and departmental commitment to hosting MOST (including financial resources and demonstrated commitment of the faculty); (6) involvement of minority faculty as site directors; and (7) the presence of white faculty who have demonstrated commitment to minority professional development.

Whereas there has been an embarrassment of riches in selecting students, the reverse has been true in selecting sites. The schools with minority faculty often do not have graduate programs; those with graduate programs often have few, if any, minority faculty. Generally speaking, we found that the more prestigious the department, the fewer minority faculty it had—a problem reproduced for MOST students when they are selecting potential graduate programs. Some departments proposed an innovative curriculum for MOST students but did not have minority faculty to serve as mentors. As a consequence, site selection is not easy. While there has been a tendency to select departments with the most prestigious graduate programs, the advisory board does not wish to exclude others. Currently, the MOST advisory board is encouraging departments to develop collaborative proposals: a department with one set of strengths might develop a summer institute proposal in collaboration with a nearby institution with complementary strengths.

Student Recruitment and Selection

Selection of students is based on academic achievement and sociological imagination, judged by the student's undergraduate record, a written essay, and letters of recommendation. Selection is made by representatives from the MOST advisory board and the site directors for the current year. Recruitment literature is mailed each year to all departments of sociology, minority advisers in historically black colleges and universities, member campuses of the Hispanic Association of Colleges and Universities, individual members of the Association for Black Sociologists and the Association for Latino/Latina Sociologists, and a list of colleges from the Bureau of Indian Affairs. Now that the program has been operating for a few years, former students also recruit new students.

The selection committee tries to balance the composition of the group by race and gender and to include a mix from different kinds of undergraduate institutions. The committee is also sensitive to selecting students with different academic backgrounds. We do not want to recruit only those already likely to be recruited by graduate schools, so we try to select students every year who appear to be more "risky" in terms of standard admissions criteria, but we have found that these students may later be disappointed by not being selected for prestigious graduate programs, even after they have participated in MOST. For example, we notice that students from less prestigious departments who have low scores on the Graduate Record Examination (GRE) seem to be eliminated from

Table 2. 1990-92 MOST program applicants

Race/ethnicity	1990		1991		1992	
	Men (32)	Women (81)	Men (28)	Women (80)	Men (32)	Women (71)
Asian	5	3	1	5	4	16
Black	18	61	20	52	20	46
Latino	7	9	6	15	6	9
Native American	2	2	1	6	2	0
Other	0	6	0	2	0	0

graduate school competition even when they have strong grade point averages and good letters of recommendation (including letters from the MOST directors). This occurs despite the fact that sociological research consistently shows a low correlation between GRE scores and success in graduate school. Research also shows that as poor as the GRE is for predicting graduate school success for white students, it is an even weaker predictor of minority student success (Taylor 1991). We urgently need to persuade admissions committees to reexamine their admissions criteria.

In the first three years of the MOST Program, there have been more than a hundred applications each year (table 2). We could easily have filled programs in several sites with students who were as interesting and talented as those we finally selected. As part of their application, students write an essay describing an experience that has influenced them and evaluating their transcripts with an eye toward assessing strengths.

These essays reveal dimensions to candidates' academic and personal attributes that are not otherwise obvious. Students' assessments of their transcripts can reveal late bloomers and the ability to overcome and learn from their experiences. The selection committee looks for the spark of a sociological imagination in student essays and has been moved and impressed by many of the responses. For example, one student wrote:

> Certainly the reason I am interested in sociology is due to my very complex past. My two younger brothers and I were placed in foster care by our biological mother when I was nine. She was deserted by my father when I was still an infant and by her second husband after they had been married for nine years. Her family offered her no support. I suspect now that their racism had something to do with it. They were working class Irish Catholic. Both my father and stepfather had been Hispanic. One of my brothers went to live with his natural father in Texas. The other brother and I were eventually adopted by a Black woman and her mother—soon to become Mom and Nana. I am just one person, and a "success story" at that. Much as I despise it, I know very well that my high school administrators and the inept foster agency

Table 3. 1990-92 MOST program award recipients

	Black		Hispanic		Asian		Native American		Other		Total
	M	F	M	F	M	F	M	F	M	F	
1990	5	13	3	5	2	2	0	0	0	0	30
1991	6	15	1	6	0	2	0	0	0	0	30
1992	3	12	4	3	1	3	2	0	0	2	30
Total	14	40	8	14	3	7	2	0	0	2	90

point to me as an example of how well "the system" is working.
Perhaps more than anything else I refuse to let irresponsible people use
my experiences to exonerate themselves.

There is little that is routine about the selection process. Students who
are selected for the MOST Program come from diverse academic and
personal backgrounds (table 3). Their backgrounds later form the foundation from which their sociological perspectives grow.

Curriculum

Each institute is unique in its curriculum and program activities, drawing
on the strengths of the different sites and program directors. At the University of Wisconsin, Madison, for example, students enrolled in existing
summer school courses, but worked with departmental faculty in ongoing research projects. At the University of Delaware, we developed a
new core course offered only to MOST students—a six-credit course on
perspectives and methodologies of sociological inquiry with a focus on
race, class, and gender. Site directors do not force minority students to
study race, although, at Delaware, we found that race—along with gender and class—was the subject that interested students the most.

Although the curriculum for the MOST summer institute varies on
each campus, it always includes concentrated work in sociological theory
and research. Faculty are both minority and majority group members
who have a demonstrated commitment to minority scholarship and professional development.

Research Evaluation

In addition to annual evaluations of the program by participants, the advisory board is implementing a longitudinal research evaluation to determine the extent to which the undergraduate training project increases the
number of minority sociologists with Ph.D.'s. Students will be tracked
over several years through an annual questionnaire designed to measure

the effect of program support and other factors (educational and family background, financial need and support, mentoring and support systems, personal aspirations) on retaining them in sociological careers. Although data from the research evaluation are not yet available, they should provide a basis for analyses that will help in future program development.

MOST Delaware

It is no exaggeration to say that in the first two years both sites proved to be very successful, but work in the MOST Program requires intense commitment and extensive time from the site directors. We summed up our first-year Delaware MOST experience by calling it a "total institution" with little division between the staff and students. As codirectors, we designed and taught the six-credit course, served as professional and personal advisers to all thirty students (including, for some, in the years following the summer program), developed and administered two major guest lecture series, participated in field trips, managed the program budget, hosted students in our homes, and coordinated an enormous amount of administrative work (including student transportation systems, housing, meals, health care, computer installations in residence halls, and myriad other things).

Over the two-year run of the program, we had thirty students from across the country, representing major research institutions, small liberal arts colleges, state comprehensive universities, and historically black colleges. We designed a program structure with the idea of developing a course on the intersection of race, class, and gender; creating a community of scholars across cohorts with similar interests; showing different paradigms of sociological methods and theory; building student research skills, including computer applications and data analysis; assisting students in selecting graduate schools; discussing life after graduate school; and reflecting upon the contradictions of minority faculty life.

In the first year, we contained these efforts in a three-hour morning session that met five days a week and a two-hour computer lab (taught by a graduate assistant) that met twice a week. In the second year, the morning sessions were reduced to four a week and the computer sessions expanded to four afternoons a week. We made this change to integrate the data analysis and methodological instruction more completely with the theoretical and conceptual component of the course.

We coupled our instruction (by a black and a white woman) with a visiting lecture series that brought to campus (in the first year) nine nationally recognized scholars whose work was in race, gender, and class.

The purpose of the visiting lectures was to expose students to a variety of research topics and perspectives within the field. On the first day, the visitors gave a public lecture based on their research; on the second day, we asked them to speak to MOST students about their lives as sociologists and, in particular, their early moments of sociological awareness. (In the second year, we truncated the visits to one day and invited fewer guests; this sacrificed the informal time students and guests shared, but gave students more time to develop research proposals.)

Ethnic, gender, and class tensions were rarely an overt concern in either year. The directors had, after all, a stated mission to produce a supportive environment. In retrospect, we think we may have unwittingly downplayed some areas of conflict. Students did point out ethnic imbalances in reading lists, gender dynamics in the classroom (particularly male attempts to dominate discussions), and the intricacies of interactions across race, ethnicity, and class. In this volatile terrain, these were relatively safe critiques, often delivered with a measure of good humor. But we all avoided the raw emotions just below the surface of interethnic relations, building instead a close-knit community in the first year and a more reserved society in the second.

Emphasizing the community theme, we also involved student mentors, both graduate and undergraduate, who assisted with instruction, met informally with the MOST students, helped with social activities, and served as advisers, friends, and colleagues to the students.[6] The extensive use of students greatly facilitated the development of community and eased the faculty directors' workload.

In the first year, we discovered that we had an extraordinarily cohesive, mutually supportive group united by common interests and the common disadvantage of trying to find interesting things to do in Newark, Delaware, in the summer. They organized trips to New York, Washington, and Rehobeth Beach and gave parties at the drop of a hat. We also often heard of the continuation of classroom discussions in the residence hall late into the night. In the second year, a less cohesive, more competitive group learned basic computer skills with some abandon; they were usually impossible to reach by phone because they were constantly connected via their telephone lines to the mainframe computer! Some of them routinely relieved tension with nightly volleyball competition.

For all of us, the program was more work than we ever imagined. The directors gave up a great deal of professional and personal time. Still, it was one of the most satisfying experiences of our careers. The simple task of describing and hearing described why and how we became sociologists forced us to view the discipline in a new and exciting light. Issues of barriers and coping strategies, conflicts and accommodations produced a constant recentering. It was thrilling to work with a truly multiracial class in which black, Latino, and Asian students together challenged and articulated sociological concepts, research, theory, the faculty, and each other. We developed relationships with students who we knew would become, in many cases, lifelong colleagues.

It was thrilling to watch students move on to graduate school and report back on what they had learned. One wrote about his first semester in graduate school that "the most fun has come from being a T.A. . . . After class last week three students came up to me and told me how much they enjoyed my class. That really made me feel good!" Another wrote, "Among the many valuable lessons from my MOST summer is the broadening of my way of thought. I am now more conscious about including race, class, and gender in my writing, my reading, and my conversation." And another student wrote:

> I really appreciate all of the support and encouragement that you gave
> me during the summer. Not only do I feel that I have a greater
> command of sociology as a discipline, but I am much more confident in
> myself since participating in the summer program. The encouragment
> that I received during the summer is definitely reflected in my school
> work. I am much more vocal in classroom discussions and often refer to
> the wealth of knowledge that I received in Delaware.

The success of the MOST Program is apparent, even in these early and anecdotal indicators of the impact on students. But, along the way, we encountered many obstacles and problems that we had often not anticipated. We learned of the enormous need for administrative support to run such a program. The second year was much smoother, although no less demanding; by then, we had the good sense to hire an administrative assistant and we knew more about what to expect.[7] As a result, we scaled back our expectations; also, Margaret Andersen had been promoted to associate provost of academic affairs, making the delivery of administrative support easier (although it created even more demands on her time). We also hired an additional faculty member in the second year—Dr. Morrison Wong, who taught and coordinated all of the quantitative and computer-based instruction.

The problems we encountered are instructive and represent important points of departure for the future. We were warned ahead of time that institutional racism would be inevitable; unfortunately, this proved to be true. We also learned that it was very difficult to get any sector of the university community to understand that MOST was not a remedial program (after all, it involved minorities). This was most apparent when the university approved our request for computer support, but excluded modems; the assumption was that students would only need the computers for word processing, that is, learning how to write. Only after careful explanation that analyzing data from the mainframe was an important part of sociological instruction were we able to add modems to the students' equipment.

Indeed, to some nothing we did seemed to count as the "real" work of the university. Colleagues from the mathematics department, who held a summer school class in the same room in the period before us, explained that their class was important and asked that our students stand in the hall every day for fifteen minutes into our period while the math students had extra time. We could make up our lost time at some other point in the day, they suggested.

Notions of a remedial program were also common among our colleagues in the discipline, who in writing letters of recommendation for potential MOST students frequently wrote comments like: "I had this wonderful student in Sociology 101. Unfortunately he/she did not write a very good paper in the course. He/she could really use your program."

While the MOST students were well aware of these things, of more direct interest to them was the fact that many wanted to study the intersection of race, class, and gender and wanted us to provide a list of the best graduate programs where they could study all three. We soon discovered this was a short list—particularly if you add the stipulations, as the students did, of the presence of minority faculty and a prestigious program from which they would acquire strong credentials. And, if they further asked for programs focusing on race, class, and gender where senior African-American or Latina women were on the faculty, we often found we could make no recommendation at all. Thus, from the first day of students' attempts to identify potential graduate programs, we found the discipline, not the students, to be deficient.

The problem was further complicated by the fact that a number of students were interested in graduate programs with some "practical" focus (such as law, urban planning, or social work). They argued that they wanted to give back something to the communities from which they came. One student wrote that "as minorities, we cannot make . . . a distinction between research and service. Perhaps an increase in minority scholars will cause a shift in focus from aloof objectivity to educated compassion." We see this tension as contributing to the exclusion of minorities from sociology. Historically, people like W. E. B. Du Bois and Jane Addams have been excluded from the canon of great sociologists, in part because they advocated an activist, community-based approach rather than taking the more abstract, elitist, and theoretical approach

characteristic of academic sociology (Deegan 1988). This pattern continues in the present. We could only say that it is possible to combine academic study with applied work, but that, frankly, community involvement is usually devalued within the field.

The students saw sociology as providing the basis for understanding
their own lives and communities. One student wrote in the application
essay:

> Most of my years as a young child were spent in the East Los Angeles
> area, where I attended school with many other people of color:
> primarily Mexican-Americans . . . [but] my parents decided to move to
> South Pasadena: a place I considered as a neighborhood of rich, stuck-up
> white kids. I was extremely afraid of this move, as I knew that I would
> be one of only a few Chicanos at the school. . . . My family would
> drive through the neighborhood on the way to visit my grandmother—I
> would scrunch down underneath the windows so that no one could see
> me. . . . It was during this period in my life in which I established the
> way I interact with the world: I learned the art of observing. Coming
> from a lower class background into a world of the middle class, I was
> able to see their world from a different perspective than they did. The
> differences and inequalities that I noticed not only intrigued, but
> angered, me and this gave me a desire to study and question our society
> so that someday I might help change the injustices that exist. I am an
> observer: of people, interactions, institutions—and I am intensely
> interested in the existing state of society and the means through which it
> endures. Because of my experiences of marginality and being
> continuously labeled as an "other," I have attained the abilities of
> perceptive observation and reflection which I believe are vital to the
> discipline of Sociology.

Other students also wrote of the intersection of race, class, and gender
in their experiences and how it shaped their sociological imaginations.
For example:

> I was one of a tiny number of minorities at a private high school. There
> were two things that I knew intuitively as a child. First, that there was
> very little that was in my immediate control. Secondly, that it was in
> my best interest to be hypersensitive to people around me, to what I
> would now call their "norms and values." I could not help but make
> what I now realize are sociological observations about *everything*. I
> remember shortly after starting high school watching television as a car
> commercial came on and realizing that they weren't interested in selling
> to me or anyone who lived within a six mile radius of me. They were
> selling to the people I went to school with. That realization had a huge
> impact on how I understood issues of class and race.

This same student spoke in class of riding the subway from Bedford-Stuyvesant to the Upper East Side of Manhattan, where she went to school; she passed the time on the train by watching changes in the dress and demeanor of the people of different social classes entering and leaving the train at different stops. She continued:

> I am a good sociologist now (or hope to be soon!) because *it was a matter of survival for me as a child*. I might as well do what I did then and eventually get paid for it. Sociology for me is a way to have power in retrospect. (emphasis added)

Another student simply wrote, "Life is sociology!"

After leaving the program, the students continued to struggle with the expectations stemming from their location in the race, class, and gender system. Many of them came from working-class families who resisted the students' leaving home to attend distant schools for graduate education. The need to support their families often interfered with their education—a situation more often faced by minority and working-class students than others. One student who had to delay applying to graduate school wrote to us in the year after she participated in the program:

> By default, I am now the housekeeper at home (my mom is working at 2 jobs and there are no other females besides me and mom). It is amazing how housework can take up all your time. I am just so slow in the kitchen. It takes me all day to clean up and prepare dinner for the family. Although I sometimes feel my brain is wasted doing house chores, I know I am helping out my mom and that keeps my brain stimulated. It's just frustrating sometimes abiding to our gender segregated roles. To keep myself entertained, I analyze the situations around me and record them. It's rather interesting reading back my analysis.

One year later, she wrote again:

> I do plan to be in graduate school despite my brother's suggestion that I should delay it again. I think if I were to, I will always have to delay it for something. I figure while I'm still upset by the sexism and racism at home, I better go before I become too tired to get upset and angry.

We were honest with students about the problems they would face as minorities and as women in academic life, although we tried not to be discouraging. These students are young, bright, energetic, and mostly female. We know that many, despite their ability, will be permanent "ABD's" (i.e., all but dissertation) or will later have trouble getting tenure as faculty members. We know that as faculty, especially the women, they will have more committee assignments and heavier student advising, lecturing, and teaching loads than the rest of their colleagues. We know that the experience of getting tenure and promotion is sometimes so humiliating for women and minorities that it can feel more like a scarlet letter than a badge of honor. We struggled with how to encourage and support them, knowing we could not say, "Come on in, the water's fine!"

We do not have easy answers to these dilemmas. We still believe that just the increase in numbers of minority scholars—all else aside—will have the positive effect of easing the pressure on some individuals and has to make things better. But we also believe that we cannot rest on the laurels of a successful MOST Program—six weeks of intensive summer academic camp. We must individually be aware of the problems in graduate training in our discipline, demand change, and continue to push for faculty recruitment—particularly in the "best" programs where the future superscholars are trained. We are unwilling to wait for students to make a better world and believe this should become a priority for the faculty now.

Lessons for the Future

The sociology profession has a long-standing commitment to the inclusion of racial and ethnic minorities. Indeed, as we talk about our experience in the MOST Program, we find that colleagues in other disciplines are often envious of our relative success in producing minority scholars. Despite the success of MOST, we still find troubled times within the discipline, and we believe that the troubles we have seen have important implications.

To begin with, the study of race and ethnicity is still largely seen as a "special interest" in graduate programs of sociology, not part of the core content. (We suspect this is true in other fields, too.) Few graduate programs in sociology have taken the study of race, class, *and* gender as a central focus in their curriculum; this problem is particularly acute in the most prestigious graduate programs, where there is a noticeable absence of curriculum change and where minority faculty, particularly women of color, are rare. Academic elitism dominates, discouraging students with more activist orientations from entering the field. Moreover, we find that few faculty in any field have any graduate training in the subject of race, yet they are expected to build race into their courses, serve as advisers to students of color, consult with campus officials about racial conflict within the university, and be able to provide informed analyses of pressing social issues.

Finally, although most departments and universities have stated commitments to minority recruitment and retention and seem genuinely to want minority students in the discipline and in their departments, few question how standard practices and assumptions are institutionalized obstacles to the achievement of these goals. For example, the admissions chair in a prestigious program told us that one of our MOST students, who had been awarded a nationally prestigious Ford Foundation Fellowship to attend any graduate program in the country, was probably too "ideological," unappreciative of quantitative methodology, and naive about the academic world to be admitted to the program. (The student was the child of academic parents.)

In the end, recruiting and retaining minority students often have a lower priority than maintaining the status quo. If the disciplines are to become truly inclusive, transformation of their content and practices must be the first priority. Even with strong efforts to recruit minorities, if people of color do not see themselves and their commitments reflected in the content of what they learn, they are likely to become alienated and will be less likely to endure the demands and insults of graduate education.

Our experience indicates that multiracial education can be achieved and that it is possible for new communities of people to come together across the divisions of race, class, and gender. But we also found ourselves working within a discipline and an institutional structure that posed considerable obstacles to a more racially inclusive and just education. If universities and their graduate programs expect to increase minority participation significantly, they will be forced to change. Our experience in the MOST Program suggests both the problems and possibilities for that transformation. As a MOST student says, "Education by neglect doesn't sound that appealing anymore."

Notes

This paper reflects what we have learned from the Minority Opportunity Summer Training (MOST) Program, but could not have been developed without the dedication, friendship, and support of those on the MOST national advisory board. It is only through their collective, collaborative, and dedicated work over the years that this project has come to fruition; we thank Chuck Bonjean, Marion Coleman, Patricia Hill Collins, Clarence Lo, Lionel Maldonado, Cora Marrett, Matt Snipp, and Howard Taylor for their many contributions to this important project. We also thank the MOST students at the University of Delaware for sharing their experiences and ideas with us and for leading the way in transforming sociology so that it can become the inclusive discipline we hope it one day will be.

1. We realize that the term "minority" is problematic both because so-called minorities are often the numerical majority and because it minimizes the contributions and activism of people of color. We use it here because of the names of both the Minority Fellowship Program and the MOST Program.

2. Funding sources include the National Institute of Mental Health, the National Institute of Education, the Sydney Spivack Foundation, and the Cornerhouse Fund.

3. The original task force was chaired by Dr. Charles Willie of Harvard University.

4. The original subcommittee included Margaret Andersen, Charles M. Bonjean, Marion Coleman, Patricia Hill Collins, Bonnie Thornton Dill, Clarence Lo, Lionel Maldonado, and Howard Taylor.

5. The MOST advisory board currently includes Dr. Howard F. Taylor, chair, (Princeton University); Dr. Duane Alwin (University of Michigan); Dr. Margaret L. Andersen (University of Delaware); Dr. Charles M. Bonjean (University of Texas, Austin); Dr. Patricia Hill Collins (University of Cincinnati); Dr. Clarence Lo (University of Missouri, Columbia); Dr. Lionel Maldonado (California State University, San Marcos); Dr. Carole Marks (University of Delaware); Dr. Sylvia Pedraza (University of Michigan, Ann Arbor); and Dr. Russell Thornton (University of California, Berkeley).

6. Our student mentors included Evelyn Chaffin (B.A. University of Cincinnati, now a Ph.D. candidate at the University of Delaware), Rachel Levy (B.A. University of Delaware, now a Ph.D. candidate at the University of Connecticut), Ramiro Martinez (B.A. Southwest Texas State University, Ph.D. Ohio State University, now an assistant professor at the University of Delaware), Valerie Moore (B.A. University of Delaware, now a Ph.D. candidate at the University of Massachusetts, Amherst), and Teri Rosales (B.A. University of Minnesota, Duluth, M.A. University of Delaware, now a Ph.D. candidate at the University of Michigan).

7. Gail Brittingham, secretary for the Black American Studies Program at the University of Delaware, gave extraordinary administrative support to the program.

References

Blackwell, James E. 1987. *Mainstreaming Outsiders: The Production of Black Professionals*. Dix Hills, N.Y.: General Hall Publishing Co.

Deegan, Mary Jo. 1988. "W. E. B. Du Bois and the Women of Hull-House, 1895–1899." *American Sociologist* 19 (Winter): 301–11.

Elson, John. 1992. "The Campus of the Future." *Time* 139 (April 13): 54–58.

Epps, Edgar. 1989. "Academic Culture and the Minority Professor." *Academe* 75 (September–October): 23–26.

Higginbotham, Elizabeth. 1988. "Integrating All Women into the Curriculum." Working paper, Memphis (Tennessee) State Center for Research on Women.

Kahn, Sy. 1991. "Multiracial Organizations: Theory and Practice." *Liberal Education* 77 (January–February): 35–37.

Madrid, Arturo. 1992. "Missing People and Others." In *Race, Class, and Gender: An Anthology*, edited by Margaret L. Andersen and Patricia Hill Collins, 6–11. Belmont, Calif.: Wadsworth.

Taylor, Howard. 1991. "Standardized Testing in America: The Matter of Gender and Race." Lecture delivered to MOST Program, University of Delaware, June.

Walker, Alice. 1983. *In Search of Our Mothers' Gardens*. New York: Harcourt Brace Jovanovich.

Chapter 10

The Politics of Curricular Change: Establishing a Diversity Requirement at the University of Massachusetts at Boston

Estelle Disch

In the spring of 1988, when a professor of history at the University of Massachusetts at Boston (UMB) got to the section on Africa in her modern world history course, two white male students told her that they did not want to learn about Africa.[1] They argued that they did not believe that Africa had contributed much to civilization. Shocked and dismayed, she began to ask students what they thought the course was about. Many, some of them seniors, said her course was the first in their college experience in which they had ever studied a non-Western culture. A week of heated classroom discussion made it clear that many students failed to understand why they should learn about non-Western cultures since other courses did not address them; the absence of attention to world cultures in the curriculum had rendered the topic unworthy of study for these students.

The incident sparked this professor's commitment to explore ways to eliminate the accidental encounter with diversity that these students had found in her course and to assess the feasibility of requiring all UMB undergraduates to study diversity before graduating. Three years later, with the support of a large contingent of faculty, students, staff, and administrators, the Faculty Council passed a diversity requirement, the first universitywide curricular mandate in UMB history.[2] The requirement was designed to affect all undergraduate students entering the university starting in the fall of 1992. The passage of the requirement occurred after a three-year process of research into how other institutions had responded to this issue, discussion of the UMB context, educating our campus about diversity issues, and negotiating among various interest groups on campus.

The grass-roots strategy we used to gain support for the requirement evolved in large part from the diversity of the campus community. We sought support for the requirement from groups of people at all levels of the university, and we won its passage in spite of the fact that many people did not agree with what we were doing. We hope that our experience will be helpful even on campuses that evolve different strategies.

The Wider Context: Nationwide Curriculum Transformation

The passage of the UMB diversity requirement occurred after more than two decades of work on curriculum transformation across the United States. Sparked especially by the civil rights and women's movements, many colleges had established courses and programs in African-American studies, ethnic studies, and women's studies, and scholars and activists had written numerous critiques of Eurocentric privileged male scholarship.[3] In fact, by 1992, Margaret Wilkerson concluded that "few campuses have a totally exclusive curriculum—one that *completely* excludes the works of non-Western cultures and of people of color and women."[4]

By the spring of 1989, when a group of UMB faculty and staff began to discuss the feasibility of instituting a diversity requirement on our campus, some other colleges had already passed such requirements. We learned that the requirements were framed in several principal ways: a long list of diversity courses from which students chose a certain number; a specific required course (or small number of courses) focused on diversity; or the integration of diversity into widely required courses such as Western civilization or English composition.[5]

Keeping in mind examples of how other diversity requirements were framed, this initial group of faculty and staff expanded, became known as the Diversity Requirement Working Group, and set as its mission the passage of a UMB diversity requirement. We struggled intensely with definitions, rationales, possible designs for the requirement, and political strategies to secure its passage.

About the University of Massachusetts at Boston

In many ways, UMB was an ideal institution in which to work for this kind of curricular change. It is a young urban university (founded in 1964) with the largest proportion of students of color of any four-year campus in New England. Many of our faculty chose UMB because they wanted to teach in an urban context. About 14 percent of our faculty and 25 percent of our staff are people of color. We have one of the most physically accessible campuses in New England, and about four hundred of our students are people with disabilities. The average age of our students is twenty-seven. And faculty attitudes at UMB are progressive on several issues related to diversity when they are compared with faculty at 347 other colleges nationwide.[6]

There are numerous student organizations on campus that represent the diversity of our student body and support students from all five colleges. The Asian Student Center, Black Student Center, Casa Latina, Disabled Student Center, Irish Club, Women's Center, and Lesbian, Gay, and Bisexual Center, among others, provide meeting places and activities focused on issues pertaining to their particular groups. In the Center for Educational Rights a multicultural group of students work for educational justice. *Prisma*, a student publication, is a multicultural, multilingual magazine that serves as a forum for cross-cultural understanding.

Many faculty and staff in all five colleges have been involved in numerous diversity-oriented projects since the founding of UMB and the mission of several of the colleges made a diversity requirement a natural fit.[7] Various institutes on campus address diversity issues as well: the Trotter Institute focuses on the study of black culture; the Gaston Institute on Latino community development and public policy; the Joiner Center on the study of war and its social consequences; and the McCormack Institute on public policy in general (housing, etc.). The Urban Scholars Program brings inner-city high school students to our campus and establishes links between high school teachers and faculty. And the *Journal of Urban and Cultural Studies*, based in the College of Arts and Sciences, addresses diversity as a major focus. In short, there was already a focus on diversity here before we started to work on the diversity requirement. While we do not know the relative benefits of the UMB context compared to those of other colleges, we knew from the beginning that we would meet many receptive people as we began to discuss the requirement. But we also knew that there would be serious resistance.

The Center for the Improvement of Teaching is staffed with funding from the office of the provost and serves faculty from all five colleges.

Established in 1983, it was originally funded by a Ford Foundation grant to provide support to faculty who wanted to work on their teaching. When Esther Kingston-Mann, the professor of history I referred to at the beginning of this essay, was invited to direct the center in the fall of 1988, she decided to focus its work on the growing national concern about diversity. She chose the theme "Teaching About Differences" as the focus for the annual semester-long faculty seminar the following year and directed the Diversity Requirement Working Group from its beginning. When I served as interim director of the center for a year starting in the fall of 1989, I ran two conferences and several faculty forums on diversity issues, providing ways for all members of the campus community to get involved in diversity discussions. In 1990-91, when Esther Kingston-Mann returned as director of the center, she concentrated on refining the proposal for a diversity requirement and lobbying for its passage and I became coordinator for diversity awareness, offering educational workshops related to diversity on campus.

Definition of Diversity

The composition of the first diversity working group, convened in February 1989, was crucial in the framing of our definition of diversity. The ten people involved represented various races, ethnicities, social classes, religions, genders, and sexual orientations, and included the director of the campus Disabled Student Center. Early on we defined diversity broadly to include race, class, gender, sexual orientation, disability, age, and culture (defined as religion, ethnicity, national origin, or a combination of these). Although no school that we knew of had defined diversity so broadly, we became convinced that an inclusive definition would be right on our campus.

Academic Rationale

After numerous discussions of the various reasons why a diversity requirement should be instituted, we decided to emphasize the educational rationale as the one that we could most effectively discuss with our faculty. Political rationales (e.g., to help students learn to fight injustice) and personal or social rationales (to help students get along better with people different from themselves or to be less prejudiced or to help a wide range of students feel more welcomed to our campus) were not the basis for our case. We argued, instead, that diversity had to be studied because learning was incomplete without it, and that students' survival in the world would be more difficult without this knowledge. Noting that the increasing diversity of the U.S. population poses a challenge to everyone who lives here, the final proposal passed by the Faculty Council states that "our goal has been to establish the university as a place where students will acquire the analytical tools and knowledge necessary to survive, prosper, and contribute to a complex and changing world."[8] The proposal further argued that the requirement would "promote the understanding of the culture, experiences and viewpoints of groups who have not previously been considered a major focus of our curriculum."[9]

In discussing these issues, the Diversity Requirement Working Group agreed with Elizabeth Minnich that we needed to change "*what* and, just as important, *how* we think so that we no longer perpetuate the old exclusions and devaluations of the majority of humankind that have pervaded our informal as well as formal schooling."[10] We further agreed with Minnich that "that which is actively excluded from—or never makes it into—the curriculum is . . . almost certain to continue being devalued, seen as deviant and marginal at best."[11]

Although many members of the Diversity Requirement Working Group felt strongly that political and social rationales were also very important, the baseline of consensus among us was the educational rationale. We believe that choosing this rationale, along with our inclusive definition of diversity, helped our campus avoid the "political correctness" debate so common on other campuses and in the media.

The Diversity Requirement

As we grappled with our definition of diversity and the rationale we would use to argue our case, we were confronted with numerous challenges about the structure of the requirement.

The Pros and Cons of a Broad Definition of Diversity

We wondered whether our broad definition of diversity would effectively water down the requirement so much as to render it meaningless. We feared that if faculty were required to address all seven areas of diversity (race, class, gender, age, sexual orientation, disability, and culture) in every diversity course, they might feel overwhelmed by the list, unaware that the intersecting identities of most people would make simultaneous attention to several of these issues inevitable in many fields (e.g., the study of race would be impossible without careful attention to the intersections of class and gender, the study of gender impossible without careful attention to the intersections of race, age, class, and sexual orientation). Yet as we agreed to limit the number of areas addressed to a minimum of two, we feared that crucial issues could be ignored. Would racism be left out? Would many faculty not address sexual orientation, disability, and age, the three areas least addressed in courses on our campus?[12] Would faculty be committed enough to locate work by people who represented a wide array of cultural differences (e.g., work by disabled lesbians of color), thus making the task of inclusiveness easier and the reality of intersecting identities more clear? These questions will remain unanswered until we are able to evaluate the requirement.

The issues of power and inequality emerged over and over again in our discussions and challenged us to find ways to address them without provoking the political correctness debate. An early version of the proposal was inspired in part by our Board of Regents Policy Against Racism. This policy recommends that educational activities specifically address prejudice and discrimination and the effects of prejudice and discrimination.[13] Ultimately, the issue of power was left to the voices of the people being studied rather than stated as an explicit aspect of the requirement. Our goal was to legitimize forms of knowledge that have been marginalized, but we left the definition of those forms of knowledge to the faculty who would teach the courses. Many of us (including me) would have preferred more explicit language requiring attention to power and inequality, but the consensus of the working group was that the less explicit wording was more likely to be accepted. That part of the final proposal reads as follows:

> A major purpose of this requirement is to promote understanding of the culture, experiences and viewpoints of underrepresented groups who have not previously been considered a major focus of our curriculum. To the extent possible, course material should be selected that expresses the direct experience of these groups in their own voices.[14]

Structuring the Requirement

We worked closely with the office of the provost and consulted with the registrar about logistical and financial constraints. We needed to assess how many students would take diversity courses, and how many sections of what size courses we would therefore need, taking into account the fact that some students would transfer out before taking the course(s), and that others might take more than the minimum if the requirement were structured in an open way. We realized early in the process that developing a single required course for all students would be financially impossible. We needed a model that would not cost money at a time when the university's budget was being drastically cut by the state.

We decided to propose a system somewhat like that at the Amherst campus, in which a substantial number of courses would be flagged as diversity courses and students could choose among them. We decided to propose a two-course requirement, one course about diversity in the United States and one about diversity in other parts of the world, the latter to include courses that compare the United States to other societies. While we were not successful in getting this two-course requirement approved by our highest governing body, which agreed to "a course requirement," the College of Arts and Sciences, the largest on campus, did accept that proposal, and the College of Public and Community Service required more than two competencies (their course equivalent) for most of their students.

In an effort to assess how much faculty support we had for teaching to meet the requirement, we asked all full-time faculty whether they had an interest in doing so. By April 1991, sixty-five faculty from the Colleges of Arts and Sciences, Public and Community Service, Management, and Nursing had expressed interest in teaching courses under the proposed requirement. Many, in fact, were already teaching courses that addressed diversity directly. That number of faculty seemed adequate to begin implementing the requirement.

Quality Control

We faced trade-offs with the decision to develop a requirement that did not involve a single required course (or a small number of required courses). Some people in the Diversity Requirement Working Group were worried that there would be little or no consistency in what students learned and that the diversity requirement would look very different from one student to another. In order to monitor how courses would be taught, we decided to propose a universitywide certification committee that would approve both courses and faculty for the requirement; thus, particular teachers would be approved to teach courses they themselves had developed. We expected to choose/approve teachers based on their expertise in multicultural/diversity teaching. This proposal met with so much resistance (in fact, overt hostility) from faculty that we were forced to structure the course approval process in a looser way, putting control of the requirement in the hands of each college and losing the opportunity to monitor teaching effectiveness at the university level. The loss of this monitoring led us to an even deeper commitment to providing support and education for faculty (see more about this later).

Ease of Access for Students

Most of our students work off campus, many have families to support, and most try to arrange a compact course schedule and leave campus to go directly to work. Severe budget cuts were already limiting students' access to courses, and we did not want to make students' lives any more difficult than they already were. We decided, therefore, to propose that diversity courses be offered at all levels of the curriculum in order to make them as accessible as possible. Students would be able to take the courses as part of core requirements, general education, majors, minors, certificate programs, or free electives. Although this proposal was modified in some colleges in the final implementation, the College of Arts and Sciences accepted it as proposed.

What Is a Diversity Course?

Throughout our discussions, people wanted to know what the Diversity Requirement Working Group meant by diversity courses. We often cited as an example a professor of English who teaches a course on Shakespeare.[15] When he teaches *Macbeth* and *King Lear* he shows films of productions of each play in two countries (England and Japan in the case of *Macbeth* and England and the Soviet Union in the case of *King Lear*) to help students understand the cultural contexts in which the plays have been interpreted. He has students read a history of the role of black actors in *Othello* and examines how racism affected decisions about whether Othello would be played by a black actor. Students see the only film available in which a black actor plays Othello. They also examine how race is represented in productions of the play, including efforts to interpret Othello as not black. Thus the canon is taught with the goal of understanding different cultural responses to a single piece of literature, and racism is addressed. If an entire course were taught in this way, the Diversity Requirement Working Group agreed that it could count as an international/comparative diversity course.

A second example of a diversity course is a core curriculum course entitled "Self in Society," taught in the sociology department, that examines the impact of the social order on a wide range of people who are struggling for empowerment.[16] Autobiographical material is combined with sociological concepts and theory to help students understand the role of social context, particularly social inequality, in shaping people's lives. The autobiographical materials are written by women and men of various races, ethnicities, social classes, sexual orientations, religions, disabilities, and ages. A third example, "Modern World History," the course I referred to in the opening of this chapter, examines how the

Industrial Revolution transformed the world, generating new forms of social, economic, racial, cultural, and national conflict. Using primary source materials to trace the emerging struggles over political power, wealth, and the meaning of freedom and justice, students examine the history of England, Ireland, China, India, Nigeria, Russia/the Soviet Union, and Vietnam. The cultural contribution of each nation is presented, and readings focus on women and men from various social classes.

Faculty Support and Training

Teaching about diversity can be extremely challenging and sometimes very stressful for both faculty and students.[17] People who are in various ways privileged often resist looking at how their privilege is a product of a social order in which certain groups are marginalized so that those in the center can enjoy their privilege, however limited it might at times be. This resistance can block communication, and the conflicts that erupt in the classroom over these issues can be difficult to manage. In addition, privileged people often find the pain of those who have been marginalized difficult to grasp.

In order to address the need for faculty support and training, we made a commitment to offering ongoing faculty forums and coordinated a successful effort to get Ford Foundation funding for faculty seminars. These seminars help faculty grapple with curriculum transformation, finding new paradigms for making sense of the world once multiple perspectives are considered. The grant will fund one course reduction for a total of thirty-two faculty (plus four faculty workshop leaders) to work on courses for the requirement. The first seminar began in January 1992 with eight members. Three other seminars followed in consecutive semesters. These seminars will augment rather than replace the ongoing series of faculty forums we have been doing (described later).

Negotiating the Final Proposal

Once the Diversity Requirement Working Group had agreed about how the requirement should be structured and how we would argue for its passage, we developed a proposal and opened discussion of the issue in March 1990 with deans, faculty, and administrators who had not been directly involved in our work. Preliminary responses told us that the proposal would probably not pass as initially framed. Since a severe fiscal crisis that year had put all curricular matters on hold, we used the intervening time to negotiate changes in the proposal and to lobby for its passage. When it finally came up for a vote in May 1991, the Faculty Council approved the proposal with two crucial changes: the council approved "a course requirement" rather than two courses, and each college was empowered to work out its own way of meeting the requirement. The wording was such that if a college wanted to incorporate more than one course, it could.

What follows is a more detailed description of the relentless effort on the part of dozens of people to win the passage of the requirement at UMB, where, given our demographics and prior commitment to diversity, it perhaps should have been easier.

Support from the Top

From the beginning of our focus on a curricular response to diversity, the higher administration provided unwavering support. UMB Chancellor Sherry Penney funded two conferences (granting honorary degrees to prominent educators of color at one of them), stipends for summer curriculum workshops for faculty (for two summers), and additional guest speaker fees.

The office of the UMB provost (held consecutively by Betty Diener, Leverett Zompa, and Fuad Safwat) provided stipends for the first diversity working group, release time for an additional faculty member to work in the center (an unprecedented move, especially since release time was being severely cut as a result of the fiscal crisis), and an operating budget (for printing, a few guest speakers, etc.).

An Open Process

After the initial Diversity Requirement Working Group spent a semester investigating what other campuses were doing,[18] the discussion of diversity education at UMB was opened to our entire campus. In the early fall of 1989 the Center for the Improvement of Teaching sponsored a campuswide conference entitled "Towards a Multicultural Curriculum at UMass/Boston—A Working Conference for the UMB Community." About seventy-five people came on a Saturday to listen to students of color and gay and lesbian students talk about their experiences on campus. At the end of the conference, those present agreed unanimously that we needed a diversity requirement and that we should increase awareness of diversity issues on campus. As a result, the Diversity Requirement Working Group expanded to include anyone who wanted to work on the requirement (ultimately, about thirty people were involved in one way or another) and a Diversity Awareness Working Group with about eight members was formed. People volunteered to be part of the groups, everyone who volunteered was allowed to join, and we reached out individually to numerous people who were members of groups usually marginalized in the curriculum.

An Intensive Education Campaign on Campus

While the Diversity Requirement Working Group wrote and rewrote the proposal for presentation to the campus and lobbied key groups and individuals, an ongoing education campaign took place. In the spring of 1990, at a conference open to the public, thirteen students of different races, social classes, genders, sexual orientations, ages, disabilities, religions, ethnicities, and national origins each spoke for five minutes about how the university could respond more sensitively to their learning needs. The audience (close to two hundred people) listened carefully to what the students said, and many people were amazed that they had never realized how insensitive our campus can be for some people.

Faculty forums focusing on curriculum integration and classroom dynamics were run every few weeks for three semesters. These forums were led by members of our own faculty who had worked on curriculum transformation, members of the student support staff who could inform faculty about the needs of particular groups of students, students who were willing to serve as educators, and a few outside experts. The cost was minimal because UMB people were willing to do these presentations free. In fact, many people welcomed the opportunity to speak and were relieved to see forums on issues that they thought should be addressed in a public way.

The Diversity Awareness Working Group led twenty diversity awareness workshops in various units of the university during the two years prior to the passage of the requirement. A wide range of people attended (the campus police, the publications office staff, students in several courses, the staff of the campus radio station, the advising center staff, etc.). Occasionally people attended sessions because our presentation was on the agenda of a staff meeting or a class. We occasionally met some resistance in these sessions, but the reception seemed very positive overall. Most of the workshops were led by racially or culturally mixed teams. Depending on what a particular group wanted, we sometimes showed a videotape about diversity at UMB and at other times did experiential exercises with people to help them look at their own attitudes about differences.

Outreach to Students

Jean Humez, a professor of women's studies, helped a group of students produce a videotape about diversity at UMB that was shown in courses, in the diversity workshops, and in public forums.[19] The idea for the video was generated in our first conference, and students received course credit for producing it.

Before the passage of the requirement, the Student Senate passed a resolution in favor of it, and a group of students gathered six hundred student signatures in support of the requirement. No student spoke publicly against it before it was passed and the few objections we heard later were by single individuals.

Even when we were not directly lobbying for the requirement, we kept educating the campus about the issue. Several hundred UMB faculty, staff, and students appeared at one event or another during the two academic years prior to the approval of the requirement. Many attended numerous events, and a genuine community of people concerned about diversity began to develop.

Toward an Inclusive Curriculum

The way we have framed our diversity requirement will make major changes in our curriculum in several ways: (1) In some colleges, there will be courses focused on diversity at all levels of the curriculum and all departments will be invited to offer diversity courses. (2) As faculty deepen their discussion of diversity courses, they appear to be thinking about this issue even for courses that will not be designed to fit the requirement.[20] Based on my conversations with numerous faculty, I am convinced that most who develop one diversity course will inevitably become more sensitive to this issue in their other courses, even if they are not diversity courses per se. (3) We expect that as students begin to take the diversity courses, they will raise questions about diversity in other courses and their feedback will help deepen faculty skills in this area. (4) Although no diversity course will be required to address all of the seven areas of diversity named earlier, many faculty want to address all seven. (5) The diverse composition of the Ford-funded faculty seminars continues to build a multiracial, multicultural base of support for this work.

We believe that the structure we have developed will benefit all students. Students who have not yet grappled with diversity will, we hope, have a positive learning experience when they do. Students who belong to groups ordinarily marginalized and often invisible in the curriculum will know where to find courses that address at least some kinds of diversity. Students who enjoy this kind of learning will know how to find additional courses since all will be flagged in the course schedules and a list of diversity courses and sections will be provided each semester.

What We Have Learned

Margaret Wilkerson in a recent article recommends several strategies that can help move curriculum in a multicultural direction:

> First, any effort to change curricula must be based on sound intellectual grounds. . . . Second, there must be institutional support from the top administrator as well as from deans and department chairs. . . . Third, opportunities for faculty to attend institutes and forums must be created so that the careful, thoughtful work of transforming courses and curricula can be undertaken with colleagues.[21]

Our experience validates much of Wilkerson's advice. We had support from the top administrators, we based our argument on intellectual grounds, and we paid constant attention to the need for faculty forums and curriculum seminars. Our experience varies from Wilkerson's advice in that we did not have the active support of deans and department chairs in the beginning. Instead, we first worked on developing a broad base of support among faculty and students, and approached the deans later, after we had a proposal drafted. The dean of our largest college (thought by many to be the most powerful dean on campus), waffled in his support of the requirement before finally backing it just in time for the vote, only to undermine it once it had passed (calling it a social rather than an educational requirement, and delaying setting up the committees that would implement it). Along the way he had argued in support of college autonomy and the canon, and his voice represented a substantial minority of faculty.

Looking back over these three years of work, we have some advice about how to do what Wilkerson describes, along with some other suggestions for campuses working toward diversity requirements.

Mobilize faculty support. Find a group of faculty committed to preparing the intellectual rationale for the requirement, making sure it is as diverse a group as possible for your campus. Individually invite faculty who are already working on diversity issues to join you, even if they are too busy to attend regular meetings. See if they will read drafts of proposals, attend crucial meetings with deans, or sign support statements. One mistake we made was not to reach out individually to some very active multicultural educators on our campus. We were not excluding them, but some of them seemed to feel that they should have been explicitly invited to participate. Later we had to convince some of them to support the proposal—not because they were against the idea of a requirement, but because they had not been part of negotiating the compromises that occurred, thought we should have designed it differently, or simply felt excluded for lack of a personal invitation.

Since curricular change has to be enacted by faculty, it is crucial to build a broad base of faculty support. We used support from the top to effectively mobilize faculty input and, eventually, support for the requirement.

Get support from the top. Ask your administration for money for release time for a couple of organizers, refreshments at faculty forums, a guest speaker fund, stipends or release time for faculty willing to participate in curriculum transformation seminars, faculty travel to conferences addressing curriculum transformation, and so forth.

Mobilize staff support. Academic support staff have direct access to students' difficulties and can help educate faculty about what certain groups of students need (understanding the impact of various learning disabilities, the needs of students with certain physical disabilities, the shyness in class of some recent immigrants to the United States, etc.).

Listen to students and mobilize student support. In numerous educational forums (conferences, faculty forums, faculty-student dialogues), faculty and staff listened to students. Since many faculty do not find regular ways to listen to student experiences, these sessions had a powerful impact.

We stayed in close touch with student leaders through this whole process. We will need to continue working with students as the requirement is implemented and inevitable resistance emerges in order to hear student feedback and keep communication open.

Keep the issue alive. Run faculty forums and sponsor guest speakers. Use your own campus resources if money is a problem. Keep the campus aware that a group of faculty, staff, and students want curricular change. Keep offering ways that members of your campus can learn more — whether or not they support the idea of a requirement. Brown-bag lunches to discuss teaching in general can serve as a forum for diversity discussions and can offer support to teachers on other issues as well.

Do your best to sidestep the "political correctness" debate.[22] Diversity education can be argued successfully on educational grounds and on the basis of responding responsibly to a demographically changing world. Even if, as many of us believe, this should have been done long ago, the current demographics in the United States make denial of the importance of this issue much harder to sustain and defend.

In addition to making the argument for the requirement on demographic and educational grounds, we discussed diversity as a process of *inclusion*, rather than exclusion. We argued that marginalized groups and issues needed to be brought into academic discourse; we did not recommend that the "canon" (whatever that means on any particular campus at any particular time) be eliminated.[23]

Stick with it, try to stay cool when you are being attacked or think you are losing, be willing to negotiate, and plan to spend a lot of time. We were constantly amazed at the number of meetings we had to attend in order to get the diversity requirement passed. The usual governance meetings were the tip of the iceberg. Lobbying individual faculty members over long lunches and phone calls became a way of life. Attending college meetings, listening to feedback, rewriting the proposal and resubmitting it for further consideration were crucial parts of the process. Rather than bring the proposal up for a vote early on, we spent a year negotiating changes so that when it came up for a vote we had enough support to win.

Once it passes, don't think you are finished. Once the requirement was passed, our central governance body appointed an ad hoc committee to report on the progress of the implementation plans in our various colleges, and to offer assistance if requested. We learned in this process that it was extremely important to monitor what was happening, especially in those corners of the university where people in power were not fully in favor of the requirement. This ad hoc committee played a crucial role in moving the process along so that implementation plans were completed in time to start the requirement in the fall 1992 semester. We have come to see the passage of the requirement as a first step in a long process.

The Wider Context: Four Years Later

Since we began to discuss the feasibility of a diversity requirement in 1988, this issue has moved to the forefront of discussion on many campuses. A recent survey of administrators, mostly deans, found that the respondents named global affairs and the influence of cultural diversity as the two issues that would most influence curriculum in the nineties.[24] According to another recent survey, more than a third of 191 colleges and universities surveyed had some form of multicultural general education requirement. The authors conclude that the debate about multicultural education has shifted away from whether we ought to do it to how it should be done.[25] And a Carnegie Foundation report found that 46 percent of the colleges surveyed required a course in world civilizations; 20 percent required a course with racial or ethnic content.[26] As more colleges implement diversity requirements, more models are available for other campuses to study and emulate.[27]

Attention to pedagogy is also growing, as more teachers grapple with creative ways to address both the material and their students. Margaret

Wilkerson calls for "new ways of teaching and learning that acknowledge collaborative as well as individual learning."[28] Jerry Gaff argues that multicultural general-education courses "cry out for more personal, experiential, interactive, and collaborative kinds of instruction."[29] Other writers offer concrete suggestions for how to implement these kinds of abstract pedagogical suggestions.[30]

Finally, publications on multicultural curriculum development abound.[31] People who want to develop this issue on their own campuses will have more resources than necessary to get started, including advice about what *not* to do.[32]

The experience of the University of Massachusetts at Boston has been gratifying thus far. Now we have the opportunity to practice what we have worked so hard to be allowed to do — to reach *all* undergraduates instead of just those who happen to take courses with those of us who think multicultural learning is at the core of what a college education, and a humane world, are all about.

Notes

The following people provided helpful information or feedback as this article was being written: Rita Arditti, Arlene Avakian, Jeremiah Cotton, Robert Crossley, Gerry Gomez, Margaret Harris, Peter Kiang, Esther Kingston-Mann, Winston Langley, Susan Radner, Tim Sieber, Becky Thompson, and Sangeeta Tyagi.

1. The teacher was Esther Kingston-Mann, professor of history and American studies and current director of the UMB Center for the Improvement of Teaching.

2. Colleges ordinarily set their own curricular standards. There are only two other UMB requirements for graduation that apply to all our undergraduate colleges: 120 credits and a 2.0 grade point average.

3. The following journals, among others, have systematically addressed these issues: *Black Issues in Higher Education, The Black Scholar, Feminist Studies, Radical Teacher, Sage, Signs, Women's Studies International Forum, Women's Studies Quarterly.* See also the publications of the following: the Project on the Status and Education of Women of the Association of American Colleges, 1818 R Street N.W., Washington, DC 20009; the American Council on Education, Office of Women in Higher Education and Office of Minorities in Higher Education, One Dupont Circle, Suite 800, Washington, DC 20036; the Center for Research on Women, Clement Hall, Memphis State University, Memphis, TN 38152. See also the following books and articles, among others: Margaret L. Andersen, "Changing the Curriculum in Higher Education," *Signs* 12 (Winter 1987): 222-54; Barry Beckham, "Strangers in a Strange Land — The Experience of Blacks on White Campuses," *Educational Record*, Fall 1987/Winter 1988: 74-78; Charlotte Bunch and Sandra Rubaii, eds., *Learning Our Way: Essays in Feminist Education* (Trumansburg, N.Y.: Crossing, 1983); Lynn Weber Cannon, Elizabeth Higginbotham, and Marianne L. A. Leung, "Race and Class Bias in Research on Women: A Methodological Note," Research Paper 5, Center for Research on Women, Memphis (Tennessee) State University, April 1987; Laurie Crumpacker and Eleanor M. Vander Haegen, "Valuing Diversity: Teaching About Sexual Preference in a Radical/Conserving Curriculum," in *Change in Education: Women as Radicals and Conservators*, ed. Joyce Antler and Sari Biklen (Albany: State University of New York Press, 1989); bell

hooks, *Feminist Theory: From Margin to Center* (Boston: South End, 1984); Cherríe Moraga and Gloria Anzaldúa, eds., *This Bridge Called My Back: Writings by Radical Women of Color* (Watertown, Mass.: Persephone, 1981); Michelle Z. Rosaldo and Louise Lamphere, *Woman, Culture and Society* (Stanford, Calif.: Stanford University Press, 1975); Gayle Pemberton, *On Teaching the Minority Student: Problems and Strategies* (Brunswick, Maine: Bowdoin College, 1988); Paula S. Rothenberg, *Racism and Sexism: An Integrated Study* (New York: St. Martin's, 1988); Gloria T. Hull, Patricia Bell Scott, and Barbara Smith, eds., *All the Women Are White, All the Blacks Are Men, but Some of Us Are Brave: Black Women's Studies* (Old Westbury, N.Y.: Feminist Press, 1982); Barbara Smith, ed., *Home Girls: A Black Feminist Anthology* (New York: Kitchen Table, 1983).

4. Margaret B. Wilkerson, "Beyond the Graveyard: Engaging Faculty Involvement," *Change* 24 (January-February 1992): 59.

5. The University of Massachusetts at Amherst, for example, had recently passed a two-course requirement with courses designated as "D" ("diversity") scattered throughout a newly designed general education curriculum. Diversity was at first defined to focus on race, ethnicity, and gender, but the definition was later refined to focus especially on people of color and women in oppressed groups (i.e., a course addressing the experiences of privileged white women alone would not be defined as a diversity course). (Personal communication with Arlene Avakian, professor of women's studies on the Amherst campus, May 12, 1992.) William Paterson College had instituted a race and gender requirement that gave students a choice of three courses: "Justice and Racism," taught in African-American studies; "Women's Changing Roles," taught in women's studies; and "Racism and Sexism," co-sponsored by the two departments (and team-taught by faculty from both departments in the early years of the requirement). Race and gender were the primary topics, with attention also given to class and sexual orientation. (Personal communication with Susan Radner, director of the Race and Gender Project, William Paterson College, May 8, 1992; see also Paula Rothenberg, "Teaching Racism and Sexism in a Changing America," *Radical Teacher* 27 [1984]: 2.) In April 1988 Stanford University revised its yearlong (fifteen-credit) required course on Western culture to include works by women, minorities, and people of color and non-European ideas and values; the course was renamed "Cultures, Ideas, and Values." (Personal communication with Margaret Harris, coordinator of the Program on Cultures, Ideas, and Values at Stanford University, May 13, 1992. According to Harris, the definition of "minorities" was not specifically stated in the Stanford proposal but has in most cases been interpreted to mean ethnic minorities.)

6. While UMB faculty surveyed ranked the importance of increasing the number of minority faculty and administrators second only to the goal of intellectual development, faculty on other campuses ranked this issue twelfth. While 22 percent of UMB faculty reported having attended a workshop on women's or minority issues, only 13 percent of other faculty studied had done so. And 88 percent of UMB faculty reported approval of programmatic efforts to focus on cultural diversity. (Higher Education Research Institute, "National Survey of Academic Personnel," Research Brief 2.90 [Summer 1990], University of California at Los Angeles.)

7. The College of Public and Community Service has been dedicated to serving urban adult students since its inception, has a long tradition of involvement in community projects, and has the largest proportion of students of color and older students among the UMB colleges. By the time the diversity requirement was accepted by the university, the College of Public and Community Service already had a diversity requirement in place. The College of Nursing prepares students for work in urban and other multicultural settings and had already integrated attention to diversity into several required courses. The College of Management prepares students for work in national and international business. The Col-

lege of Education at the time was preparing undergraduates for work in urban schools. And the College of Arts and Sciences, although not specifically career-oriented, serves students who will work in all sorts of multicultural settings.

8. Diversity Requirement Working Group, "University-Wide Diversity Requirement, Approved by the Faculty Council, University of Massachusetts/Boston, May 1991" (University of Massachusetts Boston Center for the Improvement of Teaching, 1991), 1.

9. Ibid., 7.

10. Elizabeth Kamarck Minnich, *Transforming Knowledge* (Philadelphia: Temple University Press, 1990),1.

11. Ibid., 12.

12. Peter Kiang, "Faculty Attitudes regarding a Diversity Requirement at an Urban Public University," December 1989 (unpublished paper).

13. Commonwealth of Massachusetts Board of Regents of Higher Education, "Policy against Racism and Guidelines for Campus Policies against Racism," adopted June 13, 1989. The "Guidelines for Campus Policies against Racism" suggest "a program of educational activities designed to enlighten faculty, administrators, staff and students with regard to: developing an appreciation for diversity and pluralism; developing greater awareness of the multiple ways in which racial, ethnic, religious or cultural insensitivity and hostility may be manifested; ways in which the dominant society manifests and perpetuates racism; and learning ways in which to prevent and combat racism" (2).

14. Diversity Requirement Working Group, "University-Wide Diversity Requirement," 7. Other colleges have framed the power and inequality issues more clearly. For example, the guidelines for the State University of New York at Buffalo's required sophomore-level course entitled "American Pluralism and the Search for Equality" call for "intellectual awareness of the causes and effects of structural inequalities and prejudicial exclusion in the U.S. and the processes leading to a more equitable society" (State University of New York at Buffalo, American Pluralism Course Committee, "American Pluralism and the Search for Equality," 1990). And Haverford College, after evaluating a 1984 diversity requirement, decided to revise the requirement to focus on social justice and prejudice (racism, sexism, anti-Semitism, and homophobia). (Haverford [Pennsylvania] College, Educational Policy Committee, "Revision of Haverford's Diversity Requirement," December 14, 1989.)

15. Robert Crossley, Department of English, University of Massachusetts, Boston.

16. Taught by Estelle Disch, Department of Sociology, University of Massachusetts, Boston.

17. Estelle Disch and Becky Thompson, "Teaching and Learning from the Heart," *National Women's Studies Association Journal* 2 (Winter 1990): 68-78.

18. A high point of that semester was a visit to our campus by Paula Rothenberg, who gave a lecture on the diversity requirement she had helped to develop at William Paterson College and who met with members of the Diversity Requirement Working Group and other interested people.

19. The video is entitled "Acknowledge the Other One" and is available through the Center for the Improvement of Teaching, University of Massachusetts, 100 Morrissey Boulevard, Boston, MA 02125-3393; telephone (617) 287-6767.

20. For example, a course in which the primary focus is not diversity but where a module on diversity would work effectively and present a more complete view of the subject; a math course in which the data presented for analysis relate to diversity, such as income data for people of different races and genders.

21. Margaret Wilkerson, "Beyond the Graveyard," 62.

22. Paula Rothenberg, "Critics of Attempts to Democratize the Curriculum Are Waging a Campaign to Misrepresent the Work of Responsible Professors," *Chronicle of Higher Education*, April 10, 1991: B1, B3.

23. For a more complete analysis of how UMB avoided the debate on political correctness, see Esther Kingston-Mann, "Multiculturalism without Political Correctness: The University of Massachusetts/Boston Model," *Boston Review* 17 (May-July 1992): 30-31.

24. Jerry G. Gaff, "Beyond Politics: The Educational Issues Inherent in Multicultural Education," *Change* 24 (January-February 1992): 31.

25. Arthur Levine and Jeanette Cureton, "The Quiet Revolution: Eleven Facts about Multiculturalism and the Curriculum," *Change* 24 (January-February 1992): 25-29.

26. The Carnegie Foundation for the Advancement of Teaching, "Signs of a Changing Curriculum," *Change* 24 (January-February 1992): 51.

27. See, for example, the requirements of the University of Minnesota, Twin Cities campus; St. Cloud (Minnesota) State University; the University of California at Berkeley; the State University of New York at Buffalo; and the work of 63 colleges revising curricula in order to introduce students to the study of cultural legacies under the coordination of the Association of American Colleges described in Carol G. Schneider, "Exploring the Complexities of Culture," *Liberal Education* 77 (May-June 1991): 40-60.

28. Margaret Wilkerson, "Beyond the Graveyard," 62.

29. Jerry G. Gaff, "Beyond Politics," 35.

30. Lynn Weber Cannon, "Fostering Positive Race, Class, and Gender Dynamics in the Classroom," *Women's Studies Quarterly* 1 & 2 (1990): 126-34; Elizabeth Higginbotham, "Designing an Inclusive Curriculum: Bringing All Women into the Core," *Women's Studies Quarterly* 1 & 2 (1990): 7-23; Becky Thompson and Estelle Disch, "Feminist, Anti-Racist, Anti-Oppression Teaching: Two White Women's Experience," *Radical Teacher* 41 (Spring 1992): 4-10.

31. Here are a few additional references: Carol Ascher, "Recent Initiatives to Institutionalize Pluralism on Predominantly White Campuses," *Higher Education Extension Service Review*, Spring 1990: 1-9; Jacqueline Conciatore, "Teaching the Teachers about Racism and Sexism," *Black Issues in Higher Education*, July 20, 1989: 6-7; Paula S. Rothenberg, *Race, Class and Gender in the United States: An Integrated Study*, 2nd ed. (New York: St. Martin's, 1992); Ron Takaki, "An Educated and Culturally Literate Person Must Study America's Multicultural Reality," *Chronicle of Higher Education*, March 8, 1989: B1-B2; *Transformations: The New Jersey Project Journal* (all issues are focused on this topic); "Resource List on Teaching About Diversity," available from the Center for the Improvement of Teaching, University of Massachusetts, 100 Morrissey Boulevard, Boston, MA 02125-3393.

32. Roberto Haro, "Lessons from Practice: What Not to Do," *Change* 24 (January-February 1992): 55-58.

Chapter 11

Quaking and Trembling: Institutional Change and Multicultural Curricular Development at the City University of New York

Barbara Omolade

> *For colored people to acquire learning in this country makes tyrants quake and*
> *tremble on their sandy foundations.*

—David Walker

My 1964 Queens College graduating class had about twelve hundred students, thirteen of whom were African-American.[1] Five years later a student strike and shutdown at City College in Harlem initiated open admissions, and an influx of African-American and Puerto Rican students were admitted into the colleges that constituted the City University of New York (CUNY). Since those student-led struggles, the composition of the CUNY student body has been radically changed.

Today, CUNY, which encompasses eighteen colleges and graduate, medical, and law schools, "is a sprawling hodgepodge of 21 branches with some 200,000 students, the bulk of them poor and working-class people of every imaginable minority group" (Verhovek 1992). CUNY's student body is 32 percent African-American, 22 percent Hispanic, 10.5 percent Asian-American, and 35.3 percent Euro-American or white. Sixty percent of CUNY students are women. CUNY students represent more than eighty countries (Kleinfield 1992).

On the surface, CUNY seems to be an ideal location for a truly multiethnic faculty and multicultural curriculum. New York, one of the most ethnically diverse cities in the world, is an intellectual, cultural, and financial center and port of entry for people from all over the world.

214

Nearly every major writer, thinker, artist, and world leader has visited or lived in the city.

Many of the CUNY colleges are located in internationally known communities. City College is in Harlem. Medgar Evers College is in Crown Heights, Brooklyn, the center of the largest community of people of African descent outside of Africa. The Borough of Manhattan Community College is only blocks from Chinatown and Little Italy. Queens College is near developing communities of Korean, Vietnamese, Pakistani, and Indian immigrants. Brooklyn College is close to an old and established Jewish community.

In spite of the vast community and student resources that could facilitate a multicultural, multiethnic, and nonsexist university, most knowledge being produced and reproduced in CUNY classrooms reflects the Western, male, and elite traditions common to most American colleges and universities. In the past decade CUNY has made many attempts to create a multicultural presence in its course offerings, to foster an atmosphere of racial and ethnic tolerance, and to improve opportunities for the advancement of men and women of color into administrative positions, but its senior faculty of white men has continued to dominate teaching and research.

Higher education, particularly at public colleges like CUNY, is the site of political contention between ethnic groups, races, classes, and sexes for power, money, and status. That this struggle is located in the academy among the intelligentsia does not diminish its resemblance to community, political, and workplace struggles by people of color and white women for dignity and power.

The social movements of the 1960s, along with open admissions and affirmative action policies, removed the last major legal barriers to women and people of color entering the university. Many white male faculty and administrators at CUNY are political "liberals" who were active in those movements, when white women and people of color were marginalized in the academy. During the 1970s, however, the site of college political struggles changed from struggle for admission to one of transforming the academy from within. White women and people of color are at present *inside* the university demanding equity and the power to shape the production of knowledge to better represent their perspectives and experiences.

Since 1981, I have been a counselor, administrator, and adjunct instructor at the City College Center for Worker Education, an off-campus evening college program for about eight hundred working adults. Working closely with white male City College senior faculty to establish and manage the center for students who are mainly African-American and Latin women has offered me a unique opportunity to examine firsthand the intellectual, pragmatic, and political difficulty of transforming the production of knowledge. My experiences at the center, a microcosm of the university, have been matched by my involvement in systemwide CUNY activities. I have helped to organize grass-roots initiatives such as the Friends of Women's Studies and the Medgar Evers College Center for Women's Development. I have also been consultant and adviser to two vice chancellors of academic affairs and served on the Task Force for Balancing the Curriculum for Pluralism and Diversity, which investigated the status of ethnic and women's studies and affirmative action hiring in all CUNY units.[2] My scholarship, writings, and teaching about African-American women have enabled me to conduct workshops and seminars to help CUNY faculty integrate race, class, gender, and ethnicity into their teaching.

It is interesting to me as a social scientist that there is an absence of critical discussion both within and outside CUNY about its experiences with curriculum change and affirmative action. I am writing, therefore, as a participant-observer within the CUNY system seeking to make sense of my experiences and the efforts of others to change the university.

The central concern of this essay is the struggles of white women and people of color to critically participate in teaching and transforming the existing knowledge base. I argue that there can be no multicultural curriculum without a multiethnic and diverse faculty with expertise in African-American, Caribbean and Latin American, Asian, and Native American studies and women's studies. I address these issues with a description of campaigns and struggles by women to directly confront the university's power structure and an analysis of the political impact of these struggles on African-American men and women. Three pivotal struggles in CUNY within the past decade—the Melani suit, the curriculum change work of the Friends of Women's Studies, and the sit-in at Medgar Evers College—illuminate the difficulties and successes of "grass-roots" organizing by both black and white women. During the same time period, although black men and women in the CUNY African American Network (CAAN),[3] the Lion's Rock Network,[4] and other organizations as well as in the Medgar Evers College struggle have continued to challenge the racial and gender stratification of CUNY and its faculty, the Leonard Jeffries "issue" and the continual marginalization of black women in the curriculum and faculty highlight the ways black scholars and scholarship are specifically undermined.

The Woman Question

In 1973, twenty-five white women faculty members from most of the university's colleges initiated a class action suit (Melani et al.) charging CUNY with sex discrimination in the hiring, promotion, and tenure of women (McFadden 1983). Because women were limited to the lowest ranks of the professoriat, they were paid an average of $2,000 less than men, took on average one and a half years longer to be promoted, and retired with smaller pensions (*CUNY Women's Coalition Newsletter*).[5] In 1990, "a federal judge ruled that CUNY had discriminated unlawfully against women on its teaching staff for 15 years and a settlement of $7.5 million dollars was distributed to women faculty for past inequities" (McFadden, 19).

The Melani suit forced the university to increase the hiring and promotion of women. Women are now 37.9 percent of the full-time faculty, while the entire number of men and women of color in full-time faculty positions adds up to only 21.6 percent: black 11.7 percent, Hispanic 5.6 percent, and other (Asian/Pacific Islander, American Indian, Alaskan Native) 4.3 percent. Although a decade later white males still dominate the highest levels of the professoriat, the suit helped white women to move into faculty ranks at higher rates than women and men of color.[6]

Their advancement was further facilitated by the decision of women's studies leaders to organize women's studies as programs rather than departments. They seem to have learned from the experiences of African-American studies and other fields that faculty who teach in departments of disciplines based on the "new knowledge" are more vunerable than programs to the fiscal and political power of often hostile faculty councils.[7] Rather than struggle for departments "of their own," wresting funds and recognition from senior faculty, white women faculty members receive tenure and promotions in traditional disciplines and departments by proving their competence in white male Western intellectual traditions and thereby gain recognition as "legitimate" scholars. They can, then, choose to struggle against sexism and marginalization within traditional departments while maintaining a semiautonomous space in women's studies programs. Although the feminist scholars among these women continue to challenge and critique the gender bias of the traditional disciplines, all women faculty members, almost always white, can work effectively in both the "old" and the "new" disciplines without losing professorial rank.

Although positioned between white male sexism and racial privilege vis-à-vis faculty of color, white women are at least on college faculties.

The Melani suit was won because of the systematic discrimination against white women who were in entry-level positions in many departments in the university. Men and women of color have had little opportunity to be chosen for such positions.

Having turned their position to advantage, women's studies faculty have successfully led efforts to transform the CUNY curriculum to include gender-related issues, initiated systemwide efforts to reach faculty, and pushed for greater integration of information about women of color into course content. In 1983, the Hunter College Women's Studies Collective, made up of a core of women faculty, wrote *Women's Realities, Women's Choices*, the first basic textbook for introductory women's studies courses. These efforts led to the "Hunter model" for integrating the new scholarship on women into the curriculum. Women's studies faculty at Hunter gained support from the president, deans, and department chairs to sponsor a yearlong faculty workshop. Faculty representatives were expected to change the syllabi and teaching in the introductory courses in their various disciplines and then take suggestions and ideas back to their departments. Professor Dorothy Helly, former director of women's studies at Hunter College, explains, "The supportive administration which kept a relatively low profile in order to allow faculty to deal with the issues on a peer level was the key to this approach" (see Hunter College Report 1987).

The Struggle at Medgar Evers College

While Hunter College women's studies faculty were conducting faculty development seminars and writing their textbook, faculty and students at Medgar Evers College were facing another kind of challenge. The college "employs and serves the largest concentration of Black females in the CUNY system" and is located in a community "where over 50 percent of all households are headed by females." Two-thirds of the students at the college are black and female, and 69 percent of them are single mothers (McLaughlin and Chandler 1984: 6).

On April 20, 1982, faculty and students "began a peaceful sit-in at the president's office, demanding his ouster, quality education, and an end to the racist and sexist policies of the CUNY Board of Trustees" (ibid.: 7). Appointed in 1971 over the objections of the community-based planning committee for the establishment of Medgar Evers College, the president had done little to assure the college's growth and development. Many charged the president with allowing Medgar to be stripped of its four-year status during a 1976 budget crisis to become a hybrid community college that also offered many baccalaureate degree programs. The president's unwillingness to address and discuss student and faculty concerns prompted the three-month sit-in, "the longest student takeover in the history of the United States." Students charged the president with

> generating anti-community sentiment and suppressing the academic
> freedom of students and faculty, . . . misusing grant funds, failing to
> advocate construction of an adequate physical plant, opposing Black
> Studies and childcare at the College, changing its mission to one of
> remediation, failing to have a program of academic challenge for
> exceptional students, and continuing a pattern of harassment and
> intimidation. (ibid.)

The Student-Faculty-Community-Alumni Coalition to Save Medgar Evers College, which organized the sit-in and related activities, was led by black female faculty, students, and community members. Both the college and the community were accustomed to black women who strove for education for themselves and their families in spite of their problems with "insufficient child care facilities, shortages of decent affordable housing, domestic violence . . . and inadequate financial resources." Black women in the coalition were a "determined sisterhood" who "linked the anti-racism struggle of the black movement to the anti-sexist struggle of the women's movement" and challenged the CUNY central administration and Board of Trustees (ibid.: 8).

The sit-in received national attention and gained support from a wide range of student, feminist, and community organizations. A support group of white women students and faculty at Brooklyn College was formed, and the national, state, and local black elected officials serving Central Brooklyn called for removal of the president. The trustees' effort to enjoin the sit-in was defeated in court (ibid.: 9). Student activists conducted an effective media campaign and learned to articulate their demands to powerful board members and central office administrators while informing and rallying their fellow students. The coalition was forced to organize the graduation ceremonies and summer school because the president left the college shortly after the beginning of the sit-in.

On July 6, 1982, the president resigned and a new day dawned when his office was transformed into the Baker/Romain Child Development Center, a child drop-in center that subsequently became a Head Start program. Women students, staff, and community members from the coalition soon opened the Center for Women's Development, the only university women's center initiated by black women students and faculty and directed by a black woman. In 1989, also as a result of the coalition's efforts, the college moved to a new building and campus from its shabby former location in a factory and hundred-year-old high school.

Some coalition members believed that the crisis at Medgar Evers College influenced the CUNY Board of Trustees appointment of Joseph Murphy as chancellor because of the failure of the acting chancellor and vice chancellors to contain the sit-in. Among Murphy's first appointments was the late Marguerite Ross-Barnett as the first African-American woman vice chancellor of academic affairs.

Although she held this position for only three years, Ross-Barnett was important to the development of two independent, grass-roots women's organizations: Friends of Women's Studies and the Lion's Rock Coalition. She also developed several task forces to review and assess the status of black studies and women's studies. Ross-Barnett was effective in balancing the desires of the black and women's communities for an advocate with meeting the expectations of the university's highest academic office.

Friends of Women's Studies

In 1983, Vice Chancellor Ross-Barnett met with two African-American women from the Medgar Evers College struggle: faculty member Safiya Bandele, director of the newly founded Medgar Evers College Center for Women's Development, and me. We wanted to know how she intended to help black women at CUNY. Ross-Barnett brought the Hunter College feminists and the Medgar Evers College feminists together by asking Dorothy Helly, professor of women's studies and history from the Hunter College Women's Studies Collective (who was at the time working with Ross-Barnett), to meet with us and suggested we organize a meeting of representatives from the women's studies programs and centers of the CUNY colleges to survey their work.[8] The vice chancellor called on college presidents, board members, and department chairs to support the first formal meeting about women's studies to be held at CUNY.

The major outcome of the 1984 meeting was the beginning of a CUNY women's organization, Friends of Women's Studies, which because it was open to all women regardless of rank was more like a community-based grass-roots group than a typical university organization. Full-time faculty members, adjuncts, administrators, and students participated together. The organization had little to do with promotion, tenure, career mobility, or campus and departmental politicking. Like feminist consciousness-raising groups, the organization provided its members with support and encouragement. Women faculty trying to initiate Women's History Month programs, needing help to develop women's courses, or strategizing to gain support for women's studies benefited from the informal approach. Adjunct instructors, administrators, and students also had an opportunity to voice their concerns about working conditions and student life. Friends of Women's Studies operated like a political action committee for women staff and faculty when it sponsored formal meetings such as a forum with CUNY women presidents and advocated for women's studies programs and women's centers. Although it was under the aegis of the CUNY office of academic affairs, which provided support for mailings, no one from that office influenced its activities. Without paid staff or budget, Friends was run by a core of volunteers.

In 1985 the Friends of Women's Studies and other women's groups sponsored a systemwide conference on gender and race that focused on balancing the curriculum and teaching. In 1987 representatives from Friends requested that the chancellor support the "All Women's Studies at CUNY Faculty Development Seminar," which encouraged faculty to explore "issues related to gender as it intersects with race, ethnicity, and class" and "recent scholarship about women which emphasized the issues of diversity."

At the same time, the CUNY office of academic affairs was funded by the New York State Vocational Education Act (VEA) for a faculty development seminar and conference to examine gender balancing in academic vocational programs within CUNY's community and technical colleges.[9] Since it was apparent that faculty in these colleges also needed to revise their teaching and syllabi to balance for race and ethnicity as well as gender, the academic affairs office joined the VEA seminars to the seminar sponsored by the University Faculty Development Program. Professors Dorothy Helly and Marie Buncombe and I led this joint 1987–88 faculty development seminar and in the spring of 1988 coordinated a systemwide conference entitled "Integrating the New Scholarship on Gender, Ethnicity, Race and Class into the College Curriculum."

In order to prepare for the faculty development workshops, Helly and I spent the summer of 1987 developing curriculum for the seminar: ten to twelve sets of readings on the themes of language, creativity, family, work, sexuality, health, education, religion, and difference were prepared for distribution to seminar members each week. Most readings focused on gender, feminist perspectives, and women's experiences. When Professors Joan Tronto and Altagracia Ortíz led the 1990–91 University Faculty Development Seminars, sessions on AIDS and colonialism were added. Seminar members led the weekly discussions, often adding information and concerns from their own experience and scholarship. An outside speaker occasionally attended the sessions.

After 1988, the VEA-funded faculty development seminars were separated from the university group because community college faculty teach more courses and have less release time than faculty in senior colleges. I cofacilitated the VEA seminars with Helly until 1990. About forty faculty members have attended the VEA workshops: ten black women, five Latinas, two white men, and the rest white women.

All seminars are led by a woman of color and a white woman and are a model of feminist, nonracist, and nonhierarchical academic work. The readings and discussions offered participants new information about race and gender and the experiences of women that challenged their experience and training. Leaders learned that faculty members typically find it difficult to admit their intellectual inadequacies and limitations. The seminar leaders try to present and discuss new information in ways that encourage participants to discover their own best ways to integrate the material into their work. The goal is to create a group of faculty on each campus who, after completing the seminars, will support efforts to introduce new courses or programs reflecting and including knowledge about race, gender, and ethnicity.

Although the seminars have helped many faculty members become familiar with the new scholarship, involvement with the seminars changed the Friends of Women's Studies organization. Most of its activist initiatives—the race and gender conference, the panel with CUNY women college presidents, its meetings about the difficulty in organizing women's courses and programs—occurred before the faculty seminars were initiated. From a broad-based group concerned with the issues of all CUNY women staff and faculty, Friends became more focused on the interests of its members who were full-time faculty, all of whom were white. Many of these women became participants in the first faculty development seminars, which increased their familiarity with scholarship about women of color and enhanced their work in campus women's studies efforts.

The activist thrust of the early years of the Friends of Women's Studies gave way to working for curriculum change. Some might argue that this is also activism because seminar participants were expected to become "change agents" on their campuses and help colleagues transform and reshape their course offerings and pedagogy. Before the seminar, however, black and white women adjunct faculty, black women administrators, and white women full-time faculty members were developing a common feminist practice that viewed curriculum change as only one aspect of changes needed in the university.

The seminars changed all that because participants in the university program had to be tenured faculty recommended by their departmental chair. These requirements split the organization's membership. Members who were adjunct instructors and administrators were excluded from the seminars. Participants in the VEA seminars also had to be faculty members who were recommended by the provost of their college and the chair of their department. After the development of the seminars, the Friends of Women's Studies failed to thrive, but a group of women—former members of Friends—started the Women's Political Action Group to address general issues of concern to women students, staff, and faculty members.

Between a Lion's Rock and Hard Places: Ironies of Being Black and Female at CUNY

Ironically, although I cofounded the Friends of Women's Studies, codeveloped the curriculum for the seminars, and facilitated the VEA faculty development seminars for several years, I do not qualify to participate in the seminars because I am not a member of the full-time faculty. In spite of the prominence of black women like me in the development and leadership of these efforts, black women are barely present in the teaching faculty of CUNY colleges. Most black women faculty members are confined to low-status roles at so-called minority campuses such as Hostos or Medgar Evers College or in the remedial and special departments where they are stereotypically expected to be found. Black women are also more likely to teach in the community colleges than in the four-year colleges or graduate schools.[10]

It has been easier for black women to become administrators and staff members than to become members of the faculty. This follows a national trend: black women usually work in public-sector service positions, administering agencies or programs that help poor and disavantaged people. In CUNY, black women work as secretaries and administrators in admissions, registrars', bursars', and financial aid offices. They are counselors and department secretaries. This form of "mammification" of black women's labor—while it offers more status, a higher salary, and different tasks than the demeaning work of their domestic foremothers—reifies a similar social relationship to power.

Black women support but do not participate in the major work of the university, the production and reproduction of knowledge. Black female staff can advance into administrative positions with high levels of responsibility. During the past decade there have been two black female vice chancellors of academic affairs and there are now two black women college presidents, yet these highly visible and powerful women only highlight, by contrast, black women's lack of voice in the professoriat.

Michele Wallace, a professor of English at the City College of New York, writes about this phenomenon:

> I would like to propose that the lack of black female power in academic fields of knowledge production like literary criticism (of course, the same is even more true of anthropology, history, linguistics, and so on) participates . . . in this hegemonic scheme . . . in which black women, as a class, are systematically denied the most visible forms of discursive and intellectual subjectivity. (Wallace 1990: 215)

The handful of black women with top-level positions, managers of institutions and units, have great authority and status, but little power over either the requirements or course offerings that directly affect student learning. Hence, although black women are the second-largest cohort group of all undergraduate students in the senior college, a black woman student can be admitted to the college by a black woman, be counseled by a black woman dean, have a black woman president of the college, but never be assigned to read a book by or about black women or be taught by a black woman faculty member, and cannot expect to do any significant or in-depth research about black women.[11]

While it is true that the numbers of black women with doctorates in traditional disciplines or in black studies are few, the many black women who work at CUNY as administrators, teachers in special programs, lecturers, and adjunct faculty are rarely tapped for faculty positions in spite of their graduate work. Although many of the present senior faculty earned their doctorates *while* they were teaching in college, this practice was discontinued when open enrollment and affirmative action were introduced into CUNY. It would be possible to reinstate this practice, to hire black women and other faculty of color without doctorates and provide them with mentoring and support to complete their Ph.D.'s and then retain them on the faculty in tenure-track positions. It is also necessary to recognize in terms of promotion and raises the additional extra-academic work that faculty of color perform in mentoring and supporting students of color. The rates and ways black women are hired to the CUNY faculty have been a litmus test exposing racial-gender stratification within the university.

In order for meaningful curriculum change to take place, black women scholars and scholarship must be simultaneously included in the production and reproduction of knowledge. If new scholarship is to become a legitimate part of the academy, its bearers must be recognized and subsidized in much the same way that colleges and universities treat and reward natural scientists making ground-breaking experiments in laboratories.

Two Leonards

In 1973, two men named Leonard met at a City College (CCNY) reception for newly promoted professors. Leonard Kriegel, a self-described "faculty Everyman" and a "typical New York Jewish literary intellectual" had completed a ten-year climb up from instructor to full professor in the CCNY English department, casually met Leonard Jeffries, the newly named chair of black studies, appointed to that position with tenure and full professorship (Kriegel 1992: 142). He asserts that Jeffries was hired without a track record of notable scholarship or prominence as an academic, solely because he was a black man with a Ph.D. — "his promotion predicated on dark skin and a rhetoric designed to uplift blacks."

In hiring Leonard Jeffries as he did, President Robert Marshak merely responded to the absence of African-American studies and faculty in the professorial ranks of his college and to an enraged African-American community demanding black studies. At the time Jeffries was hired, there were virtually no African-American or Africana studies departments in the country, no opportunity for graduate studies or for publishing scholarly work in the discipline. This is the real indictment against the university that should be considered, not the hiring of a black man who did not come up through ranks that at the time were closed to him and his discipline.

The notoriety of Jeffries's controversial 1991 speech[12] obscures the legitimate difficulties that faculty of color face at CCNY, with its 77 percent mainly middle-class and middle-aged white men who were educated and received their doctorates and first jobs in the college just before the emergence of the disciplines of black studies, women's studies, Caribbean and Latin American area studies, Asian studies, and gay and lesbian studies.

Black studies, the first of these newer disciplines, entered the academy at gunpoint, amidst shouts of militant protest. Pushed by extra-university forces and the newness of the disciplines, presidents and provosts initiated new departments and were forced to hire faculty outside the usual process. "A Tale of Two Leonards" is Lenny Kriegel's view of Leonard Jeffries's lack of credentials and their college's "sin against the intellect" in hiring Jeffries, an "unproven" black scholar, with tenure. But nowhere in Kriegel's tale do we hear about the sin against the intellect of black people and other people of color committed by a professoriat that continues to systematically sidestep the challenge of the new knowledge. Because Jeffries can be dismissed as a messianic anti-Semite hired only because he was black, the intellectual work and worth of all faculty of color (who are not anti-Semitic) can be dismissed and brushed aside by charging "lack of credentials."

It is important to keep in mind that faculty of color, like Jeffries, are trained scholars who have expertise in *two* disciplines. Along with their white counterparts they have completed doctoral studies in traditional disciplines. They have also constructed disciplines about the hidden knowledge and experiences of formally enslaved, colonized, and marginalized populations. Curriculum transformation has been attempted by scholars who have maintained or developed critical stances toward the canon they had been taught and socialized to master.

Traditional disciplines universalize and mute the class, race, and gendered perspectives and experiences of the scholar and subject, while the new disciplines identify the subject and the specific cultural experiences and perspectives of the people they are studying. The new disciplines attempt to create new methodologies and approaches more connected and respectful of people's actual experiences. They challenge racism and other beliefs that distort and dismiss the experiences of people of color and women. Departments based on these concepts are expected to operate like well-endowed disciplines such as English and history.

Focusing on the extremes of Jeffries's position, posture, and hiring lets the faculty, the university, and the community ignore the real issues of white power. University representatives can then "allow" the media to trivialize and sensationalize Jeffries's views, further ignoring the legitimacy of his scholarship and his charges of white racist control of knowledge. This media coverage further derails the work of creating a discipline like black studies because white senior faculty members can continue to justify their ignorance of the classic texts, issues, and content of scholarship by and about people of color. Few of them even know or care whether Jeffries's views represent the center or the fringe of Africana studies.

This fundamental contention between the dominant intellectual culture of the university and marginalized voices and cultures is the subtext of "The Tale of Two Leonards." It explains a great deal about the social context and conditions that fostered the public rage of Leonard Jeffries and the private cynicism and anger of other CUNY faculty of color. Their fight for legitimacy and power is the text in which multicultural curricula and affirmative action debates and efforts are grounded at CUNY. For if black people, for example, cannot name and describe their own lives and experiences in their own "intellectual" way without censure, then what is the meaning of multicultural, anyway? As long as faculty from the dominant intellectual culture continue to set the definitions of intellect, "sin," and credentials, faculty from the dominated intellectual cultures are expected to comply. It seems hypocritical and beside the point to decry Jeffries's anti-Semitism without also crying out against the obscenity of ignoring and obliterating the intellectual culture of people of color and their scholars.

It is significant that few male senior faculty members have attended the faculty development seminars initiated by Friends of Women's Studies or other groups in the university. The CUNY faculty pride themselves, somewhat paternalistically, on their ability to offer working-class students a college education equal to that offered in elite colleges. Granting these students access to the finest Western intellectual traditions is viewed as a way for them to overcome prejudice and bias against the intellectual abilities of stigmatized and immigrant groups. Many of these faculty members, themselves the children of working-class ethnic immigrant parents, were ostracized from the academy because it was viewed as the exclusive privilege of the native white populations of elite Anglo-Saxon Protestants. Quotas often prevented Jewish and Catholic students from even attending many colleges (see Gorelick 1982; Steinberg 1989).

These senior faculty members view academic learning through the lens of their own struggles to prove that working-class students could "master" Western culture and knowledge; hence they are apt to support students of color who can "master" that culture. Pointing with pride to programs such as the Ford Foundation-sponsored City College Fellowships and the Mellon Minority Fellowship Program, they offer "firsthand experience of humanistic scholarship and scientific research" and "a faculty mentor to specially selected students" (Pfeffer 1990). It is not that these gifted students and others cannot benefit from the expertise of the senior faculty members but that CUNY, like most American colleges, has a faculty that is too homogeneous, too provincial, too much the reflection of Euro-American ethnic perspective, too male, too white, too middle class, and even too geographically similar and that tends to represent one worldview and a single approach to learning intellectual culture. They are limited in their ability to challenge the dominant paradigm and worldview of the academy, in part because of their belief in the primacy of Western culture and in part because of their ignorance of people of color and their intellectual traditions.

Faculty development seminars have done little to change or challenge the senior faculty. What we have achieved thus far is to introduce information about the new knowledge to white women, some people of color, and a few white men. It has been important work, but it must not be falsely celebrated. Without the full inclusion of scholars and scholarship of people of color in all aspects of higher education, seminars can only offer a limited start to transforming the curriculum.

While each college has its own history and culture, the CUNY experience is instructional because it indicates that multicultural educational changes stall for reasons beyond adequate funding or lack of talented faculty of color. It is a given that senior faculty, perhaps more than administrators, tenaciously hold on to their control of the production of knowledge for political as well as intellectual reasons.

The Melani suit, Friends of Women's Studies, and the sit-in at Medgar Evers College were successful because participants understood the political dimensions of their struggle and mobilized campaigns with *political* rather than intellectual arguments and strategies. However, because affirmative action and antiracist efforts were not linked with faculty development seminars and curriculum change in a coherent set of demands for supporting women's and ethnic studies and hiring men and women of color to the faculty, these efforts have had limited impact. While white women faculty members and black women administrators benefited, teaching and learning have changed little.

A critical juncture occurred when Friends of Women's Studies abandoned its grass-roots organizing role for faculty development work. Organizers who are demanding or implementing faculty development programs at other colleges might examine more closely who benefits most from such programs. It could be that, as in CUNY's case, they might become a marginal activity that limits or isolates people rather than connecting them to other campus issues, especially challenges to racism and the treatment of people of color.

As we continue to struggle on different levels and fronts, we learn more about the potency of multicultural education and affirmative action as strategies for transformation. Each struggle has taught us something and moves us closer to understanding how to dismantle the tenacious relations that support and maintain the present academy.

Notes

1. *African-American* and *black* are used interchangeably; *African-American* is recognized as the more formal term.

2. In 1988, the CUNY Council of Presidents' ad hoc Committee on Pluralism and CUNY issued a statement of principles and recommendations reaffirming the university's commitment to a curriculum that reflects its multiethnic, multiracial, and multigenerational student population. At the recommendation of the Board of Trustees, on September 22, 1988, Chancellor Joseph S. Murphy instructed Vice Chancellor Carolyn Reid Wallace to

convene the Task Force for Balancing the Curriculum for Pluralism and Diversity. (Progress Report of the Task Force, issued June 1989 by the Office of Academic Affairs.)

3. CAAN was founded October 30, 1986, at a meeting of CUNY Black Professionals held at the Harlem State Office Building, New York City.

4. The CUNY Lion's Rock Network of black women faculty and staff was founded in March 1986 at the farewell luncheon of Dr. Marguerite Ross-Barnett, the first black woman CUNY vice chancellor of academic affairs.

5. Statistics about CUNY staff, students, or faculty, unless otherwise cited, are from the university office of academic affairs.

6. The CUNY Women's Coalition was founded to pursue the Melani suit and continues as an organization committed to "bringing about women's equal participation in all aspects of university life." In 1982, females were only 33.8 percent of full-time faculty.

7. "New knowledge" refers to scholarly research by and about people of African, Asian, and Latin descent; Native Americans; Euro-American women; and gay men and lesbians of all ethnic backgrounds.

8. Helly was working with Ross-Barnett through an American Council of Education program that supports release time for faculty to gain administrative experience in their respective universities.

9. VEA, the Vocational Education Act, sponsored by U.S. Rep. Carl Perkins, is designed to provide funding to support and expand vocational education and to increase access to vocational education for underrepresented and underserved populations. Ten CUNY colleges, including seven community colleges, were eligible for funding because of their occupational degree options. (Vocational Education at CUNY, a report of the Office of Academic Affairs, Adult and Continuing Education Division, February 1987.)

10. "Blacks in general represent 32% of CUNY students but only 12% of its faculty, and 25% of its HEO's [administrative titles]. Of the 12% Black faculty, 8.5% are employed in 'minority' institutions (with majority populations and distinct missions related to people of color), Borough of Manhattan Community College, Medgar Evers College, and Hostos Community College." ("African American Representation among Professional and Higher Education Officer Ranks within the CUNY" by Laurel N. Huggins, May 1992.) A 1985 report from the CUNY Affirmative Action Office sent at the author's request indicates that black women represented about 6 percent of the entire faculty, or about half of the black faculty.

11. In the fall of 1988, black women were the second-largest cohort of all undergraduate students in CUNY senior colleges (18.3 percent) and the largest cohort of all community college students (24 percent), but they were only 11.6 percent of the graduate school students. (Summary of reports prepared for Higher Education Data Systems by CUNY.)

12. On July 20, 1991, Professor Leonard Jeffries spoke at the Empire State Black Arts and Cultural Festival in Albany, New York. His speech was condemned by many as anti-Semitic and antiwhite. He was subsequently removed from his position as chair by the CUNY Board of Trustees. A full text of the Jeffries speech appeared in *New York Newsday* on Monday, August 19, 1991, pages 3 and 25-29.

References

City University of New York Women's Coalition Newsletter. December 1984-January 1985.

Gorelick, Sherry. *City College and the Jewish Poor: Education in New York, 1880-1924*. New York: Schocken, 1982.

Hunter College Women's Studies Collective. *Women's Realities, Women's Choices: An Introduction to Women's Studies*. New York: Oxford University Press, 1983.

Hunter College Women's Studies Program. Report on a Project to Integrate Scholarship on Women into the Liberal Arts Curriculum at Hunter College. 1987.

Kleinfield, N. R., with Samuel Weiss. "Leader Presses Changes at CUNY, but Some See Threat to Its Mission." *New York Times*, July 7, 1992: A1, B2.

Kriegel, Leonard. "A Tale of Two Leonards." *Reconstruction* 1, no. 4 (Spring 1992): 142–44.

McFadden, Robert D. "U.S. Court Rules Against City U in Sex-Bias Suit." *New York Times*, March 19, 1983: A1, 27.

McLaughlin, Andree Nicola, and Zala Chandler. "Black Women in the Frontline: Unfinished Business of the Sixties." *Radical Teacher*, November 1984: 6–11.

Pfeffer, Robert. "Professors—An Endangered Species? How CCNY Is Helping Universities Recruit Faculty for the 21st Century." *Kaleidoscope* (City College, CUNY) 6, no. 1, (Spring 1990): 7.

Steinberg, Stephen. *The Ethnic Myth: Race, Ethnicity and Class in America*. Boston: Beacon, 1989.

Verhovek, Sam Howe. "250 at CUNY Sue New York, Citing Racial Bias in Budget." *New York Times*, February 27, 1992: B1, B2.

Wallace, Michele. *Invisibility Blues: From Pop to Theory*. New York: Verso, 1990.

Chapter 12

The Diversity of California at Berkeley: An Emerging Reformulation of "Competence" in an Increasingly Multicultural World
Troy Duster

A Fierce and Angry Debate and a Poverty of Vision

The current national debate about multiculturalism, group identity, and expansion of the curriculum tends to be fierce and binary. It is saturated with a surprising level of mean-spiritedness and apocalyptic forebodings that are, on the surface, hard to explain. For example, in the *Wall Street Journal* in July 1991, Irving Kristol wrote an essay entitled "The Tragedy of Multiculturalism" in which he stated that "multiculturalism is a desperate strategy for coping with the educational deficiencies, and associated social pathologies, of young blacks." A host of commentators have summarily dismissed courses designed to include more of the contributions of ethnic, cultural, and racial groups as nothing more than "feel good courses" or a "victim's revolt" (Aufderheide 1992; D'Souza 1991).

A full cadre of critics with the peculiar self-appointed name of the National Association of Scholars made their positions public long before any could have had an opportunity to review the serious intellectual content of dozens of new and renovated courses being developed at Berkeley to satisfy a new, single-course requirement.[1] Responding primarily to the most recent push to change the New York state curriculum for a fuller multicultural content, Arthur Schlesinger, Jr., has published a short book that he entitled, with uncharacteristic hyperbole, *The Disuniting of Amer-ica: Reflections on a Multicultural Society* (1992).

Why should the growing interest in curricular expansion that would reflect a wider band of cultural experiences and perspectives have pro-duced such an emotionally charged defense of the citadel? The closest we can come to an answer is put forward by Schlesinger, who reaches back nearly to the beginning of American history to find the root of the mat-ter. In a key discussion, he invokes a famous passage from J. Hector St. John de Crèvecoeur's *Letters from an American Farmer*, first published in 1782. Crèvecoeur was a Frenchman who immigrated to America before the revolution of 1776, was assimilated into the new country, and cele-brated an important aspect of his newly adopted nation. In his Letter III, "What Is an American?," Crèvecoeur provides an image of a new melt-ing pot, a new assimilation:

> He is an American, who leaving behind him all his ancient prejudices
> and manners, receives new ones from the new mode of life he has
> embraced, the new government he obeys, and the new rank he holds.
> The American is a new man, who acts upon new principles.
> (Crèvecoeur 1904: 54–55)

Schlesinger quotes this passage, basically subscribing to this particular formulation of what it means to be an American, and goes on to invoke Crèvecoeur to decry the new fractioning and splintering of America along ethnic and racial lines:

> The "ancient prejudices and manners" disowned by Crèvecoeur have
> made a surprising comeback. A cult of ethnicity has arisen both among
> non-Anglo whites and among nonwhite minorities to denounce the idea
> of a melting pot, to challenge the concept of "one people," and to
> protect, promote, and perpetuate separate ethnic and racial communities.
> (Schlesinger 1992: 15)

While Schlesinger quotes this letter and leaves us with the impression that Crèvecoeur had an assimilationist image for the whole nation, he ne-glects to quote from Crèvecoeur's Letter IX, "Description of Charles-town; Thoughts on Slavery." In the following passage, Crèvecoeur gives us a very different image of the new American:

> While all is joy, festivity, and happiness in Charles-Town, would you
> imagine that scenes of misery overspread in the country? Their ears by
> habit are become deaf, their hearts are hardened: they neither see, hear,
> nor feel for the woes of their poor slaves, from whose painful labours
> all their wealth proceeds. Here the horrors of slavery, the hardship of
> incessant toils, are unseen; and no one thinks with compassion of those

showers of sweat and of tears which from the bodies of Africans, daily drop, and moisten the ground they till. The cracks of the whip urging these miserable beings to excessive labour, are far too distant from the gay Capitol to be heard. The chosen race eat, drink, and live happy, while the unfortunate one grubs up the ground, raises indigo, or husks the rice; exposed to a sun full as scorching as their native one; without the support of good food. (Crèvecoeur 1904: 225-26)

This version of what it means to be an American is from the same Crèvecoeur, from the same volume of letters quoted so sympathetically by Schlesinger. In Letter IX, Crèvecoeur is not the hopeful visionary; he is depressed by the "ancient prejudices" that separate white from black, free person from slave, and wealthy from impoverished—prejudices that have persisted through the end of the twentieth century.[2] His experience in Charleston is not of differences being shed to create a new, whole (hu)-man, but rather of caste, domination, and slavery and of overwhelming differences in power relations. The truth lies somewhere in between these two images of Crèvecoeur's America.

So far, we are given only two choices in this debate: either assimilation and the shedding of ethnic, religious, and cultural differences, or ethnic, racial, tribal war. The latter image—Bosnia and Lebanon—is conjured as the only alternative to assimilation. Weiner (1992) appropriately identifies this binary set of alternatives as a setup, a reduction to the absurd.[3] If we are limited to these two choices, and if only a fool or a villain would choose war, the implicit injunction is that all reasonable people would choose assimilation.

To his credit, Schlesinger does mention, however briefly, an alternative to this binary and otherwise debased debate: in 1915 Horace Kallen wrote an essay for the *Nation* entitled "Democracy versus the Melting Pot" in which he provided a sharp contrast to a "shedding of differences" and assimilationist vision of America. Kallen argued that we should not aspire to a melting away of differences, that the persistence of ethnic groups and their distinctive traditions was a potential source of enrichment.

Kallen was responsible for the metaphor of the symphony: different instruments and different parts that blend into a harmonic whole. This conception that Kallen came to call "cultural pluralism" represents neither assimilation nor enclaved warfare. While Kallen is characterized as the precursor of multiculturalism, before we cast Crèvecoeur irrevocably as an assimilationist, we may be able to rescue an important element from the famous passage quoted earlier. In strange and interesting ways that Crèvecoeur could not have imagined, there is a new outlook developing in America. It is not the assimilationist version of shedding differences; nor is it Kallen's holding onto differences in a symphonic blend of harmony. It is sometimes cacophonous and conflictual, and it is certainly quite different from mere shedding and acquisition. It is both a holding onto and something new. While the whole nation struggles with the new immigration, nowhere is the issue more self-consciously addressed than in education. It is very much a part of our current college campus scene, very much at the root of the debate over multiculturalism, and often very much obscured by the passionate adversaries in this debate, who have reduced the matter to good guys and bad guys battling an evil citadel or defending a sacred one.

Sociohistorical Context of Current Student Self-segmentation

In the past decade, the increasing social and ethnic heterogeneity of the nation's college campuses has captured the attention of media pundits, higher-education administrators, and many faculty members. Unfortunately, the troublesome aspects of this development have dominated most of the public debate. One major issue that has absorbed the media is that many students' social lives are segmented in ways that reaffirm their ethnic, racial, and cultural identities. This segmentation, now routinely referred to as "Balkanization," causes surprise, chagrin, and even some derision. It is characterized as an unseemly reversion to "tribalism" that gets in the way of the search for common ground.

There is something both old and new here. Although typically treated as a new and alarming development, segmentation is quite an old phenomenon and has been replayed throughout the history of higher education in America. Social historians who study U.S. colleges and universities know that the Hillel and Newman foundations played important roles for Jewish and Catholic students, respectively, for much of this century. With the assistance of such organizations, parties, dances, study groups, and sometimes residences were routinely "self-segregated," often in response to active discrimination against Jews and Catholics elsewhere on campus.

Todays' critics are suffering from a selective cultural amnesia when they portray African-American theme houses and Chinese student associations as newly created enclaves that destroy the search for common ground. Even into the 1980s, the most prestigious fraternities at Yale, Michigan, Harvard, and Berkeley had never admitted a Jew, much less an African-American or an Asian. The all-Jewish fraternity was common as late as the 1960s, and when a Chinese-American, Sherman Wu, pledged a fraternity at Northwestern in 1956, it was such a sensation that it made national news and generated a folk song. Over the years, some mild hand wringing occurred about discrimination, but no national campaign was launched against the "self-segregation" of the all-white, all-Anglo fraternities.

Yet, despite this long tradition, I believe something new is occurring on campuses that may help explain the hysterical response that we have been hearing. The new development is a demographic shift that the long-dominant white majority sees as a threat to its cultural hegemony. At the Berkeley campus of the University of California, the undergraduate student body has been rapidly and dramatically transformed. In 1960, more than 90 percent of the students were white. In 1980, the figure was about 66 percent. Today, it is about 45 percent. The first-year class in the fall of 1992 signaled an even more striking change for those who still think of Berkeley in 1960s terms. For the first time in history, whites did not make up the largest proportion of the incoming class; instead, it was Asian-Americans, who accounted for about 35 percent. Only 30 percent of the class were Americans of European ancestry. Nearly 20 percent of the class were Chicanos/Latinos, and nearly 8 percent African-Americans. If this pattern holds, well over 60 percent of the Berkeley students will be "of color" by the end of the 1990s.

Although it will not be quite as dramatic in some other regions of the country, this coloring of the campus landscape reflects a vital and constantly unfolding development in American social life. Although they are symbolized by the dramatic Berkeley figures, the ramifications go far beyond the percentages of different ethnic and racial groups on college campuses. The ramifications of demographic change certainly tug at the curriculum and challenge the borders of faculty turf and expertise. But the fundamental issues tapped by this change go to the heart of American identity and culture. Bubbling just beneath the surface of all the national attention devoted to "political correctness" and "quotas" is a complicated question that, stated most simply, is this: What does it mean to be an American? A related question is How does one become an American? It is a complex issue. Crèvecoeur struggled with it in the late 1700s, Kallen (1915) and Zangwill (1908) revisited it in the early 1900s, and now it is surfacing once again.

The controversy over diversity at Berkeley, much like the battle over the social studies curriculum in New York state, is a struggle over who gets to define the idea of America. Are we essentially a nation with a common—or at least a dominant—culture to which immigrants and "minorities" must adapt? Or is this a land in which ethnicity and difference are an accepted part of the whole, a land in which we affirm the richness of our differences and simultaneously try to forge agreement about basic values to guide public and social policy?

Critics of the current, visible wave of segmentation argue that "Balkanization" threatens the ties that bind civil society. But civil society in a nation of immigrants is forever in flux, and the basic issue always has been which group has the power to define what the values and structures of their common society will be. We should learn something from our history. Being an American is different from being French or Japanese or almost any other nationality because, except for Native Americans, there actually is no such thing as an American without a hyphen. We are a nation of immigrants. Generations of immigrants have struggled to balance both sides of the hyphen, to carry on some aspects of the culture of the old country while adopting the norms and customs of the new. Today, many of their descendants continue to find comfort in an identification with the old country—however tenuous it may be—that provides a sense of belonging to a recognizable collectivity. A sense of belonging, of being one with others like oneself, helps to overcome the isolation of modern life, while paradoxically also allowing a sense of uniqueness.

This is the same phenomenon we see being reenacted on campuses all over the country today, the difference being that the actors are no longer all white. At a place like Berkeley, there is no longer a single racial or ethnic group with an overwhelming numerical and political majority. Pluralism is the reality; no one group is a dominant force. This is completely new. We are grappling with a phenomenon that is both puzzling and alarming, fraught with tensions and hostilities yet simultaneously brimming with potential and crackling with new energy. Consequently, we swing between hope and concern, between optimism and pessimism, about the prospects for a common social life among peoples from different racial and cultural groups. Are members of particular groups isolated or interacting, segregating or integrating, fighting or harmonizing? Who is getting ahead or falling behind?

It may well be that we have too narrowly conceived the options as either/or. It may be that as a nation we have cast the problem incompletely and thus incorrectly.

The Diversity Project Study

The findings of the Diversity Project, a two-year study of student life at the University of California at Berkeley, strongly suggest that assimilation and enclaves are not the only two alternatives before us, that other avenues are possible. In our research, we discovered an emerging vision of a "third experience" of diversity in which the whole is greater than the sum of its various parts. Collective problem solving by individuals from different backgrounds, for example, produces superior results precisely because of the synergism that develops from different approaches being brought to bear on the same problem.

The Diversity Project was commissioned by the chancellor to be conducted at the Institute for the Study of Social Change for the purpose of finding out, up close, how undergraduate students have been experiencing the new ethnic and racial diversity on campus. As the principal investigator, I worked closely with other institute faculty and senior research staff who, like those they interviewed, were a diverse group: two Asian-Americans, one Native American, three Chicanos, seven European-Americans, and two African-Americans.[4] We made use of this staff diversity in developing the research design for the study.[5] The institute faculty and senior research staff conducted sixty-nine small-focus-group interviews with 291 students participating over a period of a year and a half, from the fall of 1989 until the spring of 1991.[6] The focus of the interviews included students' expectations about diversity in choosing to come to Berkeley; their friendships, study patterns, social lives, conflicts or positive interactions with people of different races and ethnicities; and their recommendations to administrators and faculty that might improve the experience of being on a campus of such extraordinarily rich ethnic and racial diversity. Transcriptions of more than 160 hours of these interviews were subjected to many forms of data analysis and interpretation. These data were triangulated with two other major sources of data: *Promoting Student Success at Berkeley: Guidelines for the Future*, the report on a survey conducted by the Commission on Responses to a Changing Student Body, released by the chancellor in 1991, and the 1990 Freshman Survey, conducted by the Office of Student Research at Berkeley.

Our research revealed that while the student body is segmented along racial and ethnic lines, there are some important good social relations and collective problem solving across racial and ethnic lines. The research provides specific details about the quality of life for students as they study, live, and work in an increasingly heterogeneous environment. Through the interviews, we were able to explore how and why miscommunication between ethnic and racial groups occurs. More specifically, we explored how affirmative action is differentially perceived and regarded across race and ethnicity. The research helped us better understand the ways in which passionate positions about affirmative action play themselves out in social relationships, in the ways students relate to (or avoid) each other, or are impersonal or hostile. Through this research we could explore why, although most of the students at Berkeley say they would like to meet more students from ethnic and cultural backgrounds that are different from their own, such meetings are often fraught with conflict and not nearly as frequent as one might guess. The data enabled us to define "stages" of diversity, which helps explain current conflicts and future possibilities. Finally, the study enabled us to suggest some recommendations for change that rest on the seemingly paradoxical need to support both the development and maintenance of strong ethnic and racial identities (including ethnically homogeneous affiliations and friendships) and multiracial and multiethnic contacts that enrich the public and social spheres of life. This experience is viable precisely because people bring to that public sphere the strengths of identity forged out of their unique experiences and "separateness."

External Sameness, Internal Differences

By talking directly to students for nearly two years, we were able to make a nuanced reading of how students interpret what is going on on campus, as opposed to the partial images reported in the media. We tried to come up with a systematic way to characterize the problems of group perception and came up with an analogy to how participants experience a social movement. It is axiomatic that no social movement is as incoherent as it appears from within nor as coherent as it appears from without. If you are on the left (at least in recent decades), you see such internal variation as Trotskyism, Stalinism, different versions of progressive labor, democratic socialism, and so on. But if you are on the right, you tend to see only "the left"; it all looks pink over there. And of course the opposite is also true: if you are on the right, you can identify single-issue antiabortionists, fiscal conservatives, and all kinds of other right wingers, but from the left, all you see is this thing called "the right." It is the same thing when you are studying ethnicity. Asian–Americans, for example, are likely to be aware of strong and important internal differences among them: generational differences (whether a Japanese is Nisei or Sansei), whether a person is foreign-born or native, and, of course, which Asian nationality. But if you are white, all you are likely to see are "Asians." Likewise, blacks distinguish between streetwise kids from East Oakland and the offspring of a black suburban professional, but to many Asians, whites, and Latinos, they are all just "blacks."

The closer one is to the phenomenon, the more likely one is to see internal differences. This poses an interesting paradox: while observers from the outside are likely to impute "sameness" and "self-segregation," the "group" in question may be struggling with tremendous internal differentiation, effortfully trying to forge a common identity. Ironically, critics mistake attempts to achieve community as fragmentation and as an assault upon some larger common community. Some of this concern is misplaced, if not amusing. Upon closer inspection, for example, one finds that groups such as the Asian Business Association and the Black Engineering and Science Student Association meet only a few hours a month. They have a hard time getting people to come for just these few hours. Yet they see themselves described in the media as a coherent force, excluding others from attendance. If Dinesh D'Souza and George Will and the *Economist* were at all close to the phenomenon of "student associations," they would be far from "concerned" about a few hours spent on groups whose membership may be lagging or uncommitted from the point of view of the organizers.

The Role of Associations

A registration-week visitor to Sproul Plaza, at the entrance to the Berkeley campus, is instantly struck by the large number of card tables with poster board signs that have been set up to promote student groups and organizations. There are tables for the Hiking Club, the Chinese Student Association, the Vietnamese Student Association, MECHA (an organization of Chicano and Latino students), the Bicycle Club, Cal Adventures, and so forth. Some organizations are thus clearly targeted toward specific ethnic and racial groups, others to recreational or academic interests.

The number of registered student organizations has increased noticeably in recent years, and the membership and appeal of the organizations is increasingly linked to specifically designated populations where ethnicity and race play an important role. Cultural, social, professional, academic, self-help, and interest-group organizations have emerged to respond to the diverse unserved interests and concerns of the current multicultural student body. These groups vary from strongly monoethnic or monocultural to very mixed and multicultural.

The blossoming of informal associations is very much an American tradition. Prior to the National Quota Origins Act of 1924, which placed new limits on immigration to the United States, churches, clubs, and associations served as mediating organizations for the many immigrants who had come to America to find work. In 1920, 25 percent of the population was foreign-born, and 55 percent had at least one foreign-born parent. In this environment of predominantly white ethnic diversity, voluntary groups and organizations served as islands of friendship and affiliation.[7] European ethnic groups did not disperse or merge into the mainstream until they developed sufficient economic and political power. Immigrants, in fact, tended to move to those places in the United States where there were already well-established ethnic communities from their home country to provide social, economic, and moral support.[8]

The role of voluntary associations as mediating organizations in a multiethnic society is thus a venerable American tradition. To say that this is a new development is accurate only if one has the narrow time frame of a decade or two and belies the fact that only two decades ago, most American campuses were culturally and racially homogeneous, as were most fraternities and sororities.

Converging Desire for Diversity, Diverging Conceptions

A remarkable 70 percent of all undergraduate students at Berkeley agree with this statement: "I'd like to meet more students from ethnic and cultural backgrounds that are different from my own."[9] Negotiating the terrain of interethnic relations in a situation where none is the majority is a new experience for most of the people on campus. While Berkeley's undergraduate students generally say they want interracial experiences and contacts—on or off the campus—members of different ethnic and racial groups tend to chart this terrain in different ways. In general, the desire for diversity is not being sufficiently acknowledged, much less constructively addressed, in any of the current debates about affirmative action, quotas, and self-segregation. This shared interest in diversity should be an important starting point.

Despite the variation and diversity within and across groups, there are clear distinctions in how different groups of students construct, experience, and understand their time at Berkeley and in their expressions of interest in greater interethnic, intercultural contact. More than 72 percent of African-American respondents to the Freshman Survey were "interested" or "extremely interested" in programs to promote racial understanding. In sharp contrast, only about 43 percent of white respondents expressed such an interest, and nearly 30 percent said that they were not very interested or probably would be too busy for such activities.[10] In fact, survey data show whites to be the least interested of all groups in programs meant to promote racial understanding.

Yet when we compared the Freshman Survey findings to data from our group interviews, an interesting difference in responses by ethnic and racial groups surfaced. In the group interviews, white students, with much greater frequency than African-Americans, routinely and consistently expressed interest in having more contact and friendships with African-American students, whom they experienced as being cliquish and somewhat closed to interracial contact. The white students' willingness to be friendly, indeed, "to be friends" at the personal level is prima facie evidence of goodwill and lack of racism. In contrast, African-American students most often among the ethnic groups indicated a preference for same-group friendships, and for same-group social activities and organizations. They were most likely to report these experiences as more comfortable and resonant with shared values and experiences. To generalize from the combined findings of the survey of undergraduates, the Diversity Project, and the 1990 Freshman Survey, while whites tended to express a willingness and desire to be friends with African-Americans, they were less likely to want interracial contact in the context of special programs, courses, or activities that structure interethnic contacts. At the other end, African-Americans were far more likely to want special programs and activities and less interested in developing cross-racial friendships and social activities. These three data sets suggest that while both African-American and white students want more interracial experiences and contacts, they want them on different terms. African-Americans want more classes, programs, and other institutional commitments and responses. Whites want more individual, personal contacts developed on their own.

These data suggest again the polymorphous character of interethnic relations on campus. The task is to provide all students with a range of safe environments and options where they can explore and develop terms that they find comfortable. In the absence of such opportunities, the tendencies remain for each group to see the others from a distance, in terms of images, stereotypes, stories, and myths that are not informed by direct contact and experience.

Diversity: Sometimes Zero-sum, Sometimes Mutual Enhancement

The overwhelming sense of our group discussions with students was that the students were ambivalent and contradictory when it comes to increasing ethnic and racial diversity. This ambivalence was not only within groups, but also often in the same person. White students were the most likely to give voice to the zero-sum aspect of the new diversity. When whites thought in terms of their group interest (racial or ethnic or color interests) in being admitted to college, for example, they were most likely to feel squeezed out of what they considered their slice of the pie—squeezed on the one hand by "undeserving" affirmative action admits and, on the other hand, by "overly competitive" Asian-Americans. At the same time, some white students could also see that ethnic and racial diversity in their midst enhanced their own education and ability to live in an increasingly diverse society.

Asian-American students were the most conflicted of all the groups of students about a policy to diversify the student body.[11] Chicano/ Latino Americans, African-Americans, and Native Americans voiced the strongest support for an explicit policy of student diversification via affirmative action, yet their knowledge of how and why such a policy operates was no greater than that of whites and Asians. Thus, while it can be said that students could be divided into two camps, for and against a policy of diversification, it would ultimately be inaccurate because it fails to capture the deep and gnawing reservations among the supporters and some strong sympathy even among the detractors. Therefore, implications must be drawn with sensitivity to the complexity of the situation.

Students from every group were divided about affirmative action admissions policies, and even some students who expressed strongly positive or negative views were, upon closer examination, at variance. If there is a single pattern that emerged from the study, it is that the students are deeply conflicted, disturbed, divided, and confused about affirmative action as a policy, yet they support the idea of diversity. How this value conflict unfolds in the day-to-day relations between and among students provides some of the richest material about diversity on campus.

The Academic Index:
Ambivalence, Misinformation—and Reification

There is an extraordinary dearth of information about the actual Berkeley affirmative action admissions policy, coupled with strong, even visceral opinions about it. In all of the sixty-nine groups we spoke with, fewer than a handful of students had any firm understanding of the way the policy is actually implemented. Indeed, the combination of universally strongly held opinions with either misinformation about or complete ignorance of the policy requires some explanation.

California's Master Plan for Higher Education mandates that the University of California will be the major research institution of the state and that the top 12.5 percent of the high school graduating class is eligible for admission to the university. With more than twelve hundred high schools in the state, how this top 12.5 percent is to be determined is, of course, up for interpretation and negotiation. The grade point average (GPA) is a convenient mechanism, but there is considerable variation both within and between high schools with respect to grading procedures and the strength or weakness of a teaching program in any given field. Thus, a grade point average of 3.25 may mean one thing in High School X and quite another in High School Y. Moreover, even within a single school, a student who carefully navigates through the curriculum to achieve a 3.7 GPA may not be a better or a stronger student than one with a 3.6.

Historically, the mechanism that has been used to counterbalance this problem of different high school standards and backgrounds is the standardized test. The debate over whether standardized tests are "standardized" against some abstract culture-free, class-free bias has been going on for decades and is likely to continue. The Karabel Report had this to say about diversity and the use of these tests:

> One indicator that the far-ranging diversification of the student body that has taken place in the past decade has not been at the expense of conventional academic standards is the fact that the percentage of new freshmen with combined SAT's less than or equal to 1000 declined from 24.8 per cent in 1978 to 20.5 per cent in 1987. During these same years, the proportion of freshmen with very high SAT's (defined as 1400 or more) more than doubled.[12]

Yet this does not get at the matter of ethnic and racial differences in standardized-test scores and the level of legitimacy attached to the scores. Opponents of the current admissions policy, for example, have attacked it by pointing to the variation in SAT scores between racial and ethnic groups and have argued against admitting those with lower SAT scores.

Grade inflation is only a part of the story. During the 1980s, the median GPA has steadily increased as those already eligible for admission (3.25 and above) were in competition for an increasingly scarce resource, admission to the freshman class. Indeed, the median GPA climbed from 3.7 to 3.9; the Asian-American and European-American students' GPAs climbed to a median of 4.0. Meanwhile, the median high school grade point average for African-Americans and Chicano/Latino Americans hovered at 3.4 and 3.5 throughout the decade—above the 3.25 eligibility requirement. Affirmative action admissions at the Berkeley campus can only be understood in this context: the great majority of affirmative action admissions are students who are in the top 12.5 percent. The general misunderstanding of the policy has two important features: the mistaken belief that "minority students" (especially black and Chicano/Latino) are coming from the "bottom 87.5 percent" and are therefore unqualified, and the corresponding view that these students are less qualified than Asian-American and white students. In fact, more white students than black are admitted to Berkeley's freshman class with grade point averages below 3.6. If a black student with a grade point average of 3.8 applied to engineering and computer sciences, however, she or he would be admitted to Berkeley rather than redirected to another campus because of the affirmative action admissions policy adopted in 1984. One can now begin to see that what constitutes less or more qualified is contested terrain. Is 3.9 more qualified than 3.8? Recall that there are more than twelve hundred high schools whose grading procedures vary widely.

Dinesh D'Souza, in *Illiberal Education* (1991), makes much of a particular case in a discussion of Yat-pang Au, who was not admitted to Berkeley. D'Souza reports the case in this way:

> Yat-pang's credentials were not in question. He graduated first in his class at San Jose's Gunderson High School with a Straight A average. . . . SAT scores were 1,340 . . . in the 98th percentile, considerably above the Berkeley average. . . . Yat-pang discovered that ten other students from Gunderson High were accepted at Berkeley, none of these (with) Yat-pang's roster of achievements. (24, 25)

Since Yat-pang was valedictorian, and also had a long list of extracurricular achievements, one has the impression that an obvious injustice was done. But we must remember two important things. First, students apply for admission to different majors, and some majors are extraordinarily competitive in terms of GPA and SAT scores. In computer sciences and engineering, for example, even a 4.0 (in combination with a standardized test score) would place Yat-pang in the lower half of those applying. Another student applying to study music or comparative literature, for example, might be admitted with a "mere" 3.87 GPA. Second, recall that there are 40 percent more students with straight A averages applying to enter the Berkeley freshman class than there are places in the class.

Since the great majority of the undergraduate students at Berkeley went to California high schools, they have some knowledge of how this works, even if their knowledge is limited. Thus, in our focus groups, students would often talk about their ambivalence about use of the academic index (GPA and standardized test score) as if it were a definitive mark of competence, skill, and accomplishments—let alone an indication of potential for achievement of academic excellence. Nonetheless, most of the students recognized the academic index as a valid stratifying device. To the extent that they recognized it, they gave an independent reality to the academic index and developed the language of fairness and unfairness when they described the affirmative action admissions policy.[13]

A theme heard frequently among white and Asian-American students is that affirmative action undercuts the university's traditional color-blind, equal opportunity approach to recruitment by rewarding students of color for having too much "fun" and "goofing off" in high school. This subverts the university's meritocratic principles, it is claimed, and the policy is characterized as unfairly admitting "unqualified," "unde-serving" students who thereby "steal" the spots to which qualified students are "entitled." Using the moral language of Protestantism, these students make distinctions between "deserving" and "undeserving" students based on the amount of effort exerted in high school.

Given this operating assumption among many of the white and Asian students that we interviewed, it is not surprising that black, Chicano/Latino, and Native American students routinely expressed the feeling of "not belonging" at Berkeley. One African-American undergraduate said, "I feel like I have 'affirmative action' stamped on my forehead." Another noted, "We're guilty until proven innocent." And yet another said, "There's no way to convince whites we belong here. We do back flips and they still wouldn't accept us." When these students do well in class, they report, their classmates and teachers frequently express surprise or portray them as being somehow different from other students of color, an exception to the rule. "What is your SAT score?" is a question many freshmen resent when they feel that behind the question is the assumption that they have a low score.

It is precisely this reification of the academic index that makes some of the black and Chicano/Latino students chafe at what they take to be the assumption on the part of whites that while the white and Asian-Americans "belong" on campus, blacks and Chicano/Latinos are there only because of affirmative action. It is in this sense that the general controversy over affirmative action colors much of the substance of the ethnic and racial relations within and between groups and penetrates social and academic life in diffuse and indirect ways. Reference to the legitimacy of the academic index wavered under certain conditions. White students, for example, shifted their ground and questioned the index when the idea of "Asian overrepresentation" surfaced.[14] At that point, "well-rounded-ness" emerged as a competing criterion to the academic index.

What white students overlook is that far more whites have entered the gates of the ten most elite American institutions of higher education through "alumni preference" than the combined number of all the blacks and Chicanos who have entered through affirmative action. Data for the entering freshman class at Harvard in 1988 show that alumni preference accounted for more admissions than all the African-American, Mexican-American, Native American, and Puerto Rican registrants combined.[15] At Berkeley in 1989, 24 percent of the white students were admitted based upon criteria other than or in addition to the academic index.[16]

Many students, but especially those from European and Asian backgrounds, expressed their dismay, frustration, and reservations about a race-based affirmative action policy that did not take class or socioeco-

nomic status into account. We heard the leitmotiv of resentment, the re-
frain of "lack of fairness," when a middle-class black or Chicano/Latino
student was admitted, while either a white or an Asian student with a
better academic index score or a poor white or Asian was not. There is a
tension between the feeling that middle-class Chicano/Latinos and blacks
are given unfair preference at Berkeley and the reality that on the whole,
white and Asian students come from families with significantly greater
economic resources than do African-American and Latino students.[17]
Since there are more poor white people in the United States than there are
middle-class people of color, a class-based affirmative action policy
would necessarily bring in more whites. Unless such a policy explicitly
"bumped" wealthier whites, it would reduce the number and proportion
of people of color. Thus the historical advantage of whites, codified in
law and practice for more than a century, is revisited by such a policy.

Reformulating the Experience of Diversity

Stages of Diversity

For most of the nation's history, American college campuses typically
have been remarkably homogeneous. In the past three decades, this homogeneity has begun to break down, albeit in varying degrees and at
varying speeds in different places. Yet many of our dominant assumptions are holdovers from another era, including our views about fundamental pedagogy, learning styles, and communicative expression in the
classroom and seminars—and, of course, the very nature and quality of
civil and appropriate student life. Berkeley's recent experience of diversity can be viewed as a microcosm of society at a particular stage. The
notion of stage does not imply inevitable or linear evolution. But if this is
a matter of increasing diversification, over time, then it is of more than
heuristic value to consider how the mere growth in numbers of previously underrepresented groups might influence and change the nature
and character of relations between groups.

The first stage is what I call the Australian model, in which diversity is
an option. For its first 150 years, Australia had remarkable cultural and
racial homogeneity. There was nobody besides the whites around except
the aborigines, and if the whites wanted to deal with them—wipe them
out or absorb their art and put it in the national museum—they could do
so. Whites in Australia had limited ethnic, racial, and cultural diversity
. . . only a few Aborigines in the "outback," and they could "take it or
leave it." Berkeley in the 1960s was like that. It was a much happier time,
for whites, in Berkeley's history; there was little ethnic-racial-cultural

tension because there were few ethnic-racial-cultural differences. By the mid-1980s on the Berkeley campus, no matter what whites did, others were "in your face." This is a new context for "the smoldering cauldron of ethnic-racial Balkanization." This is stage two: fights over limited, zero-sum resources, tension, and alienation. This zero-sum version of diversity is always accompanied by strife, tensions, and hostilities, as well as some compromises, adjustments, mediated settlements, and sometimes just plain détente. But the situation is volatile. Détente can easily explode into open hostility. Between 1985 and 1990 there were numerous incidents of racist graffiti, jokes, anonymous hate notes, and brawls at an estimated 175 American campuses, including prestigious schools like Smith College, Brown University, Colby College, and the Universities of Michigan and Wisconsin. Howard J. Ehrlich, research director of the National Institute Against Prejudice and Violence in Baltimore, reports that turmoil on this scale has not been seen since the 1960s.

The current friction differs from the disputes of the 1960s, when conflict typically arose between students and administrators. Recent clashes have been between students of color and white students. When students experience this "second form" of diversity, especially those who come to Berkeley with a naive and idealistic view of what cross-cultural interaction might bring, they are likely to be disappointed and disillusioned. Responding to the estrangement with sensitivity requires understanding differences in ways students of different backgrounds experience this zero-sum period. This may ultimately prove to be educational, and some of the conflicts and differences may be resolvable, even perhaps to the enhancement of the public sphere.

The third experience of diversity is both idealistic and sometimes realized: it is the experience in which people come together across different cultural backgrounds and in that coming together produce an experience that is transcendent, greater than the sum of the individual parts. It is the peculiar and unique blend of human perspectives and experiences, of insights and problem-solving strategies, of orientations and styles, that can sometimes blend in a synergistic manner. If you put all Japanese students together, they will just re-create Japanese culture. Add a few Chinese and Korean students, and you will get synergy. Multiply that by all American cultures, and you have a resurgence of America. This is considerably more than sampling the cuisines of other cultures, listening to "their music" for a change, or observing that others dress or talk differently. It means new ways of thinking about things like family life and filial piety, for example. As a fledgling freshman from a racially homogeneous high school, I suddenly learn that my Asian friend cannot come for dinner on Sunday because he may have obligations to extended kin, or my Jewish acquaintance cannot come on Friday because some part of her family is Orthodox. It is partly the accommodations and adjustments, but more importantly, it is a potential mutual enhancement that minimizes the issue of scarce resources. People can come to see one another as resources, recognizing different and complementary competencies.

What it means to be an educated American in this context is just emerging, and only recently has it been possible to see some of the likely contours of this identity. The meaning of being a citizen in a diverse society cannot be based on mindless homogenization, assimilation, or "melted down" integration. It will revolve instead around new meanings of diversity, perhaps close to Kallen's version of pluralism. In a pluralist society, ethnic and racial groups can maintain distinctive cultures, organizations, and identities while they participate in the larger community. Individual members of ethnic and racial groups may choose to live in delimited communities, marry within their own group, and sometimes even work at similar occupations. While this sustains and promotes their ethnic identity and culture, they also relate to others. This interaction between groups is often less intimate and occurs in the realm of politics, economics, and education.

Competence in the context of pluralism will mean being able to participate effectively in a multicultural world. It will mean being "multicultural" as well as multilingual. It will mean knowing how to operate as a competent actor in more than one cultural world, knowing what is appropriate and what is inappropriate, what is acceptable and unacceptable in behavior and speech in cultures other than one's own. Competence in a pluralist world will mean being able to function effectively in contexts one has until now only read about or seen on television. It will mean knowing how to be "different" and feeling comfortable about it, being able to be the "insider" in one situation and the "outsider" in another.

Defined this way, pluralism in America can be achieved only if everyone does some changing. Every group will need to learn new ways of navigating in territories in which they do not have the power to define what is normal. No one will be immune from this process. For some groups of color, this will mean learning how to be "the majority." For whites in California, it may sometimes mean learning how to be "a minority." Addressing these issues will be an important aspect of a university education in the coming decade.

When they give voice to their idealism, this is what Berkeley's undergraduates say they want. Despite the reservoir of goodwill with which they arrive on campus in that first semester, they most often come up against the second stage of diversity, the zero-summing, the socially formed sense of enclaves that are difficult to penetrate. They would, of course, prefer to get to what we have called the "third experience" and just bypass the second, but it may well be that a period of self-segregation or Balkanization may strengthen identity and community as a prerequisite to being able to bring that strength to bear on the larger communal experience.

In this third experience of diversity, the public sphere is enriched precisely because members come from heterogeneous backgrounds, ways of thinking, ways of formulating and solving problems. A special value is placed upon a contribution to the whole, or to the common collective experience, because contributing members bring something to that experience that is unique. In order to have a third stage of diversity, and in order to get to the stage in which people will come together across their differing ethnic-cultural-racial experiences and create a greater whole, each group must be able to draw upon the integrity of its own cultural experience. Each must have a sense of distinct cultural identity and carry the distinctiveness of culture, experience, space, place, perspective, and orientation in order to make its particular contribution to the larger collective enterprise.

Muting the Binary View of Race Relations

For most of the nation's history, racial and ethnic relations have been dominated by the relations between blacks and whites. For the past two centuries, blacks have been the largest single minority. During the past two decades, however, Asian immigration and Chicano/Latino immigration and migration have increasingly come to occupy an important role in the nation's consciousness. The two states with the most people, California and New York, are also among the most ethnically and racially heterogeneous. Nearly one-fifth of the people of the United States live in California and New York. These states have the heaviest concentration of Asians and a large proportion of the Chicano/Latino population. In California, Chicano/Latinos and Asians both outnumber blacks, who now constitute the fourth-largest grouping.

This development is remarkable in its significance for the transformation of consciousness about the meaning of race in these states and, ultimately, for the nation. So long as there have been only two major groupings, blacks and whites, a circumscribed and largely dualistic thought has dominated the American landscape. This discourse has influenced most of the empirical research on the topic of race and ethnicity and has shaped the public policy debates about programs, educational policy, and so forth.

As Asians and Chicano/Latinos have increasingly come to occupy this landscape, however, the old assumptions, the old pas de deux has been transformed. A trio, a quartet, even a quintet of ethnic and racial groups is changing vital conceptions of issues of race and ethnicity for both blacks and whites. An example: black students with professional parents who come from suburban areas are sometimes accused of "acting white" by their urban peers. If in a world configured by complementary identities "being black" is partially achieved by "not acting white," then African-American racial identity is partly defined in terms of this negative relief. In its extreme and pathological form, this can take the shape of "academic success" (in grammar school and secondary school especially) being defined as "white behavior," so that affirmation of black racial identity becomes academic failure. When Asians and Chicano/Latinos are part of the matrix, all this changes.

For starters, academic success, which was once assumed to be dominated by, if not the sole province of, whites, is now associated with Asians. The Asian-American rate of eligibility for admission to the University of California is more than double that of whites. Chicano/Latinos, on the other hand, share with blacks the problems of lower rates of college eligibility and high dropout rates in high school. African-Americans and European-Americans are thus suddenly in a situation in which one is no longer the audience for the other's academic success. "Being black" becomes much more complex. Indeed, the quest for identity moves from the negative of "not acting white" to some form of affirmation of the positive of a substantive identity. This might help explain the reemergence of Afrocentrism in segments of the black community. To dismiss this development as merely a retreat into enclaves is to misread the fundamentally transformative character of shifting ethnic and racial relations.

The strong entry of third and fourth parties decisively affects whites as well. With Asian-Americans in this new mix, whites are forced to rethink a unidimensional conception of "academic success." Just as gentiles had questioned the value of using only high grade point averages in the first two decades of the twentieth century, when immigrant Jews were outperforming them, so whites at Berkeley are beginning to publicly question a single definitive measure of entitlement to study at the university. But white gentiles are caught in a contradiction on this. Many would like to insist on admission based solely upon GPA and standardized tests, but since Asian-Americans excel on this score, they find themselves arguing for "other criteria" to round out the application. This is broadly what happened at Yale in the 1960s, when black demands for affirmative action produced the counterassertion of the need to admit (students) and hire (faculty) based on "individual merit and achievements." This redounded to the benefit of Jews, who were the victims of Yale's legendary anti-Semitism during the first half of the twentieth century (Oren 1985; Synnott 1979; Wechsler 1977; Karabel 1984).

New Ways of Thinking About Competence

Given conflict among interest groups and debates about legitimate criteria for university admissions and employment, it is possible to begin to rethink the value of diversity and to reevaluate pedagogical methods, reassessing the very idea of the competence of those who can teach in a diverse setting. In the American seminar room, undergraduate or graduate, for example, professors tend to evaluate dialogue—exchanges with and feedback from students—positively. Jewish students do comparatively well in this environment, in part because they are likely to come from home and cultural environments in which there is a tradition of a challenging examination of issues, dialogue, and inquisitiveness. This sometimes looks like a direct challenge to authority. In sharp contrast, Americans of Japanese, Chinese, and Korean ancestry are likely to come from backgrounds in which the challenge to elders in positions of formal authority is rarely direct, hardly ever argumentative. Such behavior is perceived as disrespectful and contentious, and even to appear to argue with a professor is unthinkable.

Asian students seen from the perspective of the dominant group may come across as lacking ideas and as deficient in the skill to engage in lively seminar exchanges, insufficiently assertive, unable to express and defend their ideas. If the faculty has reified this model as the only one, then of course those who have certain cultural backgrounds will be regarded as "brighter."

The new multiculturalism requires a new competence from professors. They can claim that competence only to the extent that they can engage both assertive students and those with other styles of expression and learning. This helps to explain faculty resistance to the challenge of diversity. As we move toward a more diverse environment, the call for a more diverse faculty with the capacity to encompass these differences becomes more comprehensible. This converts to a real need for pedagogical talents that cannot be reduced to political rhetoric, to arguments that political concerns are the driving force behind the desire for a more diverse faculty. The task of educating, of promoting and encouraging competencies on the part of both students and faculty, is thus far more complex than has been represented by the critics of diversity, who are united more by their anecdotes and their glibness than by any substantial knowledge of what is happening around them.

Many university faculty still have a 1950s version of the canon and a unidimensional image of what it means to be a good student. The more conservative faculty are still reluctant to acknowledge that there may be a need to adjust to different learning styles. They are defensive about adjustments in the curriculum, and their fears add up to a remarkably uncreative response, a narrowly conceived zero-sum version of what could instead be the rich "third experience" of diversity: Alice Walker could join—not displace—William Shakespeare as an icon of Western civilization.

A significant and visible proportion of faculty at our major institutions are circling the wagons in a last-ditch effort to fend off multiculturalism and diversity. Over half the students at Berkeley are students of color. Meanwhile, the Berkeley faculty is 89 percent white. While the student body has changed, the faculty has remained relatively static. Many of them grew up in a world that looked rather like the Australian model. Tension is building between a faculty that has remained overwhelmingly white and male and a student body that has been transformed over the past thirty years and will increasingly demand changes. The task for administrators, faculty, staff, and students is to provide all students with a greater range of environments and options in which they can explore and develop an increased, even a new, competence for dealing with an increasingly global society.

Conclusion

At the beginning of this essay, I noted that the debate about multiculturalism has been saturated with an unhappy combination of mean-spiritedness and a poverty of vision about the potential inherent in a culturally plural society. The world is reeling from events in Lebanon, Bosnia, and Somalia, from ethnic and religious tensions in the former Soviet Union, from anti-"foreigner" sentiment in Germany, and from racial tensions simmering in America in the post-Rodney King period—and the best our academics can come up with is the idea of "tolerance" of differences. It is, of course, to be preferred to fighting wars of intolerance. Racial/ethnic détente—a version of the cold war in interethnic relations—is preferable to the specter of "ethnic cleansing." But this is not the best to which we might aspire, nor even a representation of what we have already achieved. Indeed, to return to the opening frame of this essay, Crèvecoeur may have been partly right, partly visionary, in seeing a "new [hu]-man" in the American landscape. He was not right about the "shedding of differences" as a feature of the "new American," as we have seen through the small window of hope presented in this story about Berkeley's students. But there is the promise that retaining some differences may be the greatest potential for enriching public life. For reasons that he could not have known, Crèvecoeur may well have been right in forecasting that there was going to be something unique in this new American, and it would not just be the holding on to differences in ethnic enclaves that Schlesinger and other liberals deplore. (It will not have escaped the attention of social historians that there is remarkable irony, perhaps even hypocrisy, in the fact that conservatives and right-wing Americans have now joined the liberals in decrying "the new ethnic and racial enclaves." It was the right that championed and enforced restrictive covenants, and fought for all-white clubs.)

Rather, as Italian-Americans move back and forth between Bensonhurst and the larger public scene of Queens and Manhattan, they affirm their Italian heritage, their American experience, and the "common ground" that Schlesinger, and most of us, would affirm. They are one version of Crèvecoeur's "new Americans," freed from the requirement to shed differences, affirmed in their capacity to forge "newness" out of the unique conjunction of past and present, enclave and public sphere, personal and social. Glazer and Moynihan pointed out in 1970 in *Beyond the Melting Pot* how ethnic success in America is rooted in ethnic and community-based resources, in memberships and kin supports that are not barriers to but supporters of the trajectory of their members into economic and educational success. Newer work by Light and Bonacich (1988) and by Portes and Rumbaut (1990) recasts the setting, but reaffirms the message. Their potential and emerging multiculturalism in a changing social world makes the new Americans unique. We have a special contribution to make to a world that, seemingly more than ever, needs to reconfigure its understanding of ethnic, racial, and cultural relations.

Notes

Selected segments of this paper appear in the following publications: "Understanding Self-Segregation on the Campus," *Chronicle of Higher Education*, September 25, 1991; " 'They're Taking Over' and Other Myths," *Mother Jones*, September 1991; and the Diversity Project, Berkeley: Institute for the Study of Social Change, University of California, 1992 (the segments that appear here were written by the author, who was principal author of the report).

    1. The American cultures requirement at Berkeley, passed by the Academic Senate, requires that each student admitted (beginning in the fall of 1991) must take one course that compares three of five ethnic/racial/cultural groups. More than twenty-five such courses have been and are being developed. At the time when the criticism was being leveled, most of these courses were still on the drawing board, and there could have been no chance for

the critics to have reviewed syllabi, course outlines, reading lists, or general intellectual content.

2. I am indebted to Mitchell Breitweiser for this understanding of Crèvecoeur.

3. "The acrimony generated by the current debates over multiculturalism has created extreme positions in academe. At one extreme is the view that we should teach only the history and values of western civilization; at the other is the notion that we should focus chiefly on the origins and histories of particular ethnic groups. Those who refuse to subscribe to either position seem strangely paralyzed and silent. It is imperative that we find intellectual models that support cultural diversity without erecting battle lines that discourage understanding and tolerance and that breed racism" (Weiner 1992: B1, 2).

4. The academic staff included Tomas Almaguer, Bob Blauner, Gerald Berreman, Troy Duster, Hardy Frye, André Jimenez, David Matza, David Minkus, Lillian Rubin, Martin Sanchez-Jankowski, Jerrold Takahashi, Russell Thornton, David Wellman, Norma Wikler, and Deborah Woo. The graduate research assistants were Magdalena Avila, Ricky Blumenthal, Ann Ferguson, Luis Garcia, Nadine Gartell, Gautam Ghosh, Kate Howard, Maxine Leeds, Deborah Little, Wendell Thomas, and Robert Yamashita.

5. The persons who led the focus groups and were primarily responsible for analyzing the data from those interviews were of the same race or ethnicity as those interviewed. All of the transcriptions were also reviewed by the multiracial team to discern patterns and themes.

6. The focus groups included Native American, black, Chicano/Latino, Asian-American, white, "mixed" racial/ethnic, and a mixed group (where three or four different racial groups were represented).

7. "The 'Great Melting Pot' and the History of Work Place Diversity," presentation by George Strauss to the sixth annual breakfast meeting, Berkeley Campus Human Resources Council, April 25, 1991.

8. Alejandro Portes and Ruben G. Rumbaut, *Immigrant America: A Portrait* (Berkeley: University of California Press), 1990.

9. This finding is from *Promoting Student Success at Berkeley: Guidelines for the Future*, the report on a study conducted by the Commission on Responses to a Changing Student Body released by the chancellor in 1991.

10. These data are from the Office of Student Research, 1990 Freshman Survey: Berkeley's Ten Supplemental Questions by Ethnicity and Gender, February 1991. See also table 5 of the Diversity Project Final Report, 1991.

11. The more affluent and assimilated Asian-Americans had strong concerns about the *practice* of affirmative action that focused on issues of "academic standards," meritocratic criteria, and inherent problems with "race-based" policies. Other Asian-Americans argued on behalf of affirmative action as an important wedge for undoing some of the historical effects of discrimination.

12. The Karabel Report on admissions at Berkeley was released in 1989.

13. In fact, using the academic index, Berkeley is four to five times more "selective" than Harvard, which admits less than 10 percent of its students by an academic index alone. If Harvard used only an academic index, it would have only students with straight A high school grade point averages. In short, to mistake a student with a 3.7 grade point average as "better" or "more qualified" than a 3.6 student is a common fallacy of misplaced concreteness in the academy, and is the larger context for the discussion of the seething controversy over affirmative action admissions policies.

14. As Deborah Woo (1990) has pointed out, the very collapse of the category permits a conception of "overrepresentation" in the university that masks internal differentiations between Japanese-American enrollment (which declined significantly between 1980 and

1989), Korean-American enrollment (which has tripled), and Chinese-American enrollment (which has remained the same).

15. Jerome Karable and David Karen, "Go to Harvard, Give Your Kid a Break," *New York Times*, December 8, 1990.

16. Interview with Pamela Burnett, associate director, Office of Undergraduate Admission, October 17, 1991.

17. The median family income for white students is nearly double that for blacks.

References

Aufderheide, Patricia, ed. *Beyond PC: Toward a Politics of Understanding*. St. Paul, Minn.: Graywolf, 1992.

Crèvecoeur, J. Hector St. John de. *Letters from an American Farmer*. 1782. Reprint. New York: Fox, Duffield and Co., 1904.

D'Souza, Dinesh. *Illiberal Education: The Politics of Race and Sex on Campus*. New York: Free Press, 1991.

Glazer, Nathan, and Daniel Patrick Moynihan. *Beyond the Melting Pot: The Negroes, Puerto Ricans, Jews, Italians, and Irish of New York City*. Cambridge, Mass.: MIT Press, 1970.

Hall, Stuart. "Ethnicity: Identity and Difference." *Radical America* 23, no. 4 (1991).

Kallen, Horace Meyer. "Democracy versus the Melting Pot." *Nation* 100 (February 18-25, 1915): 190-94, 217-20.

Karabel, Jerome. "Status-group Struggle, Organizational Interest, and the Limits of Institutional Autonomy: The Transformation of Harvard, Yale, and Princeton, 1918-1940." *Theory and Society* 13, no. 1 (January 1984): 1-40.

Kristol, Irving. "The Tragedy of Multiculturalism." *Wall Street Journal*, July 31, 1991.

Light, Ivan, and Edna Bonacich. *Immigrant Entrepreneurs: Koreans in Los Angeles, 1965-1982*. Berkeley: University of California Press, 1988.

Oren, Dan A. *Joining the Club: A History of Jews at Yale*. New Haven, Conn.: Yale University Press, 1985.

Portes, Alejandro, and Ruben G. Rumbaut. *Immigrant America: A Portrait*. Berkeley: University of California Press, 1990.

Schechner, Richard. "An Intercultural Primer." *American Theater*, October 1991: 28-31, 135-36.

Schlesinger, Arthur, Jr. *The Disuniting of America: Reflections on a Multicultural Society*. New York: Norton, 1992.

Synnott, Marcia Graham. *The Half-Opened Door: Discrimination and Admissions at Harvard, Yale, and Princeton, 1900-1970*. Westport, Conn.: Greenwood, 1979.

Wechsler, Harold Stuart. *The Qualified Student: A History of Selective College Admissions in America*. New York: Wiley, 1977.

Weiner, Annette B. "Anthropology's Lessons for Cultural Diversity." *Chronicle of Higher Education*, July 22, 1992: B1, 2.

Woo, Deborah. "The Overrepresentation of Asian-Americans: Red Herrings and Yellow Perils." Sage Race Relations Abstracts 15, no. 2 (May 1990).

Zangwill, Israel. *The Melting-Pot, Drama in Four Acts*. New York: Macmillan, 1920.

Contributors

Margaret L. Andersen is professor of sociology and women's studies at the University of Delaware, where she also serves as associate provost for academic affairs. She is the author of *Thinking About Women*, coeditor with Patricia Hill Collins of *Race, Class, and Gender: An Anthology*, and coauthor with Frank Scarpitti of *Social Problems*. With Carole Marks she served as codirector of the MOST Program at the University of Delaware and developed an interdisciplinary course on the civil rights movement.

Derrick Bell has spent thirty-five years in civil rights work: in litigation, administration, teaching, and scholarship. He is the author of a textbook, *Race, Racism, and American Law* (1971, 1992) and two books of stories: *Faces at the Bottom of the Well: The Permanence of Racism* (1992) and *And We Are Not Saved: The Elusive Quest for Racial Justice* (1987). After an early career as a Justice Department lawyer, NAACP Legal Defense Fund staff attorney, deputy director for civil rights at the Department of Health, Education, and Welfare, and director of the Western Center on Law and Poverty in Los Angeles, Bell joined the Harvard Law School faculty in 1969 and became its first black tenured member in 1971. In 1980, he accepted the deanship of the University of Oregon Law School. He returned to Harvard in 1986 and was dismissed in 1992, when he refused to end a leave he took to protest the school's failure to hire and grant tenure to women of color on the faculty. For the past two years, he has been a visiting professor at the New York University Law School and a frequent guest on radio and television interview programs.

Lisa Kahaleole Chang Hall is a poet, essayist, and Ph.D. candidate in ethnic studies at the University of California at Berkeley. She works as the promotional director for Aunt Lute Books, a small nonprofit multicultural feminist press in San Francisco.

Estelle Disch is associate professor of sociology and coordinator for diversity awareness at the Center for the Improvement of Teaching at the University of Massachusetts at Boston. She codirects BASTA!—Boston Associates to Stop Treatment Abuse—where she works with people who have been sexually abused by health and mental health care providers.

Troy Duster, professor of sociology and director of the Institute for the

Study of Social Change at the University of California, Berkeley, has been a member of the Assembly of Behavioral and Social Sciences of the National Academy of Sciences and of the Council of the American Sociological Association. He currently serves as a member of the Association of American Law Schools Commission on Meeting the Challenges of Diversity in an Academic Democracy.

Evelynn M. Hammonds, assistant professor in the Program in Science, Technology, and Society at the Massachusetts Institute of Technology, is the author of the ground-breaking 1986 article "Race, Sex, AIDS: The Construction of Other." As an African-American feminist, she was deeply troubled by the Senate hearings on the nomination of Clarence Thomas to the U.S. Supreme Court and by the treatment of Professor Anita Hill, which she wrote about in "Who Speaks for Black Women?" (*Sojourner*, October 1991).

Ian Fidencio Haney López, assistant professor of law at the University of Wisconsin, is researching police-Chicano relations in East Los Angeles, as well as the idea of race in American law. Haney López was born and raised in Hawaii, the son of a Salvadoran mother and an ethnic Irish-American father.

Evelyn Hu-DeHart is professor of history and director of the Center for Studies of Ethnicity and Race in America at the University of Colorado at Boulder. The center is developing undergraduate and graduate programs in Afro-American, American Indian, Asian-American and Chicano studies, as well as comparative race and ethnic studies. Her research has focused on the native peoples of the Americas and on the Asian diaspora in Latin America and the Caribbean. She lectures widely on Latin American and Caribbean affairs, multiculturalism, and race relations and consults with colleges and universities on issues of curriculum, campus climate, and student and faculty recruitment and retention.

Earl Jackson, Jr., is an assistant professor of literature at the University of California, Santa Cruz. He is the author of *Strategies of Deviance: Essays in Gay Male Representational Agency* (1994). His articles have appeared in *PMLA, Theatre Journal, Harvard Journal of Asiatic Studies, differences, GLQ*, and the *Bryn Mawr Classical Review*, among other publications. His most recent play, *He Kisses Like a Danish Summer*, premiered in Santa Cruz in 1992. His pornographic texts have appeared in *Lavender Reader, Lambchop, Chinquapin*, and *Inciting Desire*.

Carole Marks, associate professor of black American studies and sociology at the University of Delaware, is the author of *Farewell, We're Good and Gone*, a sociological analysis of the Great Migration. With Margaret Andersen, she served as codirector of the MOST Program at the University of Delaware and developed an interdisciplinary course on the civil rights movement.

Chandra Talpade Mohanty teaches women's studies at Hamilton College in Clinton, New York. Her intellectual and political commitments include racial and transnational dimensions of feminist theory; the intersections of gender, race, and education; international development and postcolonial studies; and feminist and antiracist pedagogy in the U.S. academy. She is coeditor with Ann Russo and Lourdes Torres of *Third World Women and the Politics of Feminism* (1991). She has coedited (with Jacqui Alexander) a forthcoming anthology titled *Movements, Histories, Identities: Third World Feminisms, A Reader*. She is working on a book on feminist theory, race, and the politics of cross-cultural analysis.

Barbara Omolade, a social scientist who writes and teaches about race and gender, is preparing a book of essays for Routledge Press. She is coordinator of the bachelor of science education program at the City College of New York Center for Worker Education and is an organizer, an advocate, and a consultant for multicultural education at the City University of New York and elsewhere.

Becky W. Thompson, assistant professor of sociology at the Center for Research on Women at Memphis State University, was a Rockefeller Postdoctoral Fellow in African-American Studies at Princeton University for 1992-93. She has also taught at Bowdoin College in Maine and at the University of Massachusetts at Boston. She teaches feminist theory, race and ethnicity, and the sociology of law. Her published writing is in the areas of antiracist, feminist pedagogy, mental health, and the sociology of education, and she is writing a book about trauma and recovery in the lives of African-American, Latina, and white women. She also works as an antiracism activist and is compiling an anthology of autobiographical essays on racial identity development and race consciousness.

Sangeeta Tyagi, assistant professor of sociology at Roanoke College in Virginia, has also taught at the University of Massachusetts at Boston. Her teaching areas include comparative race and ethnic relations and Third World feminist theory. Her research is in the areas of sociology of education and feminist theory. She is working on a manuscript on Indian women's folk songs as a medium for a counternarrative discourse. She is also coediting (with Becky Thompson) an anthology on racial identity development and race consciousness.

Cornel West has taught at Yale, Union Theological Seminary, and Princeton, as well as at Harvard and the University of Paris. He is the author of *Prophecy Deliverance! An Afro-American Revolutionary Christianity* (1982), *Prophetic Fragments* (1988), *The American Evasion of Philosophy* (1989), *The Ethical Dimensions of Marxist Thought* (1991), *Breaking Bread: Insurgent Black Intellectual Life* (1991), and *Race Matters* (1993) and is coeditor of *Post-Analytic Philosophy* (1985) and *Out There: Marginalization and Contemporary Cultures* (1990).

Index

Diversity Project (University of
California, Berkeley), xxix, 95, 236-38
Double consciousness, 29-30
Douglass, Frederick, 74
D'Souza, Dinesh, xv, xix, xxv, 13-14,
16-17 n. 22, 67, 239, 244
Du Bois, W. E. B., xxii, 6, 25, 31, 74,
115, 189
Duster, Troy, xiv, xvi, xxix
Dworkin, Andrea, 142

Economic inequality. *See* class
stratification
Edley, Christopher, 72, 117
Eisenstein, Zillah, 59
Eliot, T. S., xxii, 22-23
English-only movement, 122, 151
Epistemology, 60
Epps, Edgar, 178-79
Equal Employment Opportunity
Commission, 69, 77
Essentialism, 140, 142, 169; critique of,
30, 96; examples of, 85-87, 91
Ethnic studies: activist roots, 162-63;
alliances with women's studies, 48;
definition of, 5; distinction from area
studies, 4; formation of, xx, 4-6, 46-47,
162; programs and departments, 5-6.
See also African-American studies;
Native American studies
Exclusionary practices, xxv, 121; in the
curriculum, 89, 177; in hiring, xvi, 94;
types of, 90, 115-16

Fanon, Frantz, xxii, 26, 31
Feminism: academic and nonacademic,
170; and the double shift, 165; feminist
critiques, 138-39; feminist pedagogy,
48-52; feminist presses, 170-71; feminist
scholarship, 43, 53, 62; and racism,
138-39
Feminist movement: racism in, 140-41;
radical feminism, 138-39, 142
Financial aid, xviii, 164
Ford Foundation, 182, 193, 198, 203, 206,
227
Ford, Richard, 105-6
Foucault, Michel, 32, 144
Frankfurt school, 27
Freedom of speech, xviii

Frye, Marilyn, 140-41, 143, 147

Gay and lesbian movement, 4, 26; sexism
and racism in, 141-42
Gay and lesbian faculty, xvi, xxx, 20, 90,
135, 136; discrimination against, 86-87,
90, 171
Gay and lesbian studies, xxi, xxx, 89,
136-37, 151, 205
Gender, definition of, 143-44
Genovese, Eugene, 13
Giroux, Henry, xvii, 52
Grass-roots organizing, 228
Greenberg, Jack, 125
Gulf War, xvii, 13
Gutiérrez, Ramón, 5

Halcon, John, 58
Hall, Lisa Kahaleole Chang, xxix
Hall, Stuart, 29-30
Hammonds, Evelynn, xxix
Harvard Law School, xvi-xvii; Coalition
for Civil Rights, xxix, 100, 116; and
hiring, 100, 129; student protests, 100-
103
Hate speech, 12
Hegemony, 235
Helly, Dorothy, 218, 221, 222
Hemphill, Essex, 141
Heterosexism, 87, 90, 93, 94, 134, 142,
171
Higginbotham, Elizabeth, xxv, 89, 96
Higher education, changes since World
War II, 24
Hill, Anita, xix, 66, 78, 119
Hillel Foundation, 234
Hip-hop culture, 27
Hispanic: inadequacy as term, 10;
percentage of faculty, 217. *See also*
Latinos/Latinas
Hispanic Association of Colleges and
Universities, 183
Hispanic National Bar Association, 116
Hofstadter, Richard, 25
Holocaust, 23, 135
Homogeneous communalism, 30
Homophobia, 87, 172. *See also*
Heterosexism
Horatio Alger myth, 69
Hu-DeHart, Evelyn, xxix, xxxi n. 5

version, 163; media assault on, xvii;
models of, 178; and national identity,
3-15, 232-33; and politics of inclusion,
90, 97; potential of, xxii, 7, 49; support
for, 12, 15, 209; undermining of, 14,
53-54, 89, 216, 228, 231; vs.
triumphalism, 14-15. *See also* Activism;
Curriculum transformation projects;
Diversity movement
Multilingualism, xxvii, 248

National Association for the Advancement
of Colored People, 120, 125
National Association of Scholars, xv, 14,
17 n. 27, 78, 231
National Endowment for the Humanities,
xiv-xv, xxi, 13-14
National Institute Against Prejudice and
Violence, 247
Nationalism, xvii, 141
National Quota Origins Act of 1924, 239
Native Americans: citizenship of, 9;
genocide of, 8-10, 152
Native American students, 242
Native American studies, 4, 216. *See also*
Ethnic studies
Naturalization Law, 10
New criticism, 24
Newman Foundation, 234
New Right, 45

Objectivity, critique of, 92, 163, 165
Olsen, Frances, 127-28
Omolade, Barbara, xxix, 215
Oppression, 128, 135, 150

Parsons, Talcott, xxii
Patterson, Orlando, 28
Pedagogy, 44, 251; decolonization of,
48-52, 61, 83. *See also* African-
American studies; Ethnic studies;
Feminism; Multicultural education;
Women's studies
Perspective theory, 84, 113-17, 121, 123,
124, 126
Plato, 137
Pluralism, 45, 63 n. 9, 236, 248; critique
of, 42, 48, 52-57, 163; cultural, 233
Police, 26, 252

Political correctness debate, ix, xv, xvii,
xix, 12-13, 68, 77-78, 199, 200, 208,
235
Politics: of dismissal, 87-89, 115-16; of
inclusion, xxvi, 89-90, 92, 96-97; of
location, 60, 62 n. 3; of representation,
xix, 31
Pomo Afro Homos, 152
Pornography, 143
Positivism, 92
Poststructuralism, 27
Prejudice, 74
Pride, 150-51
Progressive, definition of, 162
Prophetic criticism, 34
Protestant Reformation, 20
Public intellectuals, 6

Queer theory, 131

Race: consciousness, 124; definition of,
106; identity, 140, 250; industry, 45,
53-57; privilege, xiv; social construction
of, 106-7
Racial diversity, definition of, 103
Racism, 124, 126, 171-72; in the academy,
126, 188-89, 223, 247; in the classroom,
87, 116; definition of, 123-24; against
faculty of color, 58, 126; in feminism,
138-39; at Harvard Law School, 109,
116; and heterosexism, 87, 90, 93;
against people of color, 5-6; and sexism,
224; in white gay culture, 138-39; in
women's studies, xxv. *See also*
Segregation
Radical politics, 25
Rap music, 12
Reagan, Ronald, 6, 27, 58-59
Reagon, Bernice Johnson, 97
Reductionism, 34
Reproductive rights, xxiii, 163
Reverse discrimination, xix; myth of,
47-48, 71, 73; and Supreme Court,
59-60
Reyes, Maria de la Luz, 58
Rich, Adrienne, 164
Riggs, Marlon, 152
Role model theory, 84, 109-13, 121, 123,
124, 126
Rorty, Richard, 33